BIBLIOTECA DI TESTI E STUDI / 288

SERVIZI E POLITICHE SOCIALI

I lettori che desiderano
informazioni sui volumi
pubblicati dalla casa editrice
possono rivolgersi direttamente a:

Carocci editore

via Sardegna 50,
00187 Roma,
telefono 06 42 81 84 17,
fax 06 42 74 79 31

Visitateci sul nostro sito Internet:
http://www.carocci.it

Children, Young People and Families

Examining social work practice in Europe

Edited by Maria José Freitas, Günter J. Friesenhahn
Elizabeth Frost and Maria P. Michailidis

Carocci editore

Il presente volume è stato realizzato
con il contributo dell'Unione Europea - DG Istruzione e Cultura.

This volume was realised through
the EU financial support - DG Education and Training.

1ª edizione, gennaio 2005
© copyright 2005 by Carocci editore S.p.A., Roma

Realizzazione editoriale: Omnibook, Bari

Finito di stampare nel gennaio 2005
dalla Litografia Varo (Pisa)

ISBN 88-430-3265-8

Riproduzione vietata ai sensi di legge
(art. 171 della legge 22 aprile 1941, n. 633)

Senza regolare autorizzazione,
è vietato riprodurre questo volume
anche parzialmente e con qualsiasi mezzo,
compresa la fotocopia, anche per uso interno
o didattico.

Contents

Introduction. Children, Young People and Families in a European Context   9
by *Maria José Freitas, Günter J. Friesenhahn, Elizabeth Frost* and *Maria P. Michailidis*

Section A
The Context

1. **Promoting the Rights of Children and Young People**   27
   by *Jane Dalrymple*

2. **Gender and Social Work: Influences of Gender on the Process of Professionalization in Spain and Germany**   39
   by *Tomasa Báñez* and *Gudrun Ehlert*

3. **The Welfare State, Third Sector, and Family in Italy: A Comparison with the German Model**   52
   by *Vincenzo Fortunato*

4. **The Ethics and Political Function of Social Work**   69
   by *Gérard Moussu*

Section B
Practices

5. **The Relationship between Social and Spatial Exclusion in an Urban Context: Consequences for the Development and the Behaviour of Young People**   83
   by *Detlef Baum*

6. Single Mothers and the Effects of Intensive Aid on the Quality of Their Lives: The Examples of the Netherlands and Cyprus 99
by *Anne van den Berg* and *Maria P. Michailidis*

7. Current Trends in Supporting Children, Youth and their Families in Two European Urban Regions: Amsterdam and Madrid 120
by *Wilfred Diekmann* and *Agustín Moñivas*

8. Sexual Abuse and Child Protection in England, France and Germany 133
by *Rolf H. Piquardt*

9. Interdisciplinary Teams and Transdisciplinary Networks for Child and Family Inclusion: The Relevance of European Theory to Lithuanian Practice 151
by *Nijolė Večkienė* and *Julija Eidukevičiūtė*

Section C
The Profession

10. Professionalization and Status for Child Welfare Workers: A Way of Mapping a Working Area in Social Work 173
by *Peter Dellgran* and *Staffan Höjer*

11. Social Pedagogy: A Paradigm in European Social Work Education from German and Polish Perspectives 190
by *Günter J. Friesenhahn* and *Ewa Kantowicz*

12. Supervision and Training of Professionals Working with Families and Minors at Risk 207
by *Alfonsa Rodríguez, Elena Roldán, Luis Nogués* and *Teresa Zamanillo*

Authors and Editors 221

Introduction

Children, Young People and Families in a European Context

by *Maria José Freitas, Günter J. Friesenhahn, Elizabeth Frost* and *Maria P. Michailidis*

This volume is the second in a series about social work in Europe. Volume One (Campanini, Frost, 2004) offered a descriptive overview of social work in 24 EU member-States. Each author briefly reviewed the dimensions of history, education and current practice. In other words, the background picture of social work across the whole of Europe was outlined. This volume seeks to go a step further by engaging with the specific topics of social work with children, young people and families. The 12 chapters still represent every region of Europe from Scandinavia to the South and the countries of the old communist block to England. However their concerns are less with an impressionistic overview and more with a thorough academic account of a particular strand within the topic.

This book, and indeed the first, is the product of an EU funded Thematic Network project, EUSW – European Social Work: Commonalities and Differences. Beginning in 2002, the Network now boasts some 50 members representing every country in the new Europe. (Since Mr Bush has called all European countries which were not in favour of the Iraq war the "old Europe", the term "new Europe" might be ambivalent.) Contributions to the book were volunteered by member institutions with experience and interest in the field of social work with children, young people and families. As the reader will perceive, a fascinating diversity of practices and perspectives emerged, within a volume which is also able to offer insights into some of the contextualising issues of such work as well as the practice itself.

What is presented here is a radical pan-European project: a text which spans Europe within its vision of social work with child, young people and family social work. The comparative nature of the work is a particular strength. In some chapters authors representing two different countries and social work systems have written together to undertake a direct comparison of a chosen feature, whereas in others a comparative dimension is achieved by a single author drawing on social work literature to illuminate his national perspective alongside that of specific other nations. Another type of comparison deployed within the book is that of using Europe itself (European children's rights, for example, or ethics) as the contextualising framework within which comparative dimensions are then discussed.

Social work with children, young people and families is broadly defined within the book. Our interest is in the kinds of concepts and ideas that framed such work in practice, and in the professionals who undertake these activities. In keeping with this, the book comprises three sections. Section A looks at contextual issues (relating to gender, rights, theory, and policy); Section B considers forms of practice with individuals, families and communities; Section C concerns itself with professional issues such as demarcations and definitions.

This volume is intended to advance the knowledge-base about European social work issues. It is aimed at "students" of social work and other social professions and all those still engaged in learning processes. Lecturers and trainers should find it useful for introducing a European dimension in social work curricula and courses.

For social work, a European dimension is not a value in itself. Social work has to deal with the challenges and problems which will emerge from the new European developments, e.g. the enlargement process, increasing unemployment rates, migration, poverty, and changing life conditions for families, children and young people. Social work not only has the task of supporting people to cope with these new developments, but also the task of analysing and accompanying these developments critically, and making proposals for the improvement of people's life conditions. Social work has to be aware that these tasks are embedded in a European context and beyond that. Looking at European policy and social professions in Europe there are some important structural differences which have an influence on the relations between policy and social work.

In a political sense and from certain perspectives, Europe represents freedom: freedom of movement for its' inhabitants, (social) services, goods and capital. European dimensions in this sense are connected with a decrease of trade hindrances, and with a harmonisation of structures and frameworks. This idea of harmonisation of structures also plays an important role in the context of the academic training for professions, which in many countries includes social work. The so-called Bologna process will lead to compatible university systems and degrees in more than 50 European countries. Social work, however, sometimes has more to do with dealing with diversity than with harmonisation. Social work has to respect different values, different ways of living, different concepts for someone's own life or, on a more scientific level, different approaches which analyse, explain and solve social problems and challenges, and last but not least it must respect different languages.

Even if some people hope that in the end Europe will present itself as a unity – as a homogeneous structure – we must take into account that social policy, social services and social work will remain diverse and necessarily embedded in the historical, political and social contexts of each country. It is evident that in all European countries there is at some level a transfer of power and potential to the EU. However somewhat paradoxically it seems that there is no European child, youth and family policy, which is co-ordinated, task-oriented and, in terms of approaches and concepts, unified. The challenge is not the diversity, but dealing with the diversity. In all European countries social work aims at empowerment, support, and the improvement of life conditions by delivering high quality social services provided by professionals who refer to academic findings and personal engagement.

Within the European Union the so-called principle of subsidiarity leads to a situation in which the member-States remain responsible for social and youth policy and education. Nevertheless, Europe as an entity has an increasing influence on the daily life situation of European citizens, and can also be regarded as a source of new opportunities for individual chances with regard to education, training and for jobs. "Europe has become a social and political living space for children, youth and their families" (Arbeitsgemeinschaft für Jugendhilfe, 2004, p. 13). That requires both the intervention of all social work actors in relevant European policy, and taking into consideration the European dimension of local, regional and national social services and social welfare for children, youth and families. To facilitate this, is one of the fundamental purposes of this Thematic Network.

The general aim of the Thematic Network, then, is to advance an understanding of social work, in all its diversity and similarities, across the continent. Ultimately this book seeks to promote this vision for both social work education and the profession. A common denominator and major concern for social work across Europe is the family (in all its forms), its children and the young people they grow into. It may be worth pausing now to briefly consider the general position of these groups within the EU.

1
Children in Europe

Even though the numbers are dropping not increasing across Europe as populations generally become older, the children of Europe constitute a formidable force. In some other regions of the world, e.g. in North Africa, about 40% of the population is younger than 25 years old. Compared with these regions young Europeans have to cope with an aging society, which creates some specific problems e.g. with regard to social security systems, pensions etc.

Estimated at approximately 70 million under-18-year-olds in the Union prior to May 2004, children as a category have been a major focus of legislation and research emanating from the Union since its inception. For example, the European Union *Convention on the Exercise of Children's Rights* (1996) simultaneously, and effectively, placed the welfare of children at the heart of the community's ethical and belief system to encourage its translation into national policies and laws. Endorsed by virtually all countries in the international community, that children, from whatever background and in whatever circumstances have fundamental rights to, for example, safety and health and equal treatment is a highly significant EU commitment and principle. Dalrymple further discusses the issue of children's rights in CHAP. 1 of this volume.

However before examining the "European child" in more detail, it might be worth noting from the outset the impossibility of discussing "children" as a coherent group. Infancy, young childhood, older childhood and adolescence can be seen as constituting distinct groups across Europe, though quite what the demarcations should be and what kinds of culturally determined behaviours might be expected within each would be subject to some variation. And as always what we know about each of these groups is limited by the available research, which in itself may reflect regional inequalities in funding support and/or research capacity.

Research reports however provide some useful information. In 2001-2002, for example, the World Health Organisation/Europe reported on the findings from a study of health behaviour in school-aged children. Covering children aged 11-15 from 35 countries (Europe plus Canada, the Russian Federation, the Balkan countries and the United States) this collaborative survey provides a rich source of comparative information on life-styles as well as health. For social work with children and families such information is crucial.

Health, then, is a determining feature of children's life trajectories and the level of support welfare State services may need to offer. Amongst 15-year-olds, between 8 and 32% of boys, and 16-63% of girls report their health to be less than good or moderate, merely fair through to poor across the survey. However parts of eastern and central Europe showed the worse rates. Latvia and Lithuania, for example, report the highest levels of poor health for girls, at 42% (WHO/Europe, 2004). As bodies such as the EU Community Health Monitoring Programme (2002) substantiate, poor health (including mental health) in children not only connects with personal suffering/deprivation and reduced life chances, but is also part of a complex multifactorial picture of determinants, risks and outcomes. Factors such as financial support to families, day care services and social and health services form part of a protective environment for children's health in the face of family pressures such as poverty and unemployment and adverse social circumstances such as isolation and harmful environments.

Poverty is highlighted as one of the determining factors for poor health and mental health in Europe's children. Since the 1990s levels of child poverty have increased generally (Zierer, 2003) though there is wide variation across Europe. In wealthy countries such as Norway and Sweden about 15% of the population of children live in families of low affluence, whereas the proportion can be as high as 53% in eastern European countries such as Lithuania (WHO/Europe, 2004). However this pattern is not always consistent. For example of the pre-2004 EU countries, Portugal, UK, Spain, Ireland and Italy have the highest levels of child poverty. The UK managed to improve its position from having the highest levels of child poverty to fifth highest between 1998 and 2001. However Spain, Portugal and Ireland still had more than 25% of children in relative poverty (assessed as below 60% of national median income) in 2001; the EU average then was 18% (European Community Household Panel statistics, cit. in Brewer *et al.*, 2004).

Traditionally there has been a link between poverty and migration, and/or being part of a single-parent family, and this still seems to be the case across Europe (Zierer, 2003). Rates of children living in one-parent families are as high as 16-20% in western Europe, for example England, but in southern and eastern Europe, for example Greece, Italy and Balkan States, more than 90% live with two parents (WHO/Europe, 2004). Anne van den Berg and Maria P. Michailidis consider some interventions with struggling single parents in the Netherlands and Cyprus, respectively, in CHAP. 6. However the assumption of a previous generation that poverty necessarily connects with parental unemployment seems to be less the case. Certainly where *no* member of the household have an income poverty exists, but the working poor, in precarious and/or exploitative work situations, are becoming more numerous as a European (and world) phenomena. This may also correlate with immigrant status. And of course the organisation of social security and benefits within countries invariably has a profound impact on child poverty. It is worth noting that "the poverty rate for children is in reverse proportion to the share of social security benefits in the social product of a country" (Zierer, 2003, p. 16).

This is also very much the business of social work, in relation to monitoring and intervening in child poverty and its determinants and outcomes, and of social policy initiatives. Poverty, physical ill health and mental ill health, then, are some of the primary concerns that social work must engage with in relation to children across Europe. These seem to be fundamental, with "protection from abuse and exploitation" as the fourth major category of concern. It may shock many that in a UNICEF survey of 15,000 children, aged 9-17, and including central, eastern and western Europe, 6 out of 10 children say they face violence or aggressive behaviour within their families, and 11% of them says it occurs often. 1 in 6 children feels unsafe in his neighbourhoods and 2 in 10 children report having a friend or relative who has been a victim of abuse. This also shows considerable regional variation: "The proportion of children in transition countries who feel unsafe in their communities is about double that of Western Europe" (UNICEF, 2004, p. 1).

Sexual abuse of children is another important area. As well as sexual abuse within the family, a concern that has been identified and is worked with across European social work in various ways since the 1970s, sexual exploitation, including trafficking of children, has also now become a major concern. Piquardt undertakes a cross-cultural comparison in CHAP. 8 of aspects of child sexual abuse in three European countries. There is then much work for social workers in Europe, whether employed by the State or NGOs, to do with the children of Europe, to improve the basic conditions of childhood and allow them to develop their potential. Structural frameworks ratified by European countries, such as the UN *Convention on The Rights of the Child* (1989), and the European Union *Convention on the Exercise of Children's Rights* (1996), suggest an overall favourable climate of intent in which to advance children's interests. Social work in education and health, with children in families and with those separated from their families, in refugee housing and on the streets, in juvenile justice and in community projects and all the other contexts existing in the Union, have a European wide mandate for children's work. Some examples of such initiatives in Spain and in Lithuania are discussed by Rodríguez, Roldán, Nogués and Zamanillo in CHAP. 12, and Večkienė and Eidukevičiūtė in CHAP. 9.

What is also being advocated, from conventions of rights to research reports, is that the old processes of adults making decisions for and doing things for and to children is no longer an acceptable position for any adults, let alone child welfare professionals, to take. Children's voices should and must be heard. Children should be active participants in their lives and changes within them. As recommended in their report on children's mental health: "Young people need to not only be consulted but have genuine power, influence and decision making over policy and practice" (Mental Health Europe, 2002, p. 12). Social work in many parts of Europe has begun to address the notion of service user inclusion. These principles also need to be fore-grounded when the service user is a child. Dalrymple discusses some of the issues in children's participation in CHAP. 1.

2
Young People

Turning to young people in Europe, it is apparent that some European legislation is specifically targeted at them. There is art. 29 of the Treaty of Amsterdam (crime against children), art. 13 (anti-discrimination), Title XI (*Social Policy, Education, Vocational Training and Youth*) Chapter 1 (*Social Regulations*) with arts. 136-137 as well as Chapter 3 (*Education, Vocational Training and Youth*) with arts. 149-150. Beyond that the European *Charter of Fundamental Rights* puts young persons at the centre of art. 24 with the following concern: "Children shall have the right to such protection and care as is necessary for their well-being. [...] In all actions relating to children, whether taken by public authorities or private institutions, the child's best interests must be a primary consideration".

From a European perspective, taking into consideration the principle of subsidiarity, child welfare and youth policy are first of all the task and the responsibility of each member-State. "The European Union can contribute with measures when defined objectives are not going to be achieved by actions of the Member states but perhaps more usefully through community actions" (Arbeitsgemeinschaft für Jugendhilfe, 2004, p. 8). Examples might be action programmes like *Youth* (http://www.youthforeurope.org).

International networks, transnational projects and the development of international activities in the area of training are gaining more importance. This happens in the light of the globalization process, which confronts all societies with new challenges and demands. But additionally social policy and welfare models are changing their shape. The active welfare State is becoming an activating welfare State; in other words the trend can be described as: from welfare to workfare (Walther, 2003). Individualisation and privatisation of social risks are the consequences of this development accompanied by the attempt to ground youth policy (and child welfare) on market-oriented, competition-based models. However, the Council of European ministers responsible for youth did decide in May 2002 to focus on the needs and perspectives of young people in all fields of politics. It was stressed that youth policy in the EU should interface with other divisions. The standards set became the five rules of the European governance: openness, participation, responsibility, efficacy and coherence (European Commission, 2001).

Participation has become a core issue, particularly expressed in the White Paper on youth by the European Commission (http://europa.eu.int/comm/youth/whitepaper/download/whitepaper_en.pdf). Participation means that young people have to be involved in decisions which are important for their lives, and they have to be integrated in their communities. Young people have to be consulted before decisions are taken. Dalrymple and Baum's chapters in this book consider some of this range of issues (CHAPS. 1, 5). The Commission also highlighted the big five challenges for the future in relation to youth as (European Commission, 2001):
– demographic development;
– changing conditions/social constellation for the life world of young people;
– involvement of young people in public life;
– European integration;
– globalization.

Research on the social situation of young people in Europe (Walther, 2002; Chrisholm, Kovacheva, 2002) discovered that young people have to cope with overall trends which affect their lives, for example, the trend towards longer and more complex transitions to adult life, to which extended education and training contribute significantly. The authors also highlight that young Europeans are confronted with the fact that they are living in an aging society and therefore they will become a weaker electoral factor. Overall, they suggest, in the future the youth "phase" will be less standardised, and is becoming more open-ended and characterised by a plurality of life-styles. Chrisholm and Kovacheva (2002, p. 13) summarise:

We cannot know how young people will respond to all these trends, but rather than being problems and having problems in the areas of the polity, young people in twenty-first century Europe should be at the forefront of solving problems as an integral part of the polity. [...] This requires that social organisations and public policies are capable of meeting the challenges of responding proactively to young people as citizens with equal rights as those who will carry Europe's future.

Young people in Europe constitute an important part of the population. Many are confronted with a changing social constellation, with new trends in leisure-time activities and increasing demands on schooling and learning. Young people are forced to take decisions on their own, because traditions and the traditional milieu no longer serve as examples in order to cope with the future. They may be alienated from extended families or cultural traditions, and/or from the rural or urban communities to which they, if only nominally, belong. Such dimensions of integration or its opposite are raised in the essays by Diekmann and Moñivas (CHAP. 7), and by Baum (CHAP. 5).

Within most societies there is some expectation that social services for young people will have a significant role to support, to assist and to empower young people. In a report written by a group of experts from different European countries on the White Paper on youth (Gudmundsson, 2003, p. 2) they state:

Education is and should be at the centre of a holistic approach to youth affairs – but not confined to schools. Learning takes place in leisure life and at work, and not only for those who are formally labelled as students or trainees. [...] We learn in non-formal and informal settings, too (in youth clubs, in the family, in political life). Moreover, what we learn formally often only becomes meaningful and useful when it is applied in non-formal and informal contexts.

Within welfare work the role of social pedagogue often addresses the "education" of young people in this very broad social sense. Friesenhahn and Kantowicz in CHAP. 11 discuss the comparative situation for social pedagogy across Germany and Poland. There is no doubt that in all European countries young people have been and are still a special target group for social work and related welfare professions (Voland, Porteous, 2002; IARD, 2002). Perspectives and methods have changed over the last decades but, nevertheless, young people will remain a target group because they always have special needs according to their age and the tasks (transition from school to work, establishing their independent lives etc.) which belong to youth. The variety of experiences of the life-stage "youth" and the definitional problems in themselves across Europe make it difficult to analyse "European youth" as a whole, but this book attempts to at least describe some key themes and cast an interpretative eye towards the coming decades. "Evidence-based policy-making is only possible if the evidence is available and accessible in the first place" (Chrisholm, Kovacheva, 2002, p. 69). That means for social work practice in all European countries there is a need to broaden the knowledge basis in relation to such European issues (Williamson, 2002).

In the future it will be important to introduce issues into the social work curriculum which show the consequences of the European integration process for the life of young people (as well as children and families) and which analyse and accompany this process from a critical point of view. Developing a common basis for research, co-operation and training will be both the product and part of the process. In addition we must cope with relevant findings, concerning the lives of children, and youth. And it is not just the specifics of the social situations of children, young people and families that should be studied but also the broader context of this work, such as gender politics and ethical dimensions. Báñez and Ehlert, and Moussu discuss such contextualising dimensions in CHAPS. 2 and 4 respectively.

3
Families

Whether as an institution, a social network, or a system, the family has played a fundamental role as a provider of support and well-being, mainly in the education and care of children and elderly members. Of equal significance is its contribution to social cohesion, *picking up* where welfare systems often fall short. Yet, as much as it has endured over time, the family is also a dynamic entity susceptible to a changing economic, political and social environment. This flexibility can, of course, be a useful feature in a Europe of 450 million inhabitants, but it can also make the family *vulnerable* to greater, perhaps newer challenges arising in an enlarged and diversified Europe of 25 member-States.

The demographic changes in Europe have accentuated discussions on the very concept of family, its form, size and newfound connection to socio-economic struggles. And while trends like an aging population coupled with low fertility rates (European Commission, 2002), less marriages coupled with more divorces (EUROSTAT, 2003a), less young people living at home (EUROSTAT, 2003b), a growing number of single-parent homes of which 90% are women (EUROSTAT, 2004a), increased work outside normal daytime hours and during weekends (EUROSTAT, 2004b) form part of the discussion on families in Europe, the trends should not be seen as developments resulting from changes in "traditional" family models but rather as part of the same process of accommodation towards modernity.

To tackle these trends social work professionals are exploring new patterns of social welfare provision and intervention: family group conferencing and home training programmes, shifts in youth care provisions from (semi)residential care to the home, intensive aid for single parents, family preservation services and the formulation of national family policies all serve to illustrate the growing family perspective in practice. In this scenario, the family becomes not only an additional client for social workers but also a potential partner for tackling structural inadequacies – a development that places considerable pressure on social workers to intervene in ways that are as diverse and complex as the issues at hand. Some of these issues are elucidated in this volume by Večkienė and Eidukevičiūtė (CHAP. 9), Rodríguez, Roldán, Nogués and Zamanillo (CHAP. 12), and by Fortunato (CHAP. 3).

The list of problems facing family life today is long and grows in pace with the demands for economic development and global competition. The entangling of economic and social policies becomes ever more apparent and is further evidenced by the current trade-offs being made between work and family. Likewise, a conclusion of the recent European surveys on "Quality of Life in Europe" states that, of all the policy measures to support families and children, European citizens identify the reduction of unemployment and an increased employment rate as the best (social) policy for everyone – families included (Krieger, 2004).

On the whole, the pressure to *be* and *do* more in a lifetime is leading to a redefinition of values (e.g. individualisation *vs* social responsibility), to changed roles (e.g. men *vs* women) and to a further consideration of life choices (family *vs* career). These same issues pose a difficulty for policy-makers and social work professionals alike, as personal choices are sized up against risks and as differentiated policy areas try to come together. Against this backdrop and coupled with social ills the likes of child and spouse abuse, youth crime, and poverty, it becomes more and more difficult to maintain the remnants of any kind of family life. In the face of these predicaments, issues affecting families are visible on current political agendas; systems are being adapted to consider the changing face of the family, namely, more women in the labour market, care-sharing responsibilities and provisions, nurturing environments for children. The potential of the family, regardless of form, is being acknowledged as an ally to tackle the effects of a declining welfare State.

The adaptation of the Treaties of the European Union has seen a gradual development in the provision of competencies for the European institutions on policy issues including social policy. And, while the challenges of family life in post-modern societies are drawn into EU social policy, there is no legal provision for, i.e. an EU family policy. For the most part, family issues are merged with issues of social exclusion, health care, (un)employment, and equal opportunities, while remaining delicate, *non-public* matters, which may partially explain the lack of explicit European provisions. There is of course also a wide range of existing measures tackling family concerns in the various 25 European member-States that are bound to the national context, i.e. the type of welfare regime. Such policy measures take into account the member-State's specific level of economic development as well as the perception of its citizens (Fahey, Spéder, 2004), hence the limited prospective for a single, all-embracing family policy for Europe's 25.

Needless to say, the lack of a defined European policy in this domain does not preclude the efforts of the sovereign member-States on matters of the family. The importance of a family life across Europe is not really questioned but its multidimensional character and embeddedness in various areas of welfare makes it less likely to be addressed on its own merit. In the end, the family question may be nothing else but the quest for ways to encourage members of society to contribute to the quality of life in Europe more fully.

4
The Social Work Profession

How we define social work is of course contentious and subject to much regional variation. Issues common to much of Europe are for example the boundaries of the profession. Who should be called a social worker? A volunteer in an NGO? A foster parent? Only someone with a master's degree in applied social sciences? This kind of debates is familiar and addressed in this book in CHAPS. 3 and 10, by Fortunato and by Dellgran and Höjer.

There are also region-specific issues to do with terminology and tasks; for example, the notion of social pedagogy is undergoing transformation. Parts of Europe have never adopted this as a category, whereas in other areas it is securely embedded, for example: "The German tradition of social pedagogy has become associated with social work" (Smith, 1999, p. 1). In addition, the meaning and the function of the term "social pedagogy" is subject to considerable variation in the countries in which it is used e.g. the Netherlands, Switzerland, Denmark, Hungary and the Baltic States and others. Friesenhahn and Kantowicz discuss this in CHAP. 11 with regard to Germany and Poland.

Social work is not just comprehensible via a consideration of its service users or indeed its policy context; social work also exists as a diverse profession in various states of development across Europe. Issues concerning generalism within practice *vs* speciality; professionalism *vs* "anti-expertism"; the rightful location of social work in State (statutory) or voluntary organisations or as market- and profit-oriented bodies are some of the key themes in European debates. Essays such as those by Dellgran and Höjer (CHAP. 10), and Fortunato (CHAP. 3) discuss this at more length. In relation to the status of professionals for example, the desirability and indeed possibility of addressing clients as equal partners in the helping process is an aim realised to various degrees across Europe. Empowerment of service users is becoming a reality which both challenges and redefines professionalism in social work.

The conditions and context in which social work is undertaken are also a concern in this volume in terms of its status, gender issues, economic arrangements and organisational framing, all of which affect the delivery of social work. Gender issues, for example, still connect to the (low) status and the "maternal" expectations of social work in several European countries, as discussed by Báñez and Ehlert in relation to Spain and Germany (CHAP. 2). Professional issues also include the education and training of social workers. The relationship of theory to practice and the kinds of theory that can be drawn on have been a major preoccupation of social work for many years and across national boundaries. Each generation discovers new ways of approaching social problems and currently ecological systems theory, evidence-based practice and critical social work are in the ascendance, although this varies across Europe. However an overall trend from input-based education (where the focus is on what students will be taught) to competence-based learning (where the focus is on the achieved outcomes) can perhaps be discerned more generally in social work education across Europe.

5
Conclusions

As is evident from the above, then, within the book's three sections – contextual issues, practice issues and professional issues for social work with children, young people and families – many of the current debates within a European context are examined and discussed. This book, then, is very much the product of an ideological commitment to social work education in Europe, supported by the European Union's educational funding initiatives, and reflecting the aim of increasing mutual understanding and integrated proactive development in this field. In some ways this follows an easy logic. Social work is an international activity, with many of the kinds of difficulties it attempts to ameliorate being of a universal nature. However it is the differing conditions of its delivery that make pan-European engagements of this nature stimulating, enlightening and mutually beneficial. The editors and authors maintain the hope that the volume will stimulate the desire for further enquiry into commonalities and differences in social work with children, young people and their families, as it has within the Thematic Network.

Bibliography

BREWER M., GOODMAN A., MYCK M., SHAW J., SHEPHARD A. (2004), *Poverty and Inequality in Britain: 2004*, The Institute for Fiscal Studies, London.
CAMPANINI A., FROST E. (eds.) (2004), *European Social Work: Commonalities and Differences*, Carocci, Rome.
CHRISHOLM L., KOVACHEVA S. (2002), *Exploring the European Youth Mosaic: The Social Situation of Young People in Europe*, Council of Europe, Strasbourg.
EU COMMUNITY HEALTH MONITORING PROGRAMME (2002), *Child Health Indicators of Life and Development. Report to the European Commission: Executive Summary*, EUROFORUM, Luxembourg.
EUROPEAN COMMISSION (2001), *A New Impetus for European Youth-White Paper. COM 681, 21 November*, Brussels.
ID. (2002), *Family Benefits and Family Policies in Europe*, Directorate General for Employment and Social Affairs, Unit E.2, Brussels.
EUROPEAN OBSERVATORY ON THE SOCIAL SITUATION, DEMOGRAPHY AND FAMILY STUDIES (2004), *Key Family Issues in the EU Member States: Summary Reports Prepared by the National Experts*, http://europa.eu.int/comm/employment_social/eoss/downloads/kfi_2003_en.pdf.
EUROSTAT (2003a), *Statistics in Focus, Population and Social Conditions – First Results of the Demographic Data Collection for 2002 in Europe*, http://www.eustatistics.gov.uk/statistics_in_focus/downloads/KS-NK-03-020-__-N-EN.pdf.
ID. (2003b), *Statistics in Focus, Population and Social Conditions – Trends in Households in the European Union 1995-2025*, http://www.eustatistics.gov.uk/statistics_in_focus/downloads/KS-NK-03-024-__-N-EN.pdf.
ID. (2004a), *Statistics in Focus, Population and Social Conditions – Household Formation in the EU – Lone Parents*, http://www.eustatistics.gov.uk/statistics_in_focus/downloads/KS-NK-04-005-__-N-EN.pdf.
ID. (2004b), *Statistics in Focus, Population and Social Conditions – Working Times*, http://www.eustatistics.gov.uk/statistics_in_focus/downloads/KS-NK-04-007-__-N-EN.pdf.
FAHEY T., SPÉDER Z. (2004), *Fertility and Family Issues in an Enlarged Europe*, Office for Official Publications of the European Communities, Luxembourg (http://www.eurofound.eu.int/publications/files/EF03115EN.pdf).
GUDMUNDSSON G. (2003), *European Commission White Paper on Youth Consultation Process: Report of the Research Consultation Pillar*, http://www.alli.fi/youth/research/ibyr/white%20paper.htm.
IARD (2002), *Study on the State of Young People and Youth Policy in Europe*, IARD Institute, Milan (further information at http://europa.eu.int/comm/youth/doc/studies/iard/iard_en.html).
KRIEGER H. (2004), *Family Life in Europe – Results of Recent Surveys on Quality of Life in Europe*, paper from Irish Presidency Conference on *Families, Change and Social Policy in Europe*, 13-14 May, Dublin.
MENTAL HEALTH EUROPE (2004), *Children, Adolescents and Young People*, in *Mental Health Promotion and Prevention Strategies for Coping with Anxiety, Depression and Stress Related Disorders in Europe. Final Report 2001-2003*,

Federal Institute for Occupational Safety and Health, Dortmund-Berlin-Dresden (http://www.baua.de/fors/fb04/fb1011.pdf, pp. 26-80).

SMITH M. K. (1999), *Social Pedagogy*, http://www.infed.org/biblio/b-socped.htm.

TRNKA S. (ed.) (2000), *Seminar Report: Family Issues between Gender and Generations*, Office for Official Publications of the European Communities, Luxembourg.

UNICEF (2004), *Youth Speak out from Europe and Central Asia: Happiness, Unhappiness, Poverty and Hopes Highlighted*, press release of Young Voices poll, http://www.unicef.org/newsline/01pr42.htm.

VOLAND B., PORTEOUS D. (eds.) (2002), *Working with Young People in Europe: What We Can Learn from Our Neighbours*, Russell House, Lyme Regis.

WALTHER A. (2002), *Kinder- und Jugendhilfe und Europa*, in W. Schröder, N. Struck, M. Wolff (hrsg.), *Handbuch Kinder- und Jugendhilfe*, Juventa, Weinheim, pp. 1139-60.

ID. (2003), *Aktivierung: Varianten zwischen Erpressung und Empowerment. Für eine Erweiterung des Diskurses zum aktivierenden Staat im internationalen Vergleich*, in "Neue Praxis", 3-4, pp. 288-303.

WHO/EUROPE (2004), *Health Behaviour in School-Aged Children*, Fact Sheet EURO/04/04, Copenhagen-Edinburgh.

WILLIAMSON H. (2002), *Supporting Young People in Europe: Principles, Policy, and Practice*, Council of Europe, Strasbourg.

ZIERER B. (2003), *Poverty among Children in Europe*, in "Social Work in Europe", X, 1, pp. 15-9.

Section A
The Context

Section A

Promoting the Rights of Children and Young People

By Jane Fortin

I
Promoting the Rights of Children and Young People

by *Jane Dalrymple*

International recognition of children's rights began in 1924 when a *Declaration of the Rights of the Child* was passed by the Assembly of the League of Nations (known as the Declaration of Geneva). Following this the United Nations passed a *Declaration on the Rights of the Child* in 1948. These two declarations focused on the protective and developmental aspects of children's rights. A new declaration in 1959 widened the parameters of earlier declarations, moving from a mainly protective emphasis to recognising the civil right to a name and nationality as well as referring to happiness, love, understanding and rights to play and education. In 1989, after 10 years' work, the United Nations General Assembly passed the *Convention on the Rights of the Child* (Marshall, 1997). This has been described as a "discursive space" (James, Jenks, Prout, 1998, p. 6) within which young people are treated as autonomous individuals. It has also been proclaimed as a "breakthrough in society's views about the status of children" (John, 1996, p. 4), formally recognising children as a minority rights group, whose subjectiveness has been denied and whose voices have been silenced. Ratification of the *Convention* by member-States means that they have committed themselves to *listening* to children and young people as well as to protect and care for them. It has been described as a "breakthrough" in three respects (Willow, 2002, p. 7):
1. signalling a commitment by politicians of the world that the young should be given their fair share of attention and resources;
2. granting children new rights to protection from all forms of violence and mistreatment in all settings including the family home;
3. heralding the start of accepting and valuing all children as individuals worthy of fundamental human rights, including the right to express their views, the right to association and information, and the right to freedom of thought, conscience and religion.

In Europe the *Convention* was welcomed, and to help member-States fulfil their obligations as signatories as well as working towards unity within the Union, a European *Convention on the Exercise of Chil-*

dren's Rights was passed and opened for signing in 1996. However, while these instruments are a welcome step forward in promoting the participatory rights of children and young people, they do not necessarily ensure the voice and agency of children and young people within the provision and delivery of services that affect their lives.

International instruments provide frameworks for practice and for social workers the various conventions means that there is an imperative for children and young people to be involved in the decision-making processes that affect their lives. To an extent this therefore charges social workers with some responsibility for ensuring the implementation of the conventions and to promoting the rights of children and young people. This is no easy task however and there are dilemmas for social workers as adults charged with the responsibility of protecting children and young people and making decisions which children and young people in particular situations may not agree with. In this chapter I will argue that there can be difficulties with legislative mandates that promote the rights of children and young people. The chapter will start with a discussion about the United Nations *Convention on the Rights of the Child* (CRC) and go on to consider how far mechanisms such as advocacy services and children's commissioners, set up to protect the interests of children and young people, are able to enhance their status and enable them to come to voice. From this the issues for social workers will be examined.

1.1
The Impact of International Instruments

The CRC is a global statement of what children need to be happy, healthy and safe. Acknowledgement of children's rights, consolidated by the 54 articles of the CRC, has meant that governments throughout the world now have to take into account the principles of the *Convention* when considering the role of the State in providing care and services. Key to the *Convention* is the assertion that children have equal value to adults. It has been described as introducing a "new philosophy toward children" (Lansdown, 2002, p. 273) in which they are recognised as autonomous individuals whose human dignity should be respected. It recognises that children also need care and protection however and, because of their vulnerability, need support to be able to enjoy their rights. To balance these two aspects the *Convention* states that the best interests of the child must be the primary consideration in any actions relating to children and not the interests of parents, carers or the State. Linked to this is a second principle to ensure that the views of the child are respected and that they have a right to be heard and their views taken seriously, subject to their age and maturity, in all matters affecting them (art. 12). It has been suggested that this second principle "introduces a profound challenge to traditional attitudes to children in most societies in the world" (Lansdown, 2002, p. 273).

Within the enlarged European Union there are over 76 million children, who, it has been argued, have to date largely been ignored within EU policy. In the final text of the signed Oct. 2004 European Union Constitution, however, the "protection of children's rights" has been included in the internal and external actions of the Union (arts. 3.3-3.4). This has been hailed as a key starting point for the future of children's policy in the EU by EURONET (the European Children's Network which is a non-governmental organisation which was created to promote children's rights and the active participation of children and young people at an EU level). As they state, "for the first time in the history of the EU, children and their rights are getting the recognition they deserve" (EURONET, 2003). Nevertheless, they point out that children are still invisible in both EU policy and programmes and more than 21% of children in Europe lives in relative poverty in one of the richest regions of the world.

The need for campaigning organisations such as EURONET – which was formed in 1995 by a coalition of networks and organisations concerned about the "invisibility" of children within the EU – is symptomatic of how far the CRC challenges attitudes to children. The fact that implementation of the *Convention* depends upon adults is therefore problematic. Furthermore there can be tensions between adult perspectives framed in the language of protection, which exclude children and young people from public dialogue and marginalise them in decision-making processes (Roche, 1999), and liberationist perspectives which promote autonomy. Freeman (2000) points out that some provisions of the CRC (such as arts. 5, 14.2)[1] assume that adults generally and parents in particular will promote the rights of young people. However the amount of "direction" and "guidance" they should provide has to be consistent with the evolving capacities of the child, which – Freeman argues – is a difficult concept. He also notes that there is sufficient latitude in art. 12 (which grants children and young people who can form views the right to express and have their views taken into account in all matters that affect them) to result in the right to participation being undermined since "representation" by a parent in judicial or administrative proceedings could in fact satisfy the article. On the other hand there is also a need for adults to engage in promoting the rights of young people since, as Franklin (1995, p. 14) states, "children have been excluded from participation in formal decision making for so long, that it seems unlikely they could enter this arena without the initial support and advocacy of adults".

Flekkøy and Kaufman (1997) suggest that adults actually have a *responsibility* to ensure that children have opportunities to exercise their rights if they are not to be meaningless. They point out that children's rights of participation are dependent on responsible adults providing the necessary information to enable children to make choices, give consent and learn to develop the skills necessary to move from sharing decision-making to taking it over. This is important for those involved in formal systems – such as health, social care and education – where it has been suggested that adults committed to the participation rights of children need to make "a concentrated effort" to ensure that they are heard (Schofield, Thoburn, 1996). The issue for the adults (such as social workers) making that effort, and for the children and young people who are seeking to influence their own lives, is how to challenge competing discourses in order to have an impact on the provision and delivery of services. For social work educators it is therefore important to ensure that practitioners know and understand these discourses and develop the skills to both use and challenge them appropriately in their work.

The marginalisation of children and young people by adults is a relatively new European phenomenon. Other cultures and societies have involved children in the life of their communities as active citizens. This is now being considered by sociologists as enhancing their development and status in society as well as offering more protection from abuse (Jordan, 2000). Wattam and Parton (1999, p. 3) suggest that professional responses in the UK are predicated on a particular view of childhood "which is brought to the attention of the state when it is obviously contravened". Discussing responses to sexual violence to children they argue that protectionist responses are used to "preserve" childhood. Rather than interrogate the causes of sexual violence to children or young people, constraints in the name of protection are imposed, with the victim and the family coming under scrutiny. While not all European countries respond to sexual violence to children in the same way (Cooper *et al.*, 1995) the principle that children and young people should be regarded as social actors (James, Prout, 1997) is a universal one.

It can be seen then that perceptions of childhood and youth and the accompanying conflicting perceptions of children and young people as either vulnerable and dependent, or citizens to be valued and respected, have an effect on law and policy and on international instruments such as the CRC. On the one hand adults are expected to protect children and young people and act on their behalf, while on the other to recognise their rights to act for themselves. The principle that children and young people are entitled to protection as of right, and that parents/carers have obligations which accord them rights, is difficult to challenge (Lansdown, 1995). For social workers this means they have to manage the ethical dilemmas that arise as a result of the sometimes contradictory rights and responsibilities of children, their parents/carers and the State.

1.2
Developing Mechanisms to Promote Children's Rights in the United Kingdom

The *European Convention on Human Rights* (1950) has been criticised as not being "tailored to meet the breadth of children's experiences and needs" (Willow, 2002, p. 11). However it has also been used positively to change law and policy in a number of key areas such as corporal punishment in schools, access to files (social services) and criminal proceedings for young people. The UK government appears to demonstrate a commitment to children's rights by incorporating the *European Convention* into domestic law through the *Human Rights Act 1998*. This means that it is possible to go to court if rights under the *Convention* have been breached. In addition a joint committee on Human Rights was established in Parliament in 2001 to focus on the UK's compliance with the *European Convention*. This 12-member committee also monitors compliance with other international instruments including the CRC. Willow (2002, p. 11) notes that as a result "there is hope that [...] the Human Rights Act 1998 will at least be used to remedy some of the most severe breaches of children's human rights". There have been some key developments, though, in relation to promoting the participation rights of children and young people in the four nations of the UK. The first is the growth of advocacy services for children and young people looked after in state care, or defined as in need. The second is the establishment of children's commissioners in three of the four nations.

Advocacy services for children and young people in England and Wales have developed as the international instruments already described, and legislation such as the *Children Act 1989* recognised children's rights to express their views and have their wishes and feelings taken into account in decisions affecting their lives. Advocacy has been defined as one of the oldest forms of support (Brandon, 1995). It developed in a formal way in relation to legal services where the role of the advocate in court (solicitor/barrister) is to represent the interests of their client, speak up on their behalf and protect their rights (Wertheimer, 1996). However in the last decade there has been increasing recognition of the importance of involving service users in the development and delivery of services. This has subsequently become incorporated into legislation regarding all health and social care services. In relation to children and young people various reports and inquiries have recognised that if the principles of participation underpinning legislation were to become a reality for children and young people in receipt of services then they needed the support of an advocate.

Advocacy can broadly be described as enabling children and young people to "have a voice" in matters that concern them (Dalrymple, Hough, 1995). Oliver (2003, p. 45) notes that for children and young people a definition includes "speaking up for someone, understanding, talking, making other people listen and consider their views". The UK government and the Welsh government have both implemented *National Standards for the Provision of Children's Advocacy Services* which state (Department of Health, 2002, p. 1):

Advocacy is about speaking up for children and young people. Advocacy is about empowering children and young people to make sure that their rights are respected and their views and wishes heard at all times. Advocacy is about representing the views, wishes and needs of children and young people as decision makers, and helping them navigate the system.

Such definitions focus on the individual element of advocacy services where children and young people seek support for themselves in particular situations. Advocacy services also have a political element however, and so advocacy can be described as (Henderson, Pochin, 2001, p. 15):

A political act with consequences for both individuals and the community as a whole, challenging inequality, opposing racism, preventing abuse, or even introducing someone to a new opportunity or social setting – all constituting steps towards a more civil and just society.

Advocacy services have gradually developed in the UK over the last 20 years, funded or part-funded by local authority Social Services Departments. An important element of their effective functioning is that they are independent of statutory services even if they are commissioned by them to provide advocacy support for particular groups of children and young people. Their implementation has been fragmented (Atkinson, 1999; Clifton, Hodgson, 1997; Department of Health, 2000), however more recently the government has made a commitment to develop a fully comprehensive network of children's advocacy services (Department of Health, 2000, p. 15). For those children who wish to make a complaint under the procedures of the *Children Act 1989* there is now a legislative mandate that they have access to an independent advocacy service (*Adoption and Children Act 2002*). Reforms of mental health legislation for adults provide for entitlement to independent advocacy in particular situations and may also apply to young users of mental health services. Various guidance documents also identify the need for children to have advocacy support in different situations (Robbins, 1999; Department of Health, 2001). Such developments mean that advocacy has "moved from the margins to the centre of public policy debates" (Oliver, 2003, p. 7) in the last five years in relation to children and young people in receipt of services.

Despite such developments all the political parties have been indifferent to improving children's rights, which is highlighted by the fact that a campaign for a children's commissioner for the UK (Franklin, 1995) took over a decade (Rosenbaum, Newell, 1991). Further evidence is in the lack of consistency between policies of differing government departments which, it has been suggested, is built on "ambivalence and contradiction" (Payne, 1995, p. 412) about children and young people, with legislation "designed to appease public opinion" (Lansdown, 1997, p. 115). For example in youth justice the welfare of the children is missing from legislation about crime and disorder that merely "consolidates a sequence of policy and practice which will only serve to undermine child welfare and deny youth justice" (Goldson, 1999, p. 12). This means that while one government department promotes the rights of children and young people, another promotes child curfews, the naming and shaming of offenders and secure training centres (Inman, 1999). A second example is the exclusion of young people within the education system where the "disjuncture between law, convention and educational rhetoric and their everyday lived realities" (Goldson, 1997, p. 65) is evident. It is perhaps hardly surprising therefore that studies indicate a level of professional resistance to advocacy (Oliver, 2003; Dalrymple, 2004) although there are many professionals who encourage it (Boylan, Wyllie, 1999) and, once established, advocacy services can develop good working relationships with the services that commission them. However the experiences of children and young people suggest that, despite the political element outlined in the definitions above, while they identify that being involved in decision-making can have a significant impact on their lives they feel less able to influence systems (Dalrymple, 2002, 2004). It is here that commissioners for children's rights are an important development.

1.3
The Case for Children's Rights Commissioners

The Council of Europe encourages member-States to set up children's commissioners or ombudsmen to monitor the implementation of children's rights and improve the circumstances of children across Europe. The European Network of Ombudsmen for Children suggests that there are a number of common themes in the aims of children's commissioners (www.ombudsnet.org):

- to promote full implementation of the CRC;
- to promote a higher priority for children in central, regional or local government and in civil society, and to improve public attitudes to children;
- to influence law, policy and practice, both by responding to governmental and other proposals and by actively proposing changes;
- to promote effective co-ordination of government for children at all levels;
- to promote effective use of resources for children;
- to provide a channel for children's views and to encourage government and the public to give proper respect to children's views;
- to collect and publish data on the situation of children and/or encourage the government to collect and publish adequate data.

The world's first commissioner for children was established by law in 1981 in Norway. The role of this commissioner is to protect the rights of children under the age of 19. While having no executive authority, both legally and via instruction the commissioner is responsible for disseminating information about children and young people and for protecting their interests in all areas of society. The first commissioner, Målfrid Grude Flekkøy, stated that in the role she had to "keep an eye on all areas of society, give warning of developments harmful to children and propose changes to improve their conditions" (Flekkøy, 1991, p. 24). The development of children's rights in Norway is not without its critics, though. For example the Joint Custody Association of Norway (JCAN) has suggested that the rights of children as expressed in the CRC are not maintained and defended as would reasonably be expected of a frontline State in the struggle to uphold their rights (JCAN at www.f2f.no). However the work of the commissioner has clearly raised the status of children and young people both in Norway and internationally and independent evaluations of the commissioners' offices in both Sweden and Norway have shown that the commissioner is well-known and that there have been positive changes in the lives of children (Hirst at www.nspcc.org.uk). The current commissioner has had increasing international recognition as a result of the changing position of children in society and the implementation of the CRC. The new eastern European democracies have shown a particular interest in his work and have sought his advice, as have the four nations of the UK.

The need for independent commissioners has been recognised by three of the four nations of the UK. The first nation to set up an office was Wales and the commissioner started work in March 2001. The Welsh commissioner has more powers than the Norwegian one, partly as a response to recommendations of an inquiry into the organised abuse of children in local authority care in North Wales. He can review proposed legislation and policy from the National Assembly for Wales in order to consider the effect it might have on children, and can make representations to the Assembly on any matters affecting them. Before he got the job he was interviewed by children and young people as well as adults and the direct involvement of children and young people is a key element of the work of the office (*Childcare Facts*, Daycare Trust website www.daycaretrust.org.uk). In Ireland and Scotland legislation has also been enacted to create independent children's commissioners, the first in Northern Ireland being appointed in 2003 and in Scotland in 2004. However in England the government has been criticized for avoiding the debate by claiming that other mechanism exist to protect the rights of children. A group supported by over 120 organisations campaigning for a commissioner for England has consistently argued that while special posts within government structures are vital and a welcome step forward "their constitution means that they cannot meet the standard of independence from government that is a defining characteristic of a commissioner" (Children's Rights Alliance for England, 2003). While there is now a proposal to legislate for the appointment of a commissioner in England (Department for Education and Skills, 2003) the fact remains that until this time children in England do not appear to have been "important enough to have their own champion and protector" (Children's Rights Alliance for England, 2003).

Commissioners across Europe and throughout the world use the CRC as the framework for their work. They have achieved a great deal for children and young people including promoting reforms in law, advocating the views of children and young people, highlighting discrimination of vulnerable groups and increasing knowledge and understanding about children's rights (Children's Rights Alliance for England, 2003). The European Network of Ombudsmen for Children publishes annual assessments of the work of 20 institutions indicating that the appointment of commissioners clearly creates a climate of respect for children and young people, which in turn enhances their status and enables them to come to voice. Despite the fact that they exist in different legal structures and have varying roles commissioners are generally able to influence government policy and have an awareness-raising function.

1.4
Conclusions

The development of advocacy services for children and young people in the UK has been a key element in promoting their participatory rights in decision-making. This brief review has shown how advocacy has become established against a background of competing views about childhood, with varying perspectives on children's rights indicating the paradoxes that are apparent in promoting a positive rights agenda. Nevertheless the need for children and young people to have access to independent advocacy has been clearly expressed by the UK government and the expansion of advocacy services is testament to that fact. While other European countries do not have such a comprehensive practical mechanism for involving children in decision-making the development of children's commissioners provides the necessary institutions to promote and protect their rights and ensure that in the future they will have a more direct impact on the institutions that affect their lives. As a "General Comment" from the Committee on the Rights of the Child states (Committee on the Rights of the Child, 2002, p. 2),

children's development state makes them particularly vulnerable to human rights violations; their opinions are still rarely taken into account; most children have no vote and cannot play a meaningful role in the political process that determines governments' response to human rights; children encounter significant problems in using the judicial system to protect their rights or to seek remedies for violations of their rights; and children's access to organisations that may protect their rights is generally limited.

There is a key role for social workers, then, to ensure that the rights of children and young people are not violated, particularly by the systems that impinge on their lives. Hopefully the position of children and young people in Europe will keep improving as the council of Europe continues to focus on ensuring that member-States consider children and young people as members of society with rights and equal protection under the law.

Notes

1. Art. 5 is about the rights and responsibilities of families to direct and guide their children so that they learn to use their rights properly as they grow. Art. 14 states that parents should guide their children on matters about religion although they have a right to think and believe what they want and to practice their religion if they are not stopping others from enjoying their rights.

Bibliography

ATKINSON D. (1999), *Advocacy: A Review*, Pavilion, Brighton.
BOYLAN J., WYLLIE J. (1999), *Advocacy and Child Protection*, in N. Parton, C. Wattam (eds.), *Child Sexual Abuse: Responding to the Experiences of Children*, Wiley, Chichester, pp. 56-70.
BRANDON D. (1995), *Advocacy: Power to People with Disabilities*, Venture Press, Birmingham.

CHILDREN'S RIGHTS ALLIANCE FOR ENGLAND (2003), *The Case for a Children's Rights Commissioner for England's 11,3 million children*, CRAE, London.

CLIFTON C., HODGSON D. (1997), *Rethinking Practice through a Children's Rights Perspective*, in C. Cannan, C. Warren, *Social Action with Children and Families: A Community Development Approach to Children and Family Welfare*, Routledge, London, pp. 43-65.

COMMITTEE ON THE RIGHTS OF THE CHILD, GENERAL COMMENT NO. 2 (2002), *The Role of Independent National Human Rights Institutions in the Protection and Promotion of the Rights of the Child*, Office of the UN High Commission for Human Rights, Geneva.

COOPER A., HETHERINGTON R., BAISTOW K., PITTS J., SPRIGGS A. (1995), *Positive Child Protection: A View from Abroad*, Russell House, Lyme Regis.

DALRYMPLE J. (2002), *Family Group Conferences and Youth Advocacy: The Participation of Children and Young People in Family Decision Making*, in "European Journal of Social Work", V, 3, pp. 287-99.

EAD. (2004), *Professional Advocacy as a Voice for Resistance in Child Welfare*, in "British Journal of Social Work", XXXIII, pp. 1043-62.

DALRYMPLE J., HOUGH J. (eds.) (1995), *Having a Voice: An Exploration of Children's Rights and Advocacy*, Venture Press, Birmingham.

DEPARTMENT FOR EDUCATION AND SKILLS (2003), *Every Child Matters*, Stationery Office, London.

DEPARTMENT OF HEALTH (2000), *Learning the Lessons: The Government's Response to Lost in Care – The Report of the Tribunal of Inquiry into the Abuse of Children in Care in the Former County Council Areas of Gwynedd and Clwyd since 1974*, Stationery Office, London.

ID. (2001), *Quality Protects Rescare Briefings: Children's Participation*, Stationery Office, London.

ID. (2002), *National Standards for the Provision of Children's Advocacy Services*, Department of Health Publications, London.

EURONET (2003), *Children's Rights Included in EU Constitution!*, press release, Brussels 16 June, http://www.constitutional-convention.net/bulletin/archives/001617.html.

FLEKKØY M. G. (1991), *A Voice for Children: Speaking out as Their Ombudsman*, Kingsley, London.

FLEKKØY M. G., KAUFMAN N. H. (1997), *The Participation Rights of the Child: Rights and Responsibilities in Family and Society*, Kingsley, London.

FRANKLIN B. (1995), *The Case for Children's Rights: A Progress Report*, in Id. (ed.), *The Handbook of Children's Rights: Comparative Policy and Practice*, Routledge, London, pp. 3-22.

FREEMAN M. (2000), *The Future of Children's Rights*, in "Children and Society", XIV, pp. 277-93.

GOLDSON B. (1997), *From Exclusion to Inclusion: Educationally Disadvantaged Children and Young People*, in "Journal of Child Centred Practice", IV, 2.

ID. (1999), *Youth (In)Justice: Contemporary Debates in Policy and Practice*, in Id. (ed.), *Youth Justice: Contemporary Policy and Practice*, Ashgate, Aldershot, pp. 1-27.

HENDERSON R., POCHIN M. (2001), *A Right Result? Advocacy, Justice and Empowerment*, Policy Press, Bristol.
INMAN K. (1999), *Let the Children Speak*, in "Community Care", 1st July.
JAMES A., JENKS C., PROUT A. (1998), *Theorising Childhood*, Polity Press, Cambridge.
JAMES A., PROUT A. (1997), *A New Paradigm for the Sociology of Childhood*, in Idd. (eds.), *Constructing and Reconstructing Childhood: Contemporary Issues in the Sociological Study of Childhood*, Falmer Press, London.
JOHN M. (1996), *Voicing: Research and Practice with the "Silenced"*, in Ead. (ed.), *Children in Charge: The Child's Right to a Fair Hearing*, Kingsley, London, pp. 3-26.
LANSDOWN G. (1995), *Taking Part: Children's Participation in Decision-Making*, IPPR, London.
ID. (1997), *The Case for a Children's Commissioner for England*, ChildrenFirst, Winter.
ID. (2002), *The Participation of Children*, in H. Montgomery, R. Burr, M. Woodhead (eds.), *Changing Childhoods: Local and Global*, Wiley-Open University, Chichester-Milton Keynes, pp. 273-83.
MARSHALL K. (1997), *Children's Rights in the Balance: The Participation-Protection Debate*, Stationery Office, Edinburgh.
OLIVER C. (2003), *Advocacy for Children and Young People: A Review*, Institute of Education, London.
PAYNE M. (1995), *Children's Rights and Children's Needs*, in "Health Visitor", LXVIII, 10, pp. 412-4.
ROBBINS D. (1999), *Quality Protects: Transforming Children's Services*, Department of Health, London.
ROCHE J. (1999), *Children: Rights, Participation and Citizenship*, in "Childhood", VI, pp. 473-93.
ROSENBAUM M., NEWELL P. (1991), *Taking Children's Rights Seriously*, Gulbenkian Foundation, London.
SCHOFIELD G., THOBURN J. (1996), *Child Protection: The Voice of the Child in Decision Making*, IPPR, London.
WATTAM C., PARTON N. (1999), *Impediments to Implementing a Child-Centred Approach*, in Idd. (eds.), *Child Sexual Abuse: Responding to the Experiences of Children*, Wiley, Chichester, pp. 1-18.
WERTHEIMER A. (1996), *Advocacy: The Rantzen Report*, BBC Educational Developments, London.
WILLOW C. (2002), *Participation in Practice: Children and Young People as Partners in Change*, The Children's Society, London.

2

Gender and Social Work: Influences of Gender on the Process of Professionalization in Spain and Germany

by *Tomasa Báñez* and *Gudrun Ehlert*

2.1
Introduction

Although the majority of European social work practitioners are women and there are specific gender hierarchies in the profession, gender issues seem to be of minor importance in social work. As Gruber and Fröschl (2001) point out, the reflection of gender differences and the analysis of gender relations and hierarchies should be integrated in social work practice, theory and research, and education. This is necessary because conceptions of social problems, the strategies to cope with complex and problematic situations as well as social work practice are all determined by gender perceptions and by gender differences (Gruber, Fröschl, 2001, p. 13).

So, what could be the use of "gender" and what do we mean, when we talk about gender and the social work profession? Ongoing discussions in feminist theory and gender research are based on the sex/gender-differentiation whereby sex is associated with the biological difference between female and male. The term "gender" is linked to the social meanings of masculinity and femininity in each society. Gender as a theoretical category offers different perspectives for analysis: the meaning of the constructions of masculinity and femininity in the interactions of individuals and the relevance of gender in institutions and society (Becker-Schmidt, Knapp, 1995, p. 17). In the latter sense, gender is a category which indicates inequality and stratification in all societies. In this perspective hierarchies and differences are determined by gender which is interwoven with other constructions of differences like class and race (Spelman, 1988).

Since the 1990s there have been intensive debates about the relevance of gender as a useful category or concept in social sciences instead of simply highlighting differences and diversity. Knapp (2002) gives a good summary of different discourses which theorise gender and the "axes of difference". Orme (2001, pp. 32-3) has worked out the significance of changing feminist and gender discourses for social work and social care:

Attention to the diversity of women's experiences as users of social work and social care services, and how identities are structured by experiences of oppression. Such considerations have resonance with postmodernism, but the limitations of a highly theoretical and, at times inaccessible, analysis are noted. It is suggested that a more helpful approach is to recognise how different experiences of women and men as users of social work and community care services helps to clarify understandings of the constructions of masculinity and femininity.

We would add that gender is still one important marker of stratification; it is useful when analysing social inequality alongside other markers of inequality.

From our point of view, linking social work with concepts of gender is useful for the understanding of the history of the profession as well as for the current debates about theorising social work practice. Gender perspectives in social work help us understand the low status and the poor acknowledgement of social work as a profession; the institutional processes and hierarchies in social work practice; the gender specific labour divisions in social work theory, education and research; the problems of the service users and clients of social work; and the interaction between service users and professional social workers.

Social work and gender relations in different European countries demonstrate both similarities and differences. In this chapter we will discuss the influences of gender in the process of the professionalization of social work in Germany and Spain because we are writing from our own different national backgrounds. Although both countries have different historical, economic, political and social developments, it is interesting to find similar structures of gender in the respective social work professions. Our essay starts with the history of social work as a profession and the professional concept of "motherliness" which is based on 19th century gender polarities. Then we discuss changes in the process of social work professionalization and the meaning of gender differences and gender relations within the profession.

2.2
Historical and Gender Perspectives of Social Work as a Profession

As Álvarez-Uría (1985) and Friedlander (1989) have indicated, there were two important reasons for the creation of the social work profession in the North of Europe. Firstly, there were changing approaches to poverty, secondly, bourgeois women were motivated towards taking a more active role in society. At the end of the 19th century the social needs of the European population were on the increase because of the effects of industrialisation and urbanisation. The best way to meet these new social needs was to invest people with the necessary training to help solve them. In Spain the catholic Church was interested in women as the first social workers to meet the needs of poor people. But women were also interested in this new profession because they were able to take part in the public sphere by performing a female activity. As some authors have proved (Fraisse, Perrot, 2000; Rater-Garcette, 1996; Walkowitz, 1995), European women had an important and active role in the process of modernising and organising charity. Because they were social workers they had a way of taking part in the public sphere, an area which was traditionally defined as socially masculine. Other women chose other ways to take part in the public sphere in trade unions, political movements, feminism or nationalism.

The first social work school was created in Spain in the city of Barcelona in 1932, and it was a subsidiary of the Belgian schools. At this point the social and political context was characterised by the ideas of Catholicism and also by the important political changes which were introduced by the Second Republic. These improved the social rights of the poorest people and of other social groups (e.g. political and educational rights for women). But the Civil War of 1936 and the Francoist military dictatorship led to important changes in Spanish society, which entailed the disappearance of the political rights which had been introduced by the Second Republic. For this reason Caritas did not create a relevant number of social work schools in Spain until the end of the 1950s. As a result, the Spanish catholic Church decided to create social work studies for improving the charitable work of looking after and controlling poor people. Middle-class women were especially qualified to do this work by carrying out a kind of mental motherliness; they had to moralise poor people. In this way, meeting poor people's needs was possible, but without questioning the ultimate causes of social problems. At that time, the catholic Church helped poor people through charity in an individual way, but also in an organised way; first through different religious orders and afterwards, during the 1940s, through Caritas. On the other hand, the State also helped through a public welfare system which complemented that of the Church. The latter was much more substantial than the public help. In this social context, the social work profession and social work education in Spain included a lot of practice placements, little theoretical social work and much of the content about social issues had a religious bias. This was because of the influence of Francoist ideas and the spread of poverty.

Social work in Germany also has its roots in the female involvement in the caring role of the Churches. Policies against begging and poverty were a male domain whereby male volunteers worked with, and supervised unskilled male workers until the beginning of the 20th century. Social work in Germany emerged with the social changes in the 19th century: industrialisation; the foundation of the German Reich in 1871; the workers' movement; the bourgeois women's movement; and the social security acts. The growing complexity of society, of social problems and social work led to the first professional training for voluntary working women: in 1899 a one-year-course for women in the social welfare services was established in Berlin. Charity work became one option for bourgeois women. Voluntary work gave them the opportunity to work outside their private homes, and in the public sphere.

Under the direction of Alice Salomon the first Women's School for Social Welfare opened in 1908 in Berlin, and offered a two-year-programme. Social work developed from voluntary work to a (semi)profession. In the beginning, the need for education and qualification was not linked to paid work or a profession. During the World War I, the quantitative and qualitative boundaries of voluntary social work became obvious. The complexity of social problems after the war led to the need for professionalized social work, and contributed to the foundation of specialised administrative and legislative social work institutions (*Fürsorge*: Wessels, 1994, p. 28) in the Weimar Republic. You can say that social work as a profession in Germany developed as the domain of women which was then incorporated into a gendered hierarchy and division of labour. Men were the head of the administration in the developing social bureaucracy, and men controlled the female social workers who did the field work (Riege, 1996, p. 17; Fröschl, 2001, p. 288).

At the beginning of the Nazi period, social workers and educators with Jewish backgrounds were forced to leave their posts. Many of those who could leave Germany developed social work in the United States. For the German ("Aryan") population the polarity of female and male was part of the Nazi ideology and it structured the labour division between women and men. Social workers were still mainly women; some of them were directly involved in the selection and extermination politics of the national-socialist State. After World War II social work remained a female domain in the newly founded German Democratic Republic and in the Federal Republic of Germany where gender segregation contained a horizontal and a vertical dimension (Riege, 1996; Galuske, Rauschenbach, 1994).

So, as readers can appreciate, the social work profession was born in Germany and in Spain for similar reasons, but not at the same time because of historical factors related to the different political and social contexts of each country. In Spain, the catholic Church had an enormous influence, and Spain was far more traditional than Germany. In relation to new ways of meeting poverty, the German State had a more relevant role than the Spanish State. In relation to the motivation of middle-class women, at that time, Spanish women could only take part in the public sphere through religious or fascist movements. German women could use other ways to take part in the public arena, e.g. women's movements, the social-democratic and communist parties and the charity work associated with the protestant and catholic Churches. Social work as a domain for women was incorporated within gender hierarchies and the changing political systems in both countries. Gender as a stratification category led to social work as both voluntary and paid work for women on the basis of gender polarities.

2.3
Gender Polarities as the Basis of Historical Concepts of Social Work

The influence of gender in the origin of the social work profession in Germany and in Spain will now be analysed from the background of gender polarities and stereotypes in relation to the participation of women in the labour market.

During the 1870s Spanish social work was defined as an extension of the traditional role of women in the family, as a kind of "social motherliness" for middle-class women. According to the ideas of Concepción Arenal – one of the pioneers of the Spanish social work – the most important qualities for helping poor people were "charity, gentleness, firmness, exactness, circumspection, constancy, humility" (cit. in Santalla López, 1995, p. 45). In the 1970s social research into the profession (Vázquez, 1971; Estruch, Güell, 1976) indicated that at that time social work in Spain was more a religious activity than a real profession. It gave reasons to support this statement. In first place, those early social workers were women, daughters of middle-class families, who were studying social work in order to improve their own personal education rather than to find a job. In the second place, those social workers didn't have real labour and salary conditions because a salary would have implied a loss of vocation.

In Germany the process of industrialisation in the first half of the 19th century was accompanied by a gender specific and spatial division of labour with the implementation of the model of the bourgeois family. The different role models for women (motherhood; raising children; remaining inside the house to assume responsibility for the private sphere) and men (working outside to earn the families' living; having responsibility in the public sphere) had been ideologically justified by the nature of the two sexes (Fröschl, 2001, p. 286). These gender polarities were aimed especially at the bourgeois and rising middle-class women and men. Working-class women worked outside the house in different fields during the whole of the 19th and 20th centuries.

By the middle of the 19th century women were already working in the new founded kindergarten and nursery schools. According to Johann Heinrich Pestalozzi, Friedrich Fröbel and Henriette Schrader-Breymann the idea of women's nature and of women's ability for mothering, educating and caring was developed so as to train women to work in kindergarten and as nursery nurses. This concept of mental motherliness was developed by the bourgeois women's movement and became the central argument for women doing social work. Female social workers – as the mothers of the community – should care for poor people, who needed support.

Even at the beginning of the training process, the ability of women to do social work was seen as the basis for voluntary, not paid work, it was seen as a sort of "calling" for women. There is a very famous quotation from Alice Salomon (cit. in Riege, 1996, p. 29) which describes all elements of "suitability" and all the "abilities" associated with female activity:

the women's emotional life, her understanding and leniency, which help her in working with the desperate, [...] her conscientiousness and care in doing little and unimportant tasks too, which are a big advantage for the organisational tasks, at least her motherliness, her ability to transfer the motherly love from the house into the community, into the world, which needs these forces so urgently.

Nowadays there have been debates among gender researchers about the meaning of "mental motherliness". You could interpret the concept as part of the conservative gender polarity ideology, on the other hand "mental motherliness" was used as a strong argument to bring bourgeois women into the occupation, so for them it had been an emancipatory character.

After analysing the origins of the social work profession and education in Germany and in Spain we can conclude that the profession was born as a female activity in both countries. Similar arguments which are based on the gender polarity of the 19th century have been used to declare that the "natural qualities" of women were the basis for women's roles within social work. Professional training was seen as a way of improving these "qualities" and it took some time to open the training for men in both countries.

2.4
Changes in the Process of Professionalization of Social Work

Now we are going to discuss how the changes in the historical context and in the role of the State as the employer of social workers affected the profession in Germany and in Spain. As a result of these changes the labour and salary conditions have improved and social work became a more attractive activity for men.

In the case of Spain, there were a lot of changes in the Spanish social, economic and political context in the 1970s. The democratic Constitution of 1978 recognised the personal social services as social rights and the regional and local governments started to create the public personal social services system. These changes caused important transformations in the profession, and in the labour and salary conditions. Many jobs were created and the presence of professionals in responsible posts grew. So, social work improved its professionalization process.

Despite these changes, the female character of the profession remains in Spain. But the characteristics of the Spanish female social worker have changed since the birth of the profession because of associated social and historical changes. The first social workers in Spain were daughters of the middle class from large cities. Later the origin of social workers changed because improved educational opportunities enabled the daughters of the working class and women from rural areas to study social work.

In Germany, the social professions developed within two different political and economical systems between 1945 and 1990. But, as mentioned above, social work was the domain of women in both German States. In West Germany the development of the modern welfare State was the basis for increasing job opportunities for women and men in the beginning of the 1970s. Since 1971 social work/social pedagogy was part of the academic course of study at the new founded *Fachhochschulen* (universities of applied sciences). From that time, raising the status of social work was the aim of the (male) social scientists who were coming in the new posts in social work education. At least the percentage of men studying social work/social pedagogy increased too, in comparison with the 1950s and 1960s. Currently, there are about one third men to two thirds women studying social work in Germany (Scherr, 2002, p. 381; Kleibl, 1998, p. 213). In the German Democratic Republic a specialised educational system was established. The generic social work approach only existed in a very small segment of Church-related educational institutions. Nevertheless, the State-run educational and social sector had approximately 203.000 employees in 1988 (Galuske, Rauschenbach, 1994, p. 50). This figure included nursery nurses, educators and *Fürsorgerinnen*. The GDR kept this old German term for three different types of *Fürsorgerinnen*, as health, social, and youth *Fürsorgerinnen*. In East Germany approximately 95% of women and 5% of men were working in the welfare services for the young and in day nurseries in 1991 (Galuske, Rauschenbach, 1994, pp. 147 ff.). Social work has been one of the expending professions in Germany in the last two decades during which time the employment figures have trebled (Kleibl, 1998, p. 213). The percentage of two thirds women to one third men has been constant, only within the higher paid jobs the proportion of men in social work has been increasing (Kleibl, 1998, p. 213).

Political and economic changes had an important influence on the development of the welfare State and on social work as a social service profession in both countries. Expanding job opportunities and better salary conditions led to an increase of the proportion of men in social work. How this is interwoven with gender differences and relationships in social work will be discussed in the following section.

2.5
Gender Differences and Relationships in the Profession

Until now there have only been a few studies about men in female-dominated professions (Heintz *et al.*, 1997, p. 51). Research from the US (Heintz *et al.*, 1997, p. 53) indicates that men are not confronted with exclusion and disadvantage in the way that women are in male-dominated professions. As distinct from men, who see women as rivals in their professions, women don't regard men as competition but they hope that a "masculinisation" of the profession will lead to a growth of prestige. Men could take advantage of the stereotypes about masculinity which are associated with professionalism. In the sense of a "boundary work" (Heintz *et al.*, 1997, p. 52) men claim their territories in women's professions. This "boundary work" has an identity-stabilising function and it very often goes together with a promotion: «Women are more likely to be *pushed* out of male-dominated fields while men are more likely to be *pulled* out of female-dominated fields» (Jacobs, cit. in Heintz *et al.*, 1997, p. 52).

We have argued that expanding and improving working conditions have been one reason for the growth of the proportion of men in social work in Spain and Germany. The profession could provide an opportunity for men to find a job in countries where there is a high unemployment rate amongst men and women. For example in East Germany men have seen social work as an available career opportunity since unification. Another reason, which is also based on the structures of the labour market, is the anticipated promotion within the field of social work or the opportunity of upward mobility in other fields.

According to a feminist perspective, the social work profession and education process reproduce gender relations in Germany and in Spain. There are gender differences in the profession: in the conception of the profession and its workplaces, and the importance of the job in the professional's life. Male social workers occupy the traditionally male sphere which means that many male social workers are supervisors, managers, researchers etc. And for many of them social work is just a way of occupying the highest posts, even in a female sphere.

In German and Spanish social work there is a horizontal segregation between the different fields of social work, and a vertical one within the fields. Female social workers are occupied in posts dominated by face-to-face contacts whereas men are found in more formalised areas of the administration. Women do much more part-time work than men, and in social work practice men are in higher posts within the hierarchy. In social work, there is a very small percentage of women in higher management. Social work theory is male-dominated and lecturers and professors in social work education at universities (of applied sciences) and academies are mainly men. This gender segregation containing a horizontal and vertical dimension has taken place since the beginning of the profession in both countries. But there is a gap in the research about how changes in gender segregation take place.

One problem with measuring gender segregation lies in the national statistics which operate with very coarse categories. In Germany social work/social pedagogy is part of a range of social professions. Until now, it was not assumed necessary to have differentiated statistics about these professions. That means that you do not get an annual statistic about employees in social work/social pedagogy. Data has to be collected and counted and you get different figures from different calculations. One Mikrozensus survey from 1996 seems to give some evidence: there were 19,000 employed social workers/social pedagogues in 1996; of these, 65.3% was female and 34.7% was male (Scherr, 2002, p. 381).

If men enter female professions stereotypes about masculinity and vocations come into force: matter-of-factness, rationality, leadership. And if men come into female professions there is a corresponding rise in status (Heintz et al., 1997, p. 52). One effect of having more men in social work education, theory and practice, in Germany, is the growth of discourses about social workers which ignore gender totally; the social worker is a neuter. But only the knowledge about gender differences and hierarchies in the development of professions will lead to an understanding of the (de)professionalization of social work.

It was the merit of the feminist movement of the 1970s and 1980s, and the implementation of feminist theories and gender studies which broadened the perspectives of social work in West Germany. Three main subjects have been stressed and worked out: social work as a female activity; violence against women and girls; social work with young girls and women in youth work and welfare services for the young (Friebertshäuser, Jakob, Klees-Möller, 1997, p. 12). Women's projects in social work practice have been established – women supporting women on the basis of common experiences and common discrimination – with the aim of supporting women and girls in self-determination and autonomy. Many projects developed as a matter of course in social work.

In the case of Spain the incorporation of men into social work was a consequence of the professionalization of social work, and the improvement of labour and salary conditions. However, this incorporation has not changed the female character of social work, because the profession still has the same social functions and there is an important female presence – about 93% of social workers in Aragon are women, only 7% are men. In addition, male social workers are located in the areas of the profession socially defined as less female, that means that they work in child protection and mental health services and they do supervision and management from the highest posts. However, female social workers are located in jobs where caring work is very important, for example work with elderly and disabled people. In relation to professional functions, about 6% of men is in management in comparison to about 1% of women; and about 40% of men does direct work in comparison to about 70% of women. In relation to the importance of the job in their lives, men think that the job is the most important thing in their lives, but women who have family responsibilities think that both are important, and these women social workers find it difficult to combine family and professional work at the same time. Nevertheless, they recognise that these difficulties are minimised by working for the administration as civil servants, they would be far greater in the private sector.

2.6
Outlook on Gender Perspectives in Social Work

Gender issues in social work are important in understanding the process of professionalization, and they should play a central role in social work practice with all service users. It is stimulating to analyse the role of gender in the relationship of professional help. What is needed is a research perspective which analyses the gender and the attitudes of the professionals and the service users. Research studies about gender differences in the treatment of clients in welfare institutions in Scandinavian countries (Kullberg, 2001; Brunnberg, 2001), about "gender and community care" in the United Kingdom (Orme, 2001), and gender-related approaches in different fields of social work in Germany (Böhnisch, Funk, 2002) point in that direction.

Gender stereotypes play an important part in professionals' work: for example in the attribution of responsibility in the family or in the categorisation of "deviant behaviour" in young men and women. The diagnosis or the construction of mental illness is also linked to the social construction of masculinity and femininity. Girls and boys are treated with a gender specific bias by nursery nurses, at school and in all youth care institutions. The demands of "gender mainstreaming" concepts offer social workers the possibility of considering whether the service provision meets the specific needs of girls and boys, and women and men without stereotyping and overemphasising differences, and without ignoring gender differences at the same time.

In our essay we have discussed changes in the process of professionalization of social work, and the meaning of gender differences and gender relations in the profession. To summarise, we can say that it is obvious that there have been similarities and differences in the gender relations within Spanish and German social work since the 1970s. This shows the complex and contradictory development in social work in just two different European countries, and the value of doing further research on this topic in other European countries using a comparative perspective. Finally, from our point of view, the reflection of gender differences and the analysis of gender relations and hierarchies in relation with other concepts of diversity should be integrated into social work practice, theory and research, and education in all European countries.

Bibliography

ÁLVAREZ-URÍA F. (1985), *Los visitadores del pobre. Caridad, economía social y asistencia en la España del Siglo XIX*, in Id. (coord. de), *Cuatro siglos de acción social: de la beneficencia al bienestar social. Seminario de historia de la acción social*, Siglo XXI, Madrid, pp. 117-46.
BÁÑEZ T. (2004), *El trabajo social en Aragón. El proceso de profesionalización de una actividad feminizada*, tesis doctoral, Universidad Rovira y Virgili, Tarragona.
BECKER-SCHMIDT R., KNAPP G.-A. (1995), *Das Geschlechtterverhältnis als Gegenstand der Sozialwissenschaften*, Campus, Frankfurt a.M.-New York.
BÖHNISCH L., FUNK H. (2002), *Soziale Arbeit und Geschlecht. Theoretische und praktische Orientierungen*, Juventa, Weinheim.

BOUQUET B. (1998), *Féminin-masculin chez les assistant(e)s de service social*, in "Vie sociale", 3, pp. 17-36.
BRUNNBERG E. (2001), *Are Boys and Girls Treated in the Same Way by the Social Services?*, in Gruber, Fröschl (2001), pp. 329-48.
CHRISTIE A. (ed.) (2001), *Men and Social Work: Theories and Practices*, Palgrave, London.
DOMINELLI L., MACLEOD E. (1989), *Feminist Social Work*, Macmillan, London.
ESTRUCH J., GÜELL A. M. (1976), *Sociología de una profesión. Los asistentes sociales*, Península, Barcelona.
FRAISSE G., PERROT M. (2000), *Salir*, in G. Duby, M. Perrot (coord. de), *Historia de las mujeres en Occidente*, vol. IV, *El siglo XIX*, Taurus, Madrid, pp. 485-93.
FRIEBERTSHÄUSER B., JAKOB G., KLEES-MÖLLER R. (hrsg.) (1997), *Sozialpädagogik im Blick der Frauenforschung*, Deutscher Studienverlag, Weinheim.
FRIEDLANDER W. A. (1989), *Dinámica del trabajo social*, Pax, México.
FRÖSCHL E. (2001), *Beruf Sozialarbeit*, in Gruber, Fröschl (2001), pp. 285-308.
GALUSKE M., RAUSCHENBACH T. (1994), *Jugendhilfe Ost. Entwicklung, aktuelle Lage und Zukunft eines Arbeitsfeldes*, Juventa, Weinheim.
GRUBER C., FRÖSCHL E. (hrsg.) (2001), *Gender-Aspekte in der sozialen Arbeit*, Czernin, Wien.
HANMER J., STATHAN D. (1999), *Women and Social Work: Towards a Woman-Centred Practice*, Macmillan, London.
HEINTZ B., NADAI E., FISCHER R., UMMEL H. (1997), *Ungleich unter Gleichen. Studien zur geschlechtsspezifischen Segregation des Arbeitsmarktes*, Campus, Frankfurt a.M.-New York.
HUME S., BENVENUTI P., GRISTINA D., RIEGE M. (1998), *Paradox in Professional Practice – Women's Views of Social Work: A Tri-National Study in England, Germany and Italy*, in "European Journal of Social Work", 1, 1, pp. 55-70.
KLEIBL S. (1998), *Frauenkarrieren im sozialen Dienstleistungssektor: Entwicklungslinien, Gegenwartsanalysen und Zukunftsperspektiven im 21. Jahrhundert*, in U. Gintzel et al. (hrsg.), *Jahrbuch der Sozialen Arbeit 1999. Soziale Arbeit im 21. Jahrhundert*, Votum, Münster, pp. 208-21.
KNAPP G.-A. (2002), *Dezentriert und viel riskiert: Anmerkungen zur These vom Bedeutungsverlust der Kategorie Geschlecht*, in G.-A. Knapp, A. Wetterer (hrsg.), *Soziale Verortung der Geschlechter. Gesellschaftstheorie und feministische Kritik*, Westfälisches Dampfboot, Münster, pp. 15-62.
KULLBERG C. (2001), *Gender and Social Work: Research on Gender Differences in the Treatment of Clients in Welfare Institutions*, in Gruber, Fröschl (2001), pp. 309-27.
ORME J. (2001), *Gender and Community Care: Social Work and Social Care Perspectives*, Palgrave, Basingstoke.
RATER-GARCETTE C. (1996), *La professionnalisation du travail social. Action sociale, syndicalisme, formation, 1880-1920*, L'Harmattan, Paris.
RIEGE M. (1996), *Frauen in der sozialen Arbeit. Deutsche, englische und italienische Sozialarbeiterinnen im Vergleich*, Fachhochschule Niederrhein, Fachbereich Sozialwesen, Mönchengladbach.

SANTALLA LÓPEZ M. (1995), *Concepción Arenal y el feminismo católico español*, Ediciós do Castro, La Coruña.
SCHERR A. (2002), *Männer als Adressaten und Berufsgruppe in der sozialen Arbeit*, in W. Thole (hrsg.), *Grundriss soziale Arbeit. Ein einführendes Handbuch*, Leske + Budrich, Opladen, pp. 379-85.
SPELMAN E. V. (1988), *Inessential Woman: Problems of Exclusion in Feminist Thought*, Beacon Press, Boston.
VÁZQUEZ J. M. (1971), *Situación del servicio social en España*, Instituto de Sociología aplicada, Madrid.
WALKOWITZ J. R. (1995), *La ciudad de las pasiones terribles. Narraciones sobre el peligro sexual en el Londres victoriano*, Cátedra, Madrid.
WESSELS C. (1994), *Das soziale Ehrenamt im Modernisierungsprozess. Chancen und Risiken des Einsatzes beruflich qualifizierter Frauen*, Centaurus-Verlagsgesellschaft, Pfaffenweiler.

3

The Welfare State, Third Sector, and Family in Italy: A Comparison with the German Model

by *Vincenzo Fortunato*

3.1
Introduction

This chapter deals with the system of the Italian welfare State, focusing attention on the role of the actors (the State, the market, families, the third sector) and on the main characteristic features of the model as it appears after the changes which have occurred in the last few years. In particular the analysis explores the solidaristic nature of the Italian welfare State which has traditionally been based on the key role played by families. The State has completely delegated most of the care functions to families, for example, looking after elderly people, children with disabilities etc. This analysis also looks at differences between the Italian model and other European models. Bearing this in mind, this analysis also underlines the attempts of the Italian government to move from a concept of "passive" to one of "active" subsidiarity by following the German example in which families receive greater attention from the State in terms of both financial support and legal recognition. In fact this is one of the aims of the last Italian law on social work 8 November 2000, n. 328 (Maggian, 2001), which defines as a priority the family in its role as social agent.

We must also bear in mind that family policy in Germany has always been ambivalent. Whether or not the family still holds its social meaning as the classical model of reproduction is a disputed question. Also it is not always clear whether the family is a private area or whether family policy should convert the family to a collective property, which then becomes organised within the realm of public responsibility. The public interest of securing future generations comes into conflict with the private decisions of young couples to become parents. At the same time young parents become secluded, because interest in them is not socially sustained. In addition, German family policy never dropped the ideal of the housewife and marriage and did not – as French social policy did as early as the 19th century – secure future generations by recognising that having a family/being a woman and having paid work were compatible.

With everything that is produced as family-political achievements, we nevertheless can talk with Franz-Xaver Kaufmann about the structural lack of consideration of the German family and social politics in relation to families. This appears in several dimensions.

1. Children are not uncomplicatedly accepted as resources for the society, but accepted as future payer of the pensions. In the public, in the policy and in social contexts they are not perceived as participants and are at best interesting for the consumer and leisure markets.

2. The State gives little consideration to the family. Where the State does protect the family, it has a specific model on the basis of its ideas about order, namely the middle-class nuclear family: father and mother are married and they have their own birth children. Since the general Prussian land rights (*Landrecht*, 1794) and the *Allgemeine Bürgerliche Gesetzbuch* in Austria (1811), i.e. the *Code civil* (1804), what is understood by a family has been made clear – it is the middle-class family. This middle-class family is nationally protected, which does not always mean financially supported. The past achievements of the familial distribution of burdens (*Familienlastenausgleich*) have been very small.

Distribution should solve three problems:
– first, it should cover the actual costs, which families have with the education of their children;
– second, the income losses should be compensated, which usually result with the loss of an income through parenthood;
– thirdly, it should prevent or lift social inequalities, which result from the socio-economic status of families.

Within this framework we have also analysed the role and the nature of the so-called third sector (social co-operations, charity associations, families' associations, social foundations etc.) which has become one of the main actors involved in social work since the 1970s. The rise of the third sector has deeply contributed to redefine the nature of the Italian welfare State, initiating a move towards what the experts call welfare mix, in which public and private organisations work together on a social agenda.

3.2
The Welfare States in Europe

Several scholars and experts in social policy at an international level agree on the fact that in Europe there exist different models or schemes of social protection. One of the most famous attempts to classify the different national cases is that of Esping-Andersen (1990) who proposed a typology of the different social policy models within the OECD member-States. According to Esping-Andersen, European countries are grouped around clusters that he defines *The Three Worlds of Welfare Capitalism*: the liberal, the social-democratic, and the conservative-corporate. Each one of these three models is characterised by different relations and a different equilibrium between the three main actors of social policies: the State, the market and the family.

The United States, Canada and Great Britain belong to the first group. Within the liberal model the main mechanism of social integration and regulation is represented by the market; the State is considered as residual and intervenes only when both the market and the family have failed in the process of resource allocation. Thus, the welfare State is mainly constituted by programmes of social assistance addressed only to people who pass a means test related to the lack of the necessary means for subsistence. In the social-democratic model, typical of the Scandinavian countries, the main actor of social policies is the State, whereas only a marginal role is attributed to the market and to families. Social policies are eminently universalistic and consist in particularly generous monetary transfers towards the weakest and poorest categories of the population. The third model, the conservative-corporate, groups together the continental European countries such as Germany, France, Belgium, Italy etc. The main characteristic features of this model are represented by the prevalent occupational nature of social policies based on the system of compulsory social insurances, originally designed by Bismarck at the end of the 19th century. The State maintains a high capacity for regulation, but it delegates several care functions to families. Within this model the market has only a very marginal role.

The classification presented by Esping-Andersen represents, without any doubt, a significant contribution to international study on social policies and welfare models. Nevertheless, from the mid-1990s several studies and researches (Ferrera, 1993, 1998; González, Jurado, Naldini, 2000; Naldini, 2003) emerged to develop further the Esping-Andersen analysis. In particular, these authors suggest a new classification of Europe according to four, and not three, models of social protection. This is represented by a new paradigm defined familistic to which the southern European countries, such as Italy, Spain, Greece and Portugal, would belong.

Therefore, starting from the analysis of the literature on European welfare States, it is necessary to articulate clearly the reasons that led international scholars to revisit the Esping-Andersen analysis. In particular it is necessary to explain the main characteristic features of the new model as being mainly opposed to the conservative-corporate model of continental Europe. As a result, a comparison between two countries, Germany and Italy, will explain similarities and differences, and may be interesting.

The starting point of our analysis concerns above all the role played by families in both countries. In fact, as Saraceno (2003) argues, in both countries the relation between the State, the market and families, in providing services and redistributing resources, is highly unbalanced towards families. However, there are significant differences mainly related to the importance with which families are recognised and legitimated by the State as "official" care givers. In particular, in Germany the family is not only the main institution with reference to social matters, but, from an Italian point of view, it is also an institution supported by particularly generous social policies. With regard to families, the German system of social assistance includes, other than a series of fiscal exemptions for disadvantaged people, measures exclusively directed to the social protection of children. These measures concern, for example:
– family allowance (*Kindergeld*) which is paid for all children up to the age of 18 years (or if the children are studying or in training up to the age of 27 years) in order to assist the parents to maintain the children;
– education subsidy (*Erziehungsgeld*) which has been paid to parents since 1986: it is awarded for a maximum of two years if one of the parents takes care of the child and does not work more than 19 hours per week;
– the "education leave" (*Erziehungsurlaub*) guarantees specific social rights: e.g. those parents within employment can leave their job for a maximum of three years and still be protected against unlawful dismissal;
– the *Federal Educational Grants Act* (*Bundesausbildungsförderungsgesetz*), which offers grants under the condition that a student or those responsible for his/her maintenance do not have the necessary means; but these grants are mainly given as interest-free loans and they have to be paid back.

In this way, the State realises the principle which may be defined as active subsidiarity. In contrast with Italy, Germany has a written warranty on marriage and the family and it is also embedded within the welfare State. However, neither the State nor the municipality can regulate the problems that families have; that would be a public task (e.g. within the range of education).

On the contrary, the Italian situation is characterised by a different relationship between the State and the family. In fact, the family is considered as an explicit partner of the State (Saraceno, 1994) when it comes to the management of social policies. However, the family has not yet the formal acknowledgement, legitimation and, above all, financial support which it needs to carry out the many care tasks that are "delegated" to it. Hence there is only a partially accomplished subsidiarity or, better, a "passive subsidiarity" which has deep repercussions on the quality and effectiveness of social policies.

In other words, as Rossi (1998, p. 72) argues, "when we talk about care in Italy, we find ourselves talking about the family and, especially, women who, within the family, represent the main care giver". In this country, in fact, "un-marketing", that is to say rescuing a person from the dependence of the market, is still a task for families, and women in particular, when dealing with care needs of children, disabled or elderly people, who are no longer self-sufficient. However, the central role which is played by the family is not followed by an appropriate attention in terms of social policies with regard to women and families in general. On the contrary, the paradox of Italian welfare is represented by the very lack of a social policy which considers the role played by families and their needs. This is essentially due to cultural models, values and ideologies that, from time immemorial, have characterised the Italian case. For instance, Saraceno (2003, p. 15) states that the lack of a social policy on the family

may be explained as a strategy to avoid open conflicts and clear choices in a field in which there are social values and expectations which are in tension, if not contradictory, among themselves. There are, for example: conflicts between the value of gender equality (only formally acknowledged) and behaviour expectations which are still based on a gender distinction in job access; conflicts between the value of unity and family solidarity, on the one hand, and the value given to individual autonomy, on the other hand; conflicts between the value of privacy and social responsibility.

Consequently, in comparison with other European countries, in Italy policies supporting the family were often a secondary result of category policies, rather than measures exclusively thought out and aimed at satisfying family needs. Nevertheless, in recent years, it seems that something has been changing for Italian families. In fact, after the approval of the law 328/2000, on the reform of social assistance, and the law 8 March 2000, n. 53, on parental leaves, a series of interventions and measures was planned to support families. The law 328/2000, in particular, provides for fully realising the above mentioned active subsidiarity, by acknowledging, supporting and stressing the family's role as an active subject in the fields of education and care of the person, promotion of social welfare, and cohesion. In this regard, the outline law provides for both support services to the family (e.g. in order to encourage parenthood, to support families giving domiciliary assistance to elderly people etc.) and financial advantages (to the families which provide hospitality and care services to children in custody orders, disabled and elderly people etc.). The same law also provides for tax concessions on expenses for the protection and care of those members of the family who are disabled or not self-sufficient. The second difference between the Italian case, on the one hand, and the German case and corporate model, on the other hand, is represented, as Ferrera (1998) points out, by the high particularism of welfare in Italy and southern European countries. This particularism concerns both service providers and financers. The State's weakness, the high involvement of political parties and pressure groups, and the growth of nepotism are all factors which characterise this model and distinguish it from others present in Europe.

3.3
From Welfare State to Welfare Mix: The Rise of Third Sector in Italy

Both the existence of a culture which is deeply oriented towards social solidarity – typical of the so-called caring societies – and the spread of particularism played a central role in the transformation process which involved the welfare models in recent years, thus contributing to stress the peculiarity of the Italian case even further when compared to other European countries. Starting in the 1970s, the welfare State showed clear signs of a probably irreversible crisis, due to the failing of all those factors which previously had allowed its development. Those factors are full-time employment, the prevalence of paid work over care work, the gender-based division of labour, the weak citizenship of women and, finally, population stability. The State thus began a slow and gradual transformation process which resulted in a search for ways and models that allowed for the effective expression of new questions (the new poor; social exclusion due to transformations within family models and labour organisation; new forms of juvenile discomfort; new characteristics and problems due to emigration etc.). As Ascoli (1999, p. 14) points out,

> the search for new balances and instruments everywhere goes through a process of overcoming the duality between the State and the market, and the evaluation of action fields rescued both from market processes and the public authority's field. These action fields are based on charity services, reciprocity, solidarity, unmarketed 'production' of relationship and sociability.

Owing to the crisis of the welfare State, all of Europe went through a privatisation or, as some authors state, de-nationalisation process of national assistance. The consequence of this process was the increase of those collective subjects (e.g. charity groups, social co-operatives, foundations, ONLUS, self-help groups, and social associations) which fall within that category known as the third sector. The growth of third sector organisations, and also non-profit making organisations, was in fact followed by an increase in relations between these organisations and the public sector, and consequently by a gradual decrease in State intervention and a significant increase in the quantity of tasks allocated to the private social field. Hence the passage from the traditional welfare State to what literature by now calls welfare mix, that is a model of social protection which results from the interaction between the State and private individuals.

If on the one hand this trend has been common to all European countries and the United States for some years, the privatisation process assumes in Italy some distinctive features which are related to the historic and cultural characteristics of the third sector in this country. In general, when we talk of the third sector in Italy, we refer to an extremely fragmented field which finds it difficult to emerge within a context which appears hostile to the development of a ripe and wide non-profit making sector. This hypothesis is supported by some research (Barbetta, 1996; Ranci, 1999a) according to which the economic size of the third sector in Italy is rather lower than the average for other European countries: it is about 1.8% compared to 4.2% in France, 4% in Great Britain and 3.8% in Germany.

These data, however, require a more thorough and, above all, up-to-date analysis of the economic and numerical size of non-profit making organisations in our country. Even today, one of the main characteristics of the third sector is the fragmentary quality of initiatives. In fact, it is sufficient to take a look at the large number of organisations which act in the social field to account immediately for the often different objectives, models, ruling references and users. However, there are several signs which confirm the success of non-profit making organisations in Italy in terms both of their increase and legitimation on the part of the State (cf. outline law 328/2000). The third sector, indeed, includes over 220,000 different organisations with over 680,000 paid agents and 3 million volunteers (TAB. 3.1).

TABLE 3.1
Non-profit organisations in Italy (2002)

	Institutions	Paid employment	Volunteers
Social associations (cultural, recreational, sports associations)	202,061	281,099	3,039,088
Social co-operatives	6,952	196,067	15,934
Foundations	3,088	56,145	65,432
Charity organisations*	26,403	43,600	968,000
NGOs	170	–	1,526
Committees	3,832	1,813	39,224
Other typologies	7,861	146,571	94,009
Total	250,367	725,295	4,223,213

* Some charity organisations are included among social associations.
Source: CENSIS (2003).

TAB. 3.1 clearly indicates that the most significant part of the third sector is represented by social associations (90%), which have over 3 million volunteers and 281,099 paid agents. The next most significant sector is represented by charity organisations and social co-operatives. These two latter typologies, which are central to the Italian model, have deeply different characteristics. In fact, the ideal matrix of the engagement in charity services is a volunteer involvement, whereas the number of paid agents is the least. On the contrary, social co-operatives represent the most professional organisational field of the third sector and that closest to the for-profit bodies. Within it, paid staff predominates whereas volunteers represent only 7.5% of the staff used.

A particularly interesting piece of data, which characterises the Italian non-profit organisations, concerns the activities sectors in which organisations act. First of all, 38% of Italian non-profit organisations takes part in at least two activities. If we analyse in detail the social associations, which are the most numerous component of the third sector, we may note that the most consistent intervention sector (cf. TAB. 3.2) is represented by sports activities (27.7%), then cultural and art activities (19%) and finally social assistance services (7.2%). As a whole, 88% of non-profit organisations acts in sectors other than health and social assistance.

TABLE 3.2
Composition and employment of Italian non-profit organisations (2002)

Activities	Institutions		Paid employment		Volunteers	
	N.	%	N.	%	N.	%
Culture and arts	38,368	19.0	19,411	6.9	460,712	15.2
Sports	56,044	27.7	20,458	7.3	559,352	18.4
Recreation and socialisation	40,557	20.1	10,936	3.9	599,176	19.7
Education and research	8,307	4.1	50,427	17.9	59,670	2.0
Health	8,821	4.4	37,410	13.3	311,908	10.3
Social services	14,648	7.2	58,867	20.9	466,190	15.3
Environment	3,012	1.5	1,816	0.6	82,972	2.7
Economic development and social cohesion	3,244	1.6	12,400	4.4	29,540	1.0
Advocacy	6,532	3.2	11,480	4.1	206,459	6.8
Philanthropy	1,015	0.5	340	0.1	44,347	1.5
Co-operation and international solidarity	1,265	0.6	993	0.4	31,565	1.0
Religion	3,847	1.9	2,632	0.9	114,290	3.8
Business and professional	15,471	7.7	51,989	18.5	64,190	2.1
Other activities	929	0.5	1,940	0.7	8,717	0.3
Total	202,060	100.0	281,099	100.0	3,039,088	100.0

Source: CENSIS (2003).

The tendency to diversify and to widen activities in sectors other than the traditional ones of social assistance and health is also present in charity organisations. In particular, there is an increase in the number of organisations which act in the sectors of sport and recreational promotion, and in civil protection. To some extent these changes reflect a wider view of the so-called mission of the third sector. Attention is in fact moving more and more towards the context and causes of exclusion and discomfort, and less and less towards the individual. In other words, the community dimension prevails over the individual, because the system of intervention is aimed at reconstructing relationships, memberships and solidarity. So, this new view gives rise to a new non-profit making characterisation and organisation.

If we look at the composition of the German non-profit sector (TAB. 3.3) it appears that there is a similar trend towards diversification, but with some specific features which are in opposition to the Italian situation. In particular, non-profit organisations engaged in the areas of culture and recreation rank first (35.8%), but social services still have a large diffusion with 130,000 organisations (29.2%) and they play a significant role. This wider diffusion and involvement of social services organisations probably reduces the area of intervention, and affects the duties of German families who may rely on the well-established, non-profit organisations which provide professional services.

TABLE 3.3
Non-profit organisations in Germany (1997)

	Institutions	
Activities	N	%
Culture and recreation	60,100	35.8
Education and research	10,000	2.2
Health	3,600	0.8
Social services	130,000	29.2
Environment	30,000	6.7
Economic development, housing	1,500	0.3
Advocacy/civic	40,000	9.0
Philanthropy/foundations	6,000	1.3
International activities	400	0.1
Religion	30,000	6.7
Business and professional/ unions	5,000	1.2
Other activities	30,000	6.7
Total	346,600	100.0

Source: Johns Hopkins Comparative Nonprofit Sector Project, in Zimmer, Priller (2000), p. 222.

Another consideration concerns the economic size of the Italian third sector. TAB. 3.2 highlights how the number of staff engaged in the health and social assistance fields is equal to 13.3% (37,410) and 20.9% (58,867) respectively. On the contrary, if we consider the size of the German third sector (TAB. 3.4), we can see that the proportion of agents engaged in the health field increases to 30.6% (441,000), whereas that of agents engaged in social services is equal to 38.8% (559,500). In fact, as Anheier (2001, p. 81) argues, "in terms of its composition the German nonprofit sector is health and social service dominant". According to Zimmer and Priller (2000, p. 216), the prominent position of both health and social services within the German non-profit sector

is incorporated in the 'principle of subsidiarity'. The specific interpretation of this principle in German law gives preference to non-profit over public and commercial provision of core social services. Non-profit organisations active in welfare-related fields are in the majority affiliated with the German Welfare Associations, which are quite unique in terms of their history and their closeness to the State.

In other words there is a close relationship between the State and the organisations engaged in health and social services, and these organisations are strongly supported by public grants and reimbursements of social insurance.

TABLE 3.4
Composition and employment of German non-profit organisations (1995)

Activities	Paid employment		Volunteers
	N.	%	%
Culture and recreation	77,350	5.4	40.8
Education and research	168,000	11.7	1.5
Health	441,000	30.6	8.7
Social services	559,500	38.8	10.1
Environment	12,000	0.8	5.7
Economic development, housing	87,850	6.1	2.0
Advocacy/civic	23,700	1.6	5.7
Philanthropy/foundations	5,400	0.4	2.0
International activities	9,750	0.7	2.9
Business and professional/unions	55,800	3.9	4.8
Not elsewhere classified			5.8
Total	1,440,350	100.0	100.0

Source: Johns Hopkins Comparative Nonprofit Sector Project, in Zimmer, Priller (2000), p. 227.

Due to the fragmented nature of the Italian non-profit sector and the weakness of the social service's area of intervention, the actor who is gaining a more and more important role within the Italian third sector is represented by families' and friends' associations, and self-help groups. The family, in particular, has become a strategic knot of social groups, thus carrying out tasks in many social fields. In fact, according to CENSIS (2003) data, Italian families give full assistance to about 76% of not-self-sufficient elderly people and 74.3% of infirm and disabled people. In addition, 17.4% of not-self-sufficient elderly people and 24.4% of infirm and disabled people receive assistance from families with the collaboration of doctors and social agents. In terms of economic data, the monetary value of the assistance that families grant to not-self-sufficient elderly people amounts to 75 billion Euros. Within families, grandparents also play an important role, considering the fact that 40% of children up to 14 years of age, and about 50% of those up to 2 years of age are looked after by grandparents, when not by their parents. Finally, we should not disregard the so-called gift associations through which non-organised altruism and solidarity show themselves. In this way, about 34% of Italian families grants free help to other people, by providing various services such as, for instance, elderly assistance, domestic services, settlement of bureaucratic matters etc. Every year, as a whole, the help-hours which Italians grant to needy people amount to over 231 millions.

3.4
Social Workers in the Third Sector in Comparison with the Public Sector

The development and growth of the third sector in Italy and all over Europe focus attention on the different roles and professional conditions of non-profit social workers when compared to traditional workers engaged in the public sector. At this end, it is possible to reconstruct a sort of identikit of non-profit social workers, it is also possible to analyse the most significant differences between them and the social workers who, instead, work in the public sector. These differences mainly relate to social labour, the motivations on which choices are based, working conditions and the level of job satisfaction.

Data is, first of all, related to the total number of social workers who are engaged in the non-profit field. As in TAB. 3.1, there are 725,295 Italian paid workers, of whom 60.1% are women. This means that this profession mostly interests women with a medium-high education level. Most workers (37.7%) possess a diploma, whereas 16.5% has a degree and 19.5% holds a professional qualification.

As CENSIS (2003) points out, most non-profit workers engage with this profession occasionally, without a long-term plan. In fact, 30.7% of people got in touch with the body or organisation in which they informally work through a recommendation by friends or relatives, whereas 16.9% got in touch with the same organisation because they worked within the local context. Non-profit and charity bodies act as access points to the labour market, given that 27.5% of agents was unemployed whereas 31.5% was part of no labour force. Unlike the public sector, which is accessible through public competition, non-profit organisations are more flexible and dynamic, and encourage the access and above all the voluntary passage from, and to, other sectors. They, thus, give workers the possibility of more effectively reconciling their job with their own ideals and, first of all, their family needs. This greater flexibility, along with the provision of highly qualified services, is one of the main factors for the success of the Italian third sector.

However, the most significant differences between agents working in public and private social services are those with reference to motivations, working conditions and levels of personal satisfaction. As for motivations, Borzaga (2001) points out the presence of two different types of motivations. He distinguishes, in particular, two main motivations which provide the basis for the choice to work in the social field. On the one hand, Borzaga defines the interest in the social field and of the workings of the organisation as intrinsic motivations; remuneration, the need for stable employment, the possibility of reconciling job and other extra-job activities are defined as extrinsic motivations. In response, this study first of all points out that intrinsic and ideal motivations are dominant, though they do not seem exclusive. Moreover, if we go into details, we may note that those most interested in working in the social field are those who act in the non-profit sector and, in particular, in social cooperatives. The most characteristic elements of the activity of these agents concern not as much the contractual aspects of the job, but subjective perceptions of one's own job, in the meaning that the job gives to one's own activity. On the contrary, social workers in public bodies show a low level of ideal motivation. This is probably due, as Borzaga (2001, p. 85) himself argues, to the fact that "The employment in the public sector was the result of passing a public competition in which, often at least in the past, one took part without strong motivations".

Also in the German context the ideal motivation seems to prevail in non-profit organisations. This is particularly true for volunteers; in fact, according to the results of the *Johns Hopkins Comparative Nonprofit Sector Project* (Zimmer, Priller, 2000, p. 226), 'having fun' ranks first among the reasons to engage in volunteer activities. Further motivations are 'to meet people and to make friends' or 'to stay active'. Beside these rather hedonistic motivations, Germans engage in volunteering because they try 'to help other people' or because they 'want to put their knowledge to use'.

With regard to working conditions, agents of the non-profit sector work under not particularly satisfying conditions in terms of working hours, the possibility of having a successful career and, first of all, remuneration. In comparison with the public sector, indeed, working hours are longer and the average remuneration level is lower, even when workers have the same level of education and undertake the same duties.

Finally, it is particularly important to analyse the level of satisfaction of Italian social workers. From a comparison between public and private sectors, it emerged first of all that public sector workers are less motivated and are less satisfied with both their job and the organisation in which they work, although they do have higher remuneration, better career possibilities and job security. The satisfaction level of workers, on the contrary, significantly increases in the case of non-profit organisations which – as we have already said – are characterised by a higher precariousness of employment, longer working hours and lower remuneration in comparison with the public sector. What is, then, the reason for the difference in satisfaction levels between social workers in the public and private sectors? The answer to this question is to be found, in our opinion, in the relation between organisations and social workers. The satisfaction level of agents, in particular, and consequently organisation performances are strictly connected to the type of the organisation, social structure and modalities in domestic relations management. Indeed, the appeal to essentially economic incentives in public structures does not seem capable of effectively stimulating and gratifying social workers who work for organisations in which spaces for informality and autonomy decrease, whereas control increases greatly. In non-profit organisations, on the other hand, the "human factor", as Mayo (1945) saw it, is satisfied by the realisation of a more socially pleasant, harmonious and recreational work environment, by reducing tensions among workers and between workers and organisations. Non-profit agents, then, give a higher value to psychosocial elements, such as more autonomy, flexibility, a level of involvement in decision-making, than to remuneration and other structural aspects.

Such a deep gap in the satisfaction level among social workers is opposed to the argument that considers non-profit a makeshift solution on the part of those agents who have not found an employment opportunity in the public sector. In recent years, the very opposite has been happening as a consequence of organisational "managerialisation", and the rationalisation process in socio-health and socio-assistant services. This means that an increasing number of workers – above all, women – are *choosing* to leave their job in the public sector and begin a new job within the third sector.

In general, it is possible to assert that, among the most successful factors of the growing third sector, is its capacity to conciliate economic and psycho-social incentives (Barnard, 1938) or, better (Borzaga, 2001, p. 107),

the construction of a balanced series of monetary and non-monetary rewards, able to counterbalance lower remuneration (with a consequently higher rate of competitiveness in a sector where the staff represent the prevailing part of the costs) with extra-economic gratifications consisting of management-sharing, transparency and evidence of the social benefits produced.

3.5
Conclusions

This chapter tried to outline, though briefly, some of the main characteristics of the Italian welfare system, in relation to the German system and to the main social protection models in Europe, paying a particular attention to the role of social actors and, first of all, the family. In addition, I tried to describe some of the most significant changes in the social field, due to the increasing privatisation of assistance, in the attempt to identify possible implications for social development workers of the sector in question.

This chapter, first of all, highlights the peculiarities of the Italian case which may not be included within the corporate model of continental European countries. In fact, although the origins are common to the German model, as is the essentially employment-based nature of a large part of social policy, the Italian scheme has some peculiarities which make necessary a new classification of social protection models.

Apart from the influence of historic, cultural and political factors which often caused particularistic and patronage drifts in the management of public policies and, in particular, social policies, the peculiarity of the Italian welfare State comes from its deeply solidaristic nature. In other words, it is not possible to understand the peculiarity and essence of the Italian social reality (Rossi, 1998, p. 71):

If we do not consider the peculiar relation, within our context, between organised and informal solidarity; the care behaviour, which is typical of primary nets, and the inclination to a solidaristic 'solution' (which is now commonly defined as community care) within the context of social services.

Italy, thus, appears as a caring society where the family acts as the main partner of the State, with regard to social assistance, thus loading itself with a series of care tasks towards not-self-sufficient elderly and disabled people, and minors. Nevertheless, as opposed to Germany, the Italian family is a partner whose importance is only partially acknowledged since subsidiarity, that is the "proxy" to families by the State in order to carry out care tasks, neither leads in practice to the legitimation of the functions played, nor to economic aid and support services. Consequently, in comparison to the central role played by the family, the attention of the government in terms of social policies is insufficient and fragmented.

Some signs of a renewed attention to Italian families come from the law 328/2000 concerning assistance and social services reform, which puts the family, as one of main care givers, at the centre of attention. Nevertheless, given the non-implementation of this law on the part of most Italian Regions, it is still too early to make an evaluation and assert that things are really changing. Rather, important transformations concern the relation between the government and the multiplicity of those subjects, represented by civil society, which in Italy and Europe are known as the third sector. In particular, we are witnessing a slow and gradual privatisation or, better, a de-nationalisation process which finds implementation through the supply of socio-assistant services provided by third sector bodies. These organisations are financed by public institutions for all services provided by virtue of a convention mechanism (contracting-out). Hence, there has been a change in the role of the government, and public institutions, in particular, as they have moved from being suppliers of social services to be, on one the hand "enablers, that is those who help ensure the increase in the private resources able to provide services, and on the other hand, responsible for planning and financing those services" (Pavolini, 2003, p. 29).

However, one of main factors for the development of the third sector lies in this renewed and more complex function of the State. In fact, it is the insufficiently Weberian nature of the Italian government, along with the limited capacity of the public authorities to develop a form of effective regulation, less and less based on management and more and more on planning, which causes a certain amount of concern. As Ranci (1999b, p. 89) argues, the solution passes through forms of social policy and service co-planning; the novelty and the power of the welfare mix lie in

the very experiment of new forms of co-operation aimed at defining regulation forms produced through a consultation mechanism, whose respect is guaranteed not as much through the problematic application of a higher administrative control, as through the co-division of objectives and results to be reached by all actors.

Finally, it is useful to consider the role of third sector social workers as subjects who are more and more involved in playing a first-rate role in programming and managing intervention and social services, according to that provided for by law 328/2000. My analysis, indeed, highlights particularly important data. First of all, the increase in the number of social workers who choose to work in the non-profit sector. Then, the deeper motivation and, above all, the satisfaction of third sector social worker. As has already been said with regard to public structures, non-profit organisations are more flexible and characterised by a higher informality in social relations. In addition, they implement a policy of management of human capital which is able to more effectively motivate social workers through a more balanced mix of material and immaterial incentives, despite lower remuneration, more prejudicial working hours, and a higher uncertainty in terms of employment stability. As a result, third sector organisations, in relation to their nature and particular organisational structure, seem more able to increase the value of specialist knowledge and worker professionalism than the public sector and, consequently, to grant qualitatively better performances and services to users.

Bibliography

ANHEIER H. K. (2001), *A Socio-Economic Profile of the Nonprofit Sector in Germany*, in H. K. Anheier, W. Seibel (eds.), *The Nonprofit Sector in Germany: Between State, Economy, and Society*, Manchester University Press, Manchester, pp. 70-136.

ANHEIER H. K., PRILLER E., ZIMMER A. (2000), *Zur zivilgesellschaftlichen Dimension des Dritten Sektors*, in H. D. Klingemann, F. Neidhardt (hrsg.), *Zur Zukunft der Demokratie. Herausforderungen im Zeitalter der Globalisierung*, Sigma, Berlin, pp. 71-98.

ASCOLI U. (a cura di) (1999), *Il welfare futuro. Manuale critico del terzo settore*, Carocci, Roma.

BARBETTA P. (a cura di) (1996), *Senza scopo di lucro. Dimensioni economiche, legislazione e politiche del settore non-profit in Italia*, Il Mulino, Bologna.

BARNARD C. I. (1938), *The Functions of the Executive*, Harvard University Press, Cambridge (MA).

BORZAGA C. (2001), *Qualità del lavoro e soddisfazione dei lavoratori nei servizi sociali: un'analisi comparata tra modelli di gestione*, in AA.VV., *Rapporto sulla situazione del servizio sociale. 1° Rapporto, Roma 2001*, EISS, Roma, pp. 73-108.

CENSIS (2003), *Verso una nuova mappa della società italiana. Un mese di sociale 2002*, Franco Angeli, Milano.

ESPING-ANDERSEN G. (1990), *The Three Worlds of Welfare Capitalism*, Polity Press, Cambridge.

FERRERA M. (1993), *Modelli di solidarietà. Politica e riforme sociali nelle democrazie*, Il Mulino, Bologna.

ID. (1998), *Le trappole del welfare*, Il Mulino, Bologna.
GONZÁLEZ M. J., JURADO T., NALDINI M. (eds.) (2000), *Gender Inequalities in Southern Europe: Women, Work, and Welfare in the 1990s*, Frank Cass, London.
MAGGIAN R. (2001), *Il sistema integrato dell'assistenza. Guida alla legge 328/2000*, Carocci, Roma.
MAYO E. (1945), *The Social Problems of an Industrial Civilization*, Division of Research, Graduate School of Business Administration, Harvard University, Boston.
NALDINI M. (2003), *The Family in the Mediterranean Welfare State*, Frank Cass, London.
PAVOLINI E. (2003), *Le nuove politiche sociali. I sistemi di welfare fra istituzioni e società civile*, Il Mulino, Bologna.
RANCI C. (1999a), *La crescita del terzo settore in Italia nell'ultimo ventennio*, in Ascoli (1999), pp. 59-93.
ID. (1999b), *Oltre il welfare state. Terzo settore, nuove solidarietà e trasformazioni del welfare*, Il Mulino, Bologna.
ROSSI G. (1998), *Il caso italiano*, in P. Donati (a cura di), *Sociologia del terzo settore*, Carocci, Roma, pp. 61-85.
SARACENO C. (1994), *The Ambivalent Familialism of the Italian Welfare State*, in "Social Politics", 1, pp. 60-82.
EAD. (2003), *Mutamenti della famiglia e politiche sociali in Italia*, Il Mulino, Bologna.
ZIMMER A., PRILLER E. (2000), *The Third Sector and Labour Market Policy in Germany*, in "German Policies Studies/Politikfeldanalyse", 1, 2, pp. 209-38.

4
The Ethics and Political Function of Social Work

by *Gérard Moussu*

4.1
Introduction

When analysing the areas of activity in which the social worker is involved it is perfectly legitimate to approach the question in one of a variety of ways, these can be either rational or economic, ethical or political. In this chapter I will analyse why there have been changes in the way social work is viewed and considered, in particular, why examining the question in the context of an "ethical interrogation" has given an entirely new perspective to our definition of social work. This analysis is based on historical and sociological references in a European context.

First I will analyse the transformations that have occurred in the definition of social work, and put forward the following hypothesis: a reaffirmation of the basic tenets of social work has occurred as a result of the application of critical sociology and moral and political philosophy, all of which place justice, equity and the individual subject at the heart of the matter. Next I will present a comparative analysis to examine whether this hypothesis can be sustained in European countries characterised by distinct histories and social and political realities.

Over and above differences associated with economic and social development models, I will try to demonstrate that there is a common trend in Europe concerning the reaffirmation of professional conceptions of social work. The model that emerges can be seen to emphasise the importance that should be given to the choices of individuals and groups affected by social work. It is therefore the ethical dimension that is established as the central point of reference, enabling us to apply therapeutic, social or educational responses. We are about to witness a major transformation in the way in which social work is defined, with the ethical standpoint being a political resource to promote action for the benefit of different public groups: families in difficulty, young people, the disabled etc.

4.2
Between Norms and Strategies:
The Question of Ethics in Social Work

The areas of activity that fall into the domain of social work are always challenged, and rightly so, and over the last ten years this questioning has been more critical, based on rational, ethical or political approaches.
– *Rational*: as with education or health, we wonder what benefits have been derived from allocating more and more resources to social work over the last twenty years. The fashion for evaluating public policies has had a series of repercussions on the effects of technical decisions taken in one sector or other: hostel or host family; help at home or specialised placement; targeted prevention or cultural mediation; type of social support for those on minimum income levels. For each of these ways of dealing with a social problem there is the question of how to measure the effects of the choices made.
– *Ethical*: many professionals are now more and more anxious to compare the conceptions underlying their practices with a philosophical viewpoint which is totally separate from immediate political issues.
– *Political*: one of the effects of decentralisation in particular has been to bring together those who implement decisions and the elected representatives, and thus stimulate reflection on the political aspects of social work in a context that is less ideologically predefined than was the case in the 1970s. At that time the influence of critical sociology prevented any socio-political analysis of social work that was not based on the conceptions of social control and social monitoring.

During the 1990s a series of studies was produced in relation to the second type of approach: ethical concerns have replaced the radical critique that predominated in the 1970s. In this respect, the most often quoted theoretical references say a lot about this movement of ideas. In France the 1970s were dominated by critical sociology and psychoanalysis; Michel Foucault and Jacques Lacan were the key references of this period. In the 1980s the Bourdieu movement stood out, then shared its influence with a philosophical type of questioning with Paul Ricoeur, Emmanuel Lévinas and John Rawls gradually becoming the acknowledged predominant figures[1].

The following is an outline of my analysis based on a new conception of our understanding of social work. It falls into three parts:
– first, an analysis of the reasons why the thinking behind social work has changed, and in particular why passing via an "ethical questioning" is a necessary though insufficient step, enabling us to renew the context in which our thinking of the "social" takes place;

- second, a brief description of some perspectives underlying a new comprehension of social work, especially the relationship between reflexive ethics and the political function of social work;
- finally, a comparison of some of the principles applied in some European countries.

4.3
Changes in the Thinking behind Social Work

When we consider the different analyses of social work produced between 1970 and 2000, what strikes us immediately is the constant critical discourse on the identity crisis in the social professions and the always keenly felt need to affirm a new set of skills, inspired by models that are more administration-oriented [2]. This is therefore an approach to identity that is essential to the profession in that it extends the identity confusion of the 1970s which was triggered by the critical discourse inspired by Foucault. After this wave of weakening identity, the beginning of the 1980s saw an administrative and technocratic rhetoric gradually gained ground. The watchword in those years of crisis was to transform every social worker into a project designer, always concerned about evaluating the results of his/her action.

As a reaction to this technocratic approach, there emerged the notion of the social, taking its references from the ideas of those philosophers and sociologists who deal with questions of justice, equality/equity and the construction of the subject [3]. This discussion, which has stirred up some fresh thinking in the field of human sciences, has consequences for social work, as the new definition of the actor completely shakes up and overturns the representations that had previously predominated. These previous representations saw the subject as dominated, incapable of any social reaction or action.

The concepts of anomie, alienation, domination, maladjustment, and deficiency that used to be applied more or less systematically to some of the people that social workers had to deal with are now giving way to representations in which the dominated actors are able to construct their own social responses with or without the support of the social worker [4]. It is in this context that we look at the question of ethics and the place of moral philosophy in the references underlying the concepts of social work.

The hypothesis that I put forward is as follows: the basic tenets of social work have been renewed by turning, sometimes quite involuntarily, to themes borrowed from moral and political philosophy which place questions of justice, equity and the subject at the heart of the matter.

Thus ethical thought leads to social and political considerations that modify the concepts underlying the professional practices of social work, while forming part of a reaction to the technically biased injunctions of some decision-makers[5].

4.4
What Lies behind the Interest in Ethics?

The "demand" for ethics springs from the social and cultural changes that have affected industrialised societies for the last thirty years. After a period marked by confidence in the future – the Glorious Thirty Years after World War II – there followed a period marked by uncertainty. There were major risks resulting from technological choices (nuclear, biological, food etc.), the "damage caused by progress", and the risk-society replaced the happiness that had been programmed for the end of the 20th century.

The weakening of ideologies and of the integrating role of major political and religious discourses gave way to an anxiety about the future of individuals who are plunged into an "acceleration of history" and confronted with the need to achieve and to perform (Ehrenberg, 1999). This process of "disenchantment with the world" and secularisation accompanied the rise in unemployment and the disintegration of the working-class way of life during the 1970s and 1980s[6].

These phenomena, which are extensively described and analysed in the social sciences, gave rise to an increase in uncertainties and expectations in the area of social action. The all-providing State does not fade away – far from it –, it spreads its all-embracing net to the "normal supernumeraries" (people who are unemployed). At the same time, we witness the substituting of charitable values, which have characterised social work since its creation, by preoccupations in which the subject, then the citizen become the "targets". A revival in reflection into professional deontology translates as a search for shared values amongst social workers.

There has also been an increase in ethics in many sectors of social life: economy, business, sport, medicine, science, politics, and the media. No sector lies beyond the range of questions as to the aims of different activities and the measures put in motion to implement them, with the risk of mistaking an indispensable step in "reflexive ethics" for a shift that is simply searching for what is politically or morally correct. Social workers do not escape this questioning into their working practices: how families are described; the temptation to "penalise" certain types of family behaviour by suspending benefits; the confidentiality of information given to social workers and professional confidentiality; the denunciation of ill-treatment; the social support for subjects in difficulties. These situations lead to social responses based on convictions and values, and not only on technical, rational and legal dimensions[7]. It is at this level that ethical and political interrogation appears and manifests itself.

4.5
Can Social Work Do without Norms?

The definition of social action that follows from the previous reflection raises numerous questions. First of all, the one that torments observers of the "loss of social points of reference": can social work become part of a logic of reconstruction and the restoration of social bonds by freeing itself from the demands of social integration contrary to the expression of the subject? This representation places the social worker in the position of the expert who can – and should – assess the level of "need" amongst the populations for whom he/she is responsible in order to determine the type of aid or support that will be most effective, or least determine what will be unsuitable.

Whatever ideological conception underlies these representations, social work is clearly always to be found in a context where the connection between a given situation with "commonly accepted norms" in a given society is inevitable. But the confrontation with a norm that has to be imposed is always the result of an interpretation where the amount of adjustment made to fit a rule or a law is only possible through the organisational context in which the norms are expressed. Apart from the cases where the actor has almost no room for manoeuvre because of a very "tight" control, "concrete action systems", to use Crozier and Friedberg's (1977) expression, enable social workers to adapt a rule as closely as possible to the interests of the populations concerned.

For all that, social workers can direct their action with a view to facilitating the social integration of their different publics but also with reference to principles or "internal imperatives" (Touraine, Khosrokhavar, 2000, p. 105) such as: respect for one's fellow man, dignity, and solidarity. In this case, social work calls on a strategy of "conflictuality" which enables the actor to define himself within social relations marked by domination. But this also constitutes a principle of resistance on the basis of which can develop what Touraine calls the "positive affirmation of self" (Touraine, Khosrokhavar, 2000, p. 144).

If we consider things thus, a reversal of the usual postulate of social work, then by refusing social integration in this way the individual creates a form of conflictuality enabling him/her to transform him/herself into a subject. In other words, protest, refusal, and anger must be considered as strong points from which the individual can question the norms that compel him/her to "integrate" in a way that he/she rejects. Thus recent research into those receiving income support benefits shows that some of those surveyed vigorously refused to enter into any relationship with the social worker as long as the relationship was viewed as an obligation to subject themselves and their existence to a form of scrutiny. It is when this refusal becomes reality by a distancing from the integrating norm that the individual mobilises him/herself most actively. Thus the social worker acts as a foil which, paradoxically, improves the mobilisation of the individual's resources (Dubet, Veretout, 2003).

All the art of the social worker is thus concentrated on being able to be free from normalising restraints in order to maintain a space where the social reaction of the subject can manifest itself. In this instance, social support is not synonymous with revealing dependency but is a confirmation of the subject's capacity for self-affirmation. This desire to act forms part of a professional action which calls on a reflection that associates the desire for an ethical approach with political effectiveness, thus reshaping the definition of social work.

4.6
Ethics and Social Work in Europe:
Ethical Codes and Deontology

4.6.1. Ethical Codes

In 2003 the International Federation of Social Workers proposed an ethical code in social work, and this code was a continuation of the document drawn up at its 1994 Congress in Sri Lanka. In a *Preamble*, this document specified that an ethical conscience is indispensable for any social worker practising professionally, and that is expressed as a respect for the ethical codes specific to each national culture. However, two principles are fundamental to all ethical codes: the principles of human rights and social justice. International conventions constitute the common norm to be applied and stipulate the rights accorded by the world community.

For each of these two principles there are corresponding determined objectives.
1. *First Principle: Human Rights and Human Dignity*. Objectives:
   - to respect the right to self-determination;
   - to defend the right to participation;
   - to treat everyone as an entire person;
   - to identify and develop personal capacities.

2. *Second Principle: Social Justice*. Objectives:
- to challenge negative discrimination;
- to acknowledge diversity;
- to distribute resources equitably;
- to challenge unjust policies and practices;
- to work for solidarity.

These objectives are then translated into general guidelines and transferred in case work methods that can be used in teaching practical ethics for the social professions.

If we keep to the wording of these principles, we can see that it is a straightforward matter to examine professional practices as to their pertinence in relation to these orientations. What is important to note is that this ethical code constituted a universal reference-base that is applied to cultural specificities. Of course the question of the legitimacy of such an ideological declaration has to be asked, but this takes us back to the principles of drawing up norms for action by resorting to the principle of ethics in the discussion by Jürgen Habermas (1986).

Ethics cannot be dissociated from their representation as rights and it is at this level that the political function comes into play because the affirmation of specific rights enables us to bring professional procedures into the decision-making context which has most to gain in relation to social action. This is in agreement with Rawls who says that a decision is just if it improves the situation of the one who has been allocated the least (Rawls, 1971).

Among the rights that we can identify and which can be applied to children and adolescents are the following:
- the right to control one's life;
- the right to privacy;
- the right to protection;
- the right to freedom;
- the right to integrity;
- the right to confidentiality.

Of course, these rights constitute objectives to be respected and also guidelines for action, and the social work professional must take inspiration from them and adapt them to each encountered situation. This implies that the ethical code constitutes to some extent a code of reference for action, entitling us to lay down certain legal principles to be respected and promoted.

Research into the available literature that was carried out while preparing this article showed that many countries in Europe and Latin America, the United States or even Canada adopt ethical codes that guide the professional acts of social work with all sections of the public:

families, children, handicapped people, the mentally ill. We find the same values underlying the deontological codes: social justice, solidarity, equal conditions/equity, refusal of negative discrimination. This is like a normative order of human societies with the notion of justice as the main concept (cf. Pharo, 2004, p. 316).

From the literature there emerges a notion that seems to be shared by all practitioners and researchers: social work is essentially a moral enterprise. The term "moral" relates to the normative dimension of the action undertaken and depends on a deliberation based on values adopted by the actor (cf. Bouquet, 2003, p. 69). But we can also refer to the reflective practitioner with Schön, and with the ability to reflect both in action as does Banks with the use of learning journals in fieldwork practice (Banks, Nohr, 2003). The principle to which the professional refers is the same as that described by Habermas (1986, p. 135) in relation to Kant, the principle of universalism that is written thus:

every valid norm should satisfy the condition according to which the consequences and the secondary effects which, in a foreseeable way, derive from the fact that the norm has been universally observed with a view to satisfying the interests of all, can be accepted without constraint by all those concerned.

It would appear that ethical questions are to be found in the practical-normal area that is subjected to reason, for moral judgements have a cognitive content that one can and must question. For Habermas, it is in this condition that one distances oneself from a moral scepticism and a moral relativism.

The question of the responsibility undertaken by all professionals is frequently dealt with; it is in this area that social work is continually crossed with ethical questions because decision-making and action have practical and symbolic effects which often have immediate effects on the public concerned. Thus, "Ethics is a practical wisdom *in situ*", according to Ricoeur, and "moving from values to ethics, is to move towards carrying out the act" (Bouquet, 2003, p. 65).

The practical implementation of an intention and a decision is indeed what characterises the ethical dimension of human action in general. For as Canto-Sperber (2001, p. 86) emphasises,

The quality of intentions rarely guarantees in itself the quality of results, if these intentions are not first screened by critical reflection [...] reflection also obliges us to carry out some work of legitimisation, since the reasons used to justify action have to be clearly defined. In all of this, ethical reflection remains closely related to action.

The question of ethical conflicts is also raised in some situations: every time one meets cultural specificity in relation to educational norms. There are many subjects that stir up debate in professional circles, especially in France. For example, questions concerning the respect for secularism and the use of religious symbols, also questions relating to family customs inspired by cultural codes that differentiate between gender and establish a hierarchy of masculine and feminine roles. Here the difficulties that arise for the professional pertain to cultural relativism: the dilemma with which social workers are confronted with is not to give way to a form of ethnocentrism, or inversely not to sacrifice a principle because of pressure from cultural relativism, often put forward with the best of intentions.

4.6.2. Are the Values of Social Work Threatened?

This question has been posed by several authors from various countries, in conjunction with one another regarding the effects of the social choices made by some governments. This is particularly the case in Great Britain where, despite reassuring declarations by political leaders, according to some commentators, working conditions for social workers are deteriorating and some principles are being threatened (Steele, 2001).

As well as the reduction in material resources for economic reasons, professional social workers are also highlighting the consequences of legal changes in penal matters because these may have professional repercussions. The conditions under which social workers exercise their profession may be modified and the deontological codes challenged by these changes. This would not be a change in values but a professional and political matter pitting a profession against the policy-makers. The matter of the treatment of juvenile delinquents is the best example of this opposition between preventive and repressive measures that are the subject of contradictory debates on the values underlying the different notions. The policies implemented in many countries, such as Great Britain or France, illustrate these conflicts of values which put social workers and political decision-makers in opposition to each other.

The concepts developed by social actors are based on a group of considerations which give an important place to ethical aspects. The simple questions that are asked are based on the notion that there is always "one best way": in other words, in certain situations there is a best response that should be offered. How, for instance, can educational and judicial forms of response be combined without the latter taking precedence? Social work is directly questioned as to its efficiency and the clash between values and the need for results can lead sometimes to lively arguments between these two concepts. Yet the key values are not withdrawn from professional arguments, they are, on the contrary, mobilised as resources for action. In this way, the values appear like professional aids supporting technical and/or political positions for practising social workers.

However, the social polices that are implemented in the countries of Europe are, in whatever country they are to be found, subjected to an imperative of results and no longer judged only according to means because of the economic constraints and social transformations following current societal changes. The intervention of social workers in families that are disadvantaged as a result of unemployment, the treatment of poverty and its consequences, problems of socialisation encountered by children and adolescents in housing redevelopment zones etc. bring to the fore the ethical reference points of these professionals in order to strengthen a position that is sometimes weakened by the constraints that we have just described. Thus we believe that the values of commitment or "moral entrepreneurship" are now more than ever at the heart of the professional issues involved in social work, and that they constitute a political issue in the sense that they contribute to promoting practices that place the subject at the centre of the action, while the normative demands of the powers that be (whether administrative, political or relating to public opinion and the obsession with safety) are relegated to the background.

Notes

1. Cf. particularly Ricoeur (1990); Société philosophique de Louvain, Société philosophique de Bruxelles (1984); Rawls (1971).

2. Although there has been a change in the general view taken of the social work professions in terms of confirmed "skills", a doubt still hovers over them to the extent that they are sometimes called semi-professions (cf. Autès, 1999).

3. I am thinking in particular of the themes developed by Rawls (1971) and Walzer (1983), and the directions suggested by Alain Touraine and François Dubet over the last ten years around this question and the role of experience in constituting the subject (cf. Touraine, 1992; Dubet, 1994).

4. Thus the Restos du Cœur, the DAL (Association droit au logement), the movement of illegals, AC (Act up) will enable "users" to be associated with social workers who figure among the volunteer staff for these associations.

5. As an example of this type of reaction, take those social workers who, when confronted with the computerisation of their departments, set up an ethical and deontological line of enquiry which enables them to "query" the underlying intentions behind this kind of change in professional practices.

6. For the effects of these processes on the construction of identities, cf. Dubar (2000). Concerning the consequences of modernity on individual choice and social cohesion, cf. Martuccelli (2000); Kaufmann (2001).

7. A sociological type of reasoning is imperative according to the terminology borrowed from Max Weber and taken up by Boudon (1999).

Bibliography

AUTÈS M. (1999), *Les paradoxes du travail social*, Dunod, Paris.
BANKS S., NOHR K. (2003), *Teaching Practical Ethics for the Social Professions*, FESET, Copenhagen.
BOUDON R. (1995), *Le juste et le vrai. Études sur l'objectivité des valeurs et de la connaissance*, Fayard, Paris.
ID. (1999), *Le sens des valeurs*, PUF, Paris.
BOUQUET B. (2003), *Éthique et travail social. Une recherche de sens*, Dunod, Paris.
CANTO-SPERBER M. (2001), *L'inquiétude morale et la vie humaine*, PUF, Paris.
CROZIER M., FRIEDBERG E. (1977), *L'acteur et le système. Contraintes de l'action collective*, Seuil, Paris.
DUBAR C. (2000), *La crise des identités. L'interprétation d'une mutation*, PUF, Paris.
DUBET F. (1994), *Sociologie de l'expérience*, Seuil, Paris.
ID. (2002), *Le déclin de l'institution*, Seuil, Paris.
DUBET F., VERETOUT A. (2003), *Why Go off French Welfare? Inactivity "Traps" and Strategies of Actors*, in "Revue française de Sociologie", 44, supplément, pp. 79-108.
EHRENBERG A. (1999), *L'individu incertain*, Hachette, Paris.
HABERMAS J. (1986), *Morale de la communication*, Flammarion, Paris.
ID. (1992), *De l'éthique de la discussion*, Éditions du Cerf, Paris.
KAUFMANN J.-C. (2001), *Ego. Pour une sociologie de l'individu*, Nathan, Paris.
LADRIÈRE P. (2001), *Pour une sociologie de l'éthique*, PUF, Paris.
MARTUCCELLI D. (2000), *Dominations ordinaires. Explorations de la condition moderne*, Balland, Paris.
MOUSSU G. (2001), *Entre normes et stratégie: la fonction de l'ethique dans le travail social*, in "Vie sociale", 3.
PHARO P. (2000), *Le sens de la justice. Essais de sémantique sociologique*, PUF, Paris.
ID. (2004), *Morale et sociologie. Le sens et les valeurs entre nature et culture*, Gallimard, Paris.
PHARO P., QUÉRÉ L. (éds.) (1990), *Les formes de l'action*, Éditions de l'EHESS, Paris.
RAWLS J. (1971), *A Theory of Justice*, Belknap Press of Harvard University Press, Cambridge (MA).
RICOEUR P. (1990), *Soi-même comme un autre*, Gallimard, Paris.
SOCIÉTÉ PHILOSOPHIQUE DE LOUVAIN, SOCIÉTÉ PHILOSOPHIQUE DE BRUXELLES (1984), *Justifications de l'éthique*, Éditions de l'Université de Bruxelles, Bruxelles.
STEELE L. (2001), *Are Social Work Values under Threat?*, in "The Guardian", 12 April.
TOURAINE A. (1992), *Critique de la modernité*, Fayard, Paris.
ID. (1997), *Pourrons-nous vivre ensemble? Égaux et différents*, Fayard, Paris.
TOURAINE A., KHOSROKHAVAR F. (2000), *La recherche de soi. Dialogue sur le sujet*, Fayard, Paris.
WALZER M. (1983), *Spheres of Justice: A Defense of Pluralism and Equality*, Basic Books, New York.

Section B
Practices

5

The Relationship between Social and Spatial Exclusion in an Urban Context: Consequences for the Development and the Behaviour of Young People

by *Detlef Baum*

5.1
Introduction: General Remarks

The connection between spatial separation and social exclusion is a social policy problem in most modern cities. This is because urban societies have a limited capacity for integration, and social work has been increasingly faced with the problems of individuals or groups being excluded by spatial conditions and structures. The problems have become even more advanced in large cities, and this has led to divisions between very privileged and very deprived areas. In this context, my thesis is that there is an interdependence between advantage and deprivation, and consequently between inclusion and exclusion. We do not have deprivation *in spite of* the advantageous, but *through* the advantageous. All of the conditions which are necessary for integration are, at the same time, conditions of exclusion.

In European societies, more and more people are being excluded from important areas of social life, from the possibilities for action, from the opportunities of participation in urban life. All in all, more and more people are being excluded from the average living conditions prevailing amongst the country's population. These processes of exclusion no longer follow the logic of social stratification. There is no longer an "up and down", but an "inside and outside". People are included if they fulfil the conditions of participation and interaction in urban contexts, namely integration within urban public spaces and in the urban markets. Of primary importance are the labour market and the housing market (Kronauer, 2002).

These processes have dramatic consequences for young people's development. Growing up in an urban context without having the opportunities or the resources to access urban public spaces, or to experience urbanity in general, means that young people cannot conceive of their identities under urban conditions. Yet this is a primary condition for ensuring identity in the psychological development of young people. In order to develop, it is essential that young people participate fully in an urban society. Therefore, they need not only money but also social status, resources, competencies and, above all, a psycho-social disposition towards successful interaction and behaviour. In this context, young people must attain a level of education and a job. Having a job is necessary for securing social status, for learning certain patterns of behaviour and interaction, and for acquiring a certain reputation, which ensures integration. Having social status means that someone is accepted by significant others, and young people are passing through a phase in which they are discovering their own identities by discovering why they are accepted by others, and who will accept them.

The socio-spatial division of cities leads to a division of the conditions in which young people grow up and act as individuals. Young people normally know what somebody needs in order to be integrated or accepted, and they also know that there are differences between their own possibilities and opportunities, and the possibilities and opportunities available to those on the other side of the socio-spatial divide. Also, there are now a growing number of young people who lack the socio-spatial basis for learning the norms and values which are so important for both integration and identity.

5.2
The Practical Background

I would like to discuss the questions of social inclusion and exclusion on the basis of long years of experience in practical social work with young people in deprived areas, and of research into the conditions of their lives, their behaviour and self-awareness. Also, on the basis of what they know and think, and what they expect from the future (Baum, 1996a, 1996b, 1999). My students and I have founded and organised a youth centre in a highly deprived neighbourhood, comprising of about 2,600 inhabitants in 700 flats. There is no urban structure; the distance to the city is 2.5 kilometres. The neighbourhood is separated from the city by a river and an industrial area. There is nothing else except for one supermarket. There are no doctors or other services, there is nothing here to indicate that the local people live in an urban context – except a studio for sun-tanning! The population of this area is not socially mixed, and there is no functional mixture of commerce, business, and public and private services. These conditions explain why this neighbourhood is socially, culturally and economically divided from the centre. Furthermore, this neighbourhood has a particular reputation which means that the physical distance to the centre of the city has become a symbolic distance. The spatial exclusion is reinforced by the symbolic exclusion because structurally there is no easy way to move from such a deprived neighbourhood to other parts of the city (Kronauer, 2002; Dangschat, 2000; Farwick, 2001; Bremer, 2000).

The area is part of the city without being urban. Most of the adults are unemployed or are working in low-paid jobs without prospects. A great number of them are dependent on the social support of the community. There is a high percentage of under-18-year-olds, most of whom have attended the local low-level secondary school. These young people generally find it difficult to integrate into the labour market because they cannot find places for training or for professional work. Furthermore, this area also includes a significant number of migrants, largely people who have come from Russia.

5.3
The Theoretical Background

My theoretical background is the approach of the Chicago School, a socio-ecological approach, developed in the United States in the 1920s (Burgess, Park, 1925; Wirth, 1938). My background has also been influenced by discussions of this approach which have featured in sociological literature in recent years (Friedrichs, 1995; Löw, 2001; Vortkamp, 2003).

In the 1920s and the 1930s, Chicago was very strongly influenced by the processes of migration. People from very different – but mostly European – countries came to Chicago, a city with a very highly developed industrial region. Social workers and sociologists discovered special processes and special patterns of distribution within the population. People of the same culture met each other in the same neighbourhoods. As a result, there was a specific logic of integration, but there was also disintegration in the New World. Furthermore, social workers and sociologists found out that the spatial distribution of a population reflects the social stratification of a society in a certain area, so that the particular problems of particular groups depend on the social structure of the neighbourhood on the one hand, and on the character of its space on the other hand. It was especially noticeable that a higher rate of deviant behaviour was typical in particular areas where people lived in poverty. In such areas, people could not fulfil the conditions necessary for integration, and so were overtaxed by the attendant demands and therefore forced into deviant behaviour (Burgess, Park, 1925).

Most importantly, this research demonstrated that the frame of reference for the explanation of urban social change and its associated problems lays in the socio-spatial context, and the conditions it provided for growing up, for life in general and for the reproduction of life. In this respect, the meaning of the question is important. Above all, how young people take possession of the space, so that physical spaces become social contexts in which young people live and interact. In an urban context this process of taking possession of a space develops another quality. If we agree to the premise of the Chicago approach, namely that the patterns of population distribution lead to mainly homogenous neighbourhoods, it is easy for young people to feel that "the neighbourhood is our neighbourhood", because here they are able to fulfil norms and values, and they are consequently accepted. Yet this provokes a further question: what can young people do outside of their own neighbourhoods? This is a very valid question in deprived areas – and the answer is important for explaining why young people are able to say "this is my area!". Later on I will describe reasons for this phenomenon and the consequences for the behaviour of young people.

In my point of view, this approach and its further development in the sociological discussion of the last ten years provide us with the most important theory for explaining the relationship between social exclusion and spatial segregation, and for the consequences of these processes for individuals. The space itself produces privileges and deprivations or problems, but the structures of the space also produce conditions for thinking and behaving. Spatial structures include the arrangement and the quality of the buildings, the streets, the places etc., and the space is affected by the varied character of the structures, by borders and by the opportunities for crossing over into other areas. All of these spatial conditions explain why young people can grow up in different ways whilst living within the same city.

Based on these general remarks and the practical and theoretical backgrounds I would like to discuss the following matters.

1. First I would like to discuss the consequences of these processes, and how they affect the development and the behaviour of young people, particularly with regard to identity and status.

2. Furthermore, I would like to compare these conditions and experiences with other modern western European societies with a similar social history and cultural background (France, Great Britain), and I would like to reflect on these processes before the background of experiences in eastern Europe, especially in Russia and the Czech Republic.

3. Lastly, I would like to outline some consequences for the social professions, especially for those involved with local social policy and community work.

In this context it is necessary to compare the situations in each country, bearing in mind the following questions.

a) What is the cultural and socio-economic background of a country's social problems; how are they defined, identified, and which strategies are developed for their solution?
b) What is the function of social work in this context, in the context of social policy, and in problem-solving strategies?

Society's reactions to these processes of social exclusion by spatial segregation depend upon an understanding on two levels:
– on the understanding of what we mean by the social integration of young people;
– on the understanding of the function of social policy: why must a society improve the conditions of life for young people? This depends on how the society understands childhood and youth.

5.4
The Relationship between Spatial and Social Exclusion

When and under what conditions does spatial segregation in an urban context lead to social exclusion, and what are the associated consequences for young people's identity, for their behaviour and for the conditions in which they grow up? I would like to discuss this question by reflecting upon the results of our own research.

Generally, socio-spatial exclusion results in a very particular experience of exclusion. We noticed that young people lost some of their capacity for action when they were unsuccessful in the public sphere, or when they failed in other areas or institutions of integration, such as schools, job training schemes or in jobs themselves. Such failures meant that young people felt deprived, and they felt that nobody needed them. These experiences of deprivation outside of the immediate environment lead to a retreat into the neighbourhood, and to an increased identification with it. If inhabitants of such areas cannot be assured of their identity outside the neighbourhood, they can receive assurances from within it because there they know and fulfil the values and the norms which are shared with significant others. As a result, they are accepted by the people within their own neighbourhoods, they are considered as integrated – it is their own area and so they feel that they belong (Dubet, Lapeyronnie, 1994; Baum, 1996b, p. 54).

What does this mean for young people who are forced to remain in their own neighbourhoods because they are unsuccessful outside of them? They are excluded from life outside of their immediate neighbourhoods but their own areas are deprived of all the dimensions of urban life. Youth in an urban context does not just mean that young people grow up in a city or in an urban area. Above all it means that young people are shaped and formed by the urban life-style; they are young people *of* the city, growing up under conditions of urbanity. This is important, because young people living in deprived urban areas are suffering due to the fact that they are living in a socio-political and socio-cultural context of a city – they belong to a certain city or part of the city – without growing up in an infrastructural arrangement which we call urban.

In this context, socio-spatial exclusion means that young people in particular are missing the access to areas of urban public space. This access is an important part of the socialisation process, and is an important condition for growing up. These young people feel the discrepancy between the possibilities that others have and the ones that are available to them. In their own neighbourhood they do not learn what it means to interact in an urban public space, or how to act reasonably under the condition of "uncompleted integration" (Bahrdt, 1971, p. 63). Yet this is an essential condition of acting in urban public spaces. It means that a person is only successfully integrated into a special social context with a particular role, and not with his/her whole personality. That person is therefore only able to interact reasonably if he/she can play the role and fulfil the expectations of the public space by incomplete integration. Inhabitants of deprived areas do not have the experience of this form of integration in a public context, and do not know how to maintain their identity under such conditions. That is one of the reasons why young people fear the city centre as a social space for special experiences or for acting. As a result of this fear, young people retreat to the nearer environment of their neighbourhoods, because there they can present their identity successfully and so gain acceptance. As a result, they often have no interest in visiting the city, they do not have any thematic access to the urban life-style, and the public space remains an unknown space. They feel the potential discrimination by others, because of the reputation of their locality (Baum, 1996b, p. 55).

We should consider another issue which is important to the central meaning of integration, namely labour or employment. In a modern society, having a job is the key to integration because having a job means earning wages and living without anyone else's support. Yet our research has indicated that integration by labour is only one part of the wider process of integration. Being unemployed is a necessary, but not a primary, condition of exclusion. Young people in this deprived situation do not believe that success in school or in vocational training is necessary for every aspect of their life, or for the reproduction of life. Somebody needs money but whether or not it is one's own money, which one has earned, appears to be unimportant. These attitudes were typical at the beginning of the industrialisation process, and within industrial societies. Exclusion from labour did not always mean an exclusion from all the conditions of reproduction. But in modern societies, integration via the conditions of life and reproduction is growing increasingly more important. Meanwhile, housing conditions, the neighbourhood and its infrastructure, health, education and social security are factors of inequality and are therefore criteria for inclusion or exclusion. What is important now is one's inclusion in relevant social processes, social interactions, public communications, and the possibility of achieving certain essential social goals – this form of inclusion depends more and more on how and where people live, and not on how people work.

If all the essential characteristics of a neighbourhood indicate that the people who live there are unable to manage without social and financial support, that they are unemployed and depend on State or community benefits, then the people concerned cannot develop an urban life-style. Urbanity then disintegrates because such people are unable to realise the interests and attain the goals essential to integration in an urban context. Consequently the urban structure is not needed and the city administration has no interest in maintaining it. So the missing urbanity in this quarter is a direct result of the inhabitants' missing resources and, at the same time, urbanity cannot be developed. Young people grow up and act with the feeling, that they do not belong to the city as a total social system, and therefore the spatial distance to the city is no longer just a symbol of exclusion, but together with the missing urbanity it is its central condition. We therefore cannot discuss the social exclusion of young people by only considering whether or not they are unemployed. We also have to consider a wider integration: are they integrated into the behaviours and interaction of the main fields of urbanity? I repeat: having a job may be a necessary condition of inclusion, but it does not explain social inclusion at all, and it is not the main condition of integration for young people in a deprived urban situation.

For other young people living in other social contexts, the question of integration has a meaning over and above whether or not they have a job. One of our central experiences in our work with young people is that the main condition for integration is that people must take possession of the social space – I have mentioned this already. Social spaces are taken by individuals from the inside acting in a special way. Through this process individuals interpret the space according to their interests, needs, awareness and knowledge. In order to do that, structures for stimulation, suggestion, participation, the possibilities for alternative thinking and other experiences are required. Individuals in such social spaces will only become active creators of this space if they have taken possession of it. That means that the individuals concerned must be able to realise their interests in the space, and use its structure accordingly. They do not become active creators if they have just adjusted to the circumstances. Yet if they already consider that the space conforms with their interests or needs, why should they change it?

The concept of possessing the space precedes the premise that young people must give meaning to objective things. They must learn that all objective things, social relations, and spaces have meaning only within their social, cultural and historical context. When children and young people discover their environment, they must understand that this environment is a historical product, made by members of society in a particular historical period (Deinet, 1993; Leont'ev, 1973, p. 451):

From the beginning the child is living in an objective world, created by people. To this world belong things that are needed daily, such as clothes, and simple tools, but also language, by which images and ideas will be reflected. Even nature considers the child under the conditions created by men.

Young people must learn that the objective world, the environment of their own neighbourhood and their relationship to the city, is created by people who are dependent on, and influenced by, their historical experiences and the social conditions and circumstances in which they live. Therefore, young people themselves must be able to understand that the world is changeable and that they have the opportunity of changing it.

But which perspective should parents and other adults give to the younger generation if they themselves have adjusted to their lives, if they do not believe that they can change their own situations by taking possession of their space? If parents and others do not see any future for themselves, how should they communicate the feeling that their children are a resource for themselves and for society? They must create the experience of being needed and therefore valued. Otherwise it is impossible to take possession of a space.

More and more, our societies allow disastrous processes to ignore people who are not needed – and spatial exclusion is the symbolic expression for not being needed. We even consider these people as troublesome, they are a burden on the social security system and they are turned away from the city's public spaces. Capitalistic societies do not need such groups and their number is increasing. People are needed only if they fulfil the norms and values of work, consumption and housing. Moreover, these people are mostly parents preparing children and young people for the future! Why should young people agree to the conditions of their life, why should they possess the environment as their social space, why should they share the values and norms of a society which refuses their integration?

5. THE RELATIONSHIP BETWEEN SOCIAL AND SPATIAL EXCLUSION

Above all young people are in the process of discovering their own identity – based on the feeling of being needed. If young people grow up with the feeling that they are not needed, their identity is threatened at the very point at which the personality is developing. The whole socialisation process, both in the family and at school, is aimed at integrating young people into the central markets of our society. The process should enable them to define their own cultural and social accesses to society through work, through their personal aims, and through their patterns of consumption. Young people in deprived areas are denied these experiences, not in addition to their social and spatial situation, but because of it. However, we will not assess all the consequences of this dynamic process and its attendant threats at this time.

The discussion of exclusion in France – based on empirical studies (Dubet, Lapeyronnie, 1994) – raises further questions about this issue. To repeat the statement, people are more or less forced to remain within their own neighbourhoods because they are not able to act and interact successfully outside of them. In their own neighbourhoods they are assured of their identity and their status. They are able to fulfil norms and expectations. Therefore the neighbourhood and its relations are vital for the constitution of young people's identity and status.

So what happens when the young inhabitants of these neighbourhoods are threatened by strangers, by those from other neighbourhoods who want to occupy their social area as a space of experience, of interaction and as a social space by which they ensure their identity? Referring back to the social research studies undertaken in the suburbs of the French metropolis (Dubet, Lapeyronnie, 1994; Paugam, 1991), we can see that young people will defend their area with the utmost intensity, even with violence, against anyone who wants to occupy it. It is *their* area. They are included in an area, which has all characteristics of exclusion. They are included not *in spite of* exclusion, but *by* exclusion. Young people feel that they are excluded by race or ethnic origin or by social status, and this condition is at the same time a condition for their social integration. In these cities, urban development leads to neighbourhood divisions where, on the one hand, inhabitants are privileged because their neighbourhoods are secure, and on the other hand people have to fear for their lives. Both areas integrate their populations under special conditions. Young people act not only under the condition of deprivation but also under the condition of exclusion, of being not needed by society. What alternatives do they have? They are faced with strange and unknown expectations and norms which they cannot fulfil, and with goals which they cannot attain because they do not have the resources to attain them legally. Yet, at the same time, they have to obtain these goals to become socially integrated, to become accepted by others and to establish their own identities.

Of course the French situation explains a process which is typical of France (Wacquant, 2004). We do not find this process in the industrial regions of Great Britain or Germany where the relationship between youth and labour is different. In the so-called red belt of French industrial regions and the metropolis, the life of the working classes was completely taken up by work. All the conditions of life and reproduction seemed to be a consequence of the organisation of work. So a young person also had an identity as worker. Now young people are unemployed and looking for jobs. So they have lost their identities as workers without losing their identities as inhabitants of the red belt. As a result, they now need the nearby neighbourhood as source of solidarity. In these areas there is a very close connection between production and reproduction, between life-style, communication and public space, between interaction and work, and between workers' organisations (trade unions) and local government. These connections enable a sense of solidarity so that local people can act against institutions like the police, schools, entrepreneurial organisations and the administration. Young people are aware that they are socially excluded, but all of them are in the same situation and the deprivation reinforces all forms of deviance.

5.5
The Comparison with Eastern European Development

When considering the situation in eastern Europe we must rely mainly upon the discussion papers produced by eastern European experts, most of whom are responsible for city development or local social policy. Regarding the Russian situation, the case is that, with the exception of some research projects carried out by the Russian Academy of Sciences, there is no new research regarding the specific questions mentioned here. My analysis therefore is based partly on my own research or observations, and partly on unpublished discussion papers. With regard to the Czech situation, we have the same problem. Our analysis is therefore based on observation and discussion, as well as on papers which have been prepared for discussions with experts.

Generally, modern western societies have more or less the same processes of exclusion. We have the same relationships between spatial segregation and social exclusion; these are based on similar processes of modernisation, social stratification and differentiation, and the same logic of capitalistic development. Therefore, throughout the societies of

5. THE RELATIONSHIP BETWEEN SOCIAL AND SPATIAL EXCLUSION

western Europe, there are similar consequences for young people and they grow up in similar conditions. We even share the phenomenon of cities divided into privileged and deprived areas.

We find other processes in the urban history of the East. One reason for this is the separate historical development of cities and of urbanity in eastern Europe, e.g. in Russia. Another reason lies in the way in which eastern societies developed under communism. Step by step we can see the development and formation of the middle class, a characteristic point for the historical evolution of western European cities (Vozmitel, 2004; Golod, Klezin, 2004; Golenkova, 2004). In the socialist period, neighbourhoods in Russian cities were functionally and socially mixed. We find other forms of segregation, but these types of segregation do not lead to exclusion by characteristics of social structure or stratification. It is more of a segregation by political processes. We notice deprived areas because housing is in a poor condition, but both groups live in these areas; that is those who are well situated and those who are deprived and poor. The access to an urban life-style depends on economic recourses and cultural resources as well. Therefore, only the smaller part of the population – but this part is increasing – really has access to urban life and is able to act successfully in an urban context. But this form of exclusion does not have its roots in spatial segregation.

However we observe the developments of modernisation too. We have found the initial developments of yet another form of population distribution throughout the social space of the city. Young people are not just suffering as a result of living in deprived areas, but they face other kinds of deprivation too. They have other problems of identity, and Russian society is facing difficulties in ensuring the social integration of young people (Shubkin, 2004). This means that urban society in Russia, particularly in the large cities and the metropolitan centres of Moscow and St. Petersburg, is suffering from serious disintegration. This is because an increasing number of urban inhabitants are unable to acquire the gains which secure social integration and security. More and more, young people and older children are becoming part of this excluded group. They live on the streets without any prospects and without support from either family or local government. Their families urgently need support from the State or from local government because, on the whole, the young people support their families. Families need things for their daily lives, even for their survival, and it is the young people who provide them. These parents do not have the psychological resources required to educate their children. They are busy enough trying to cope with a normal day at home. They do not have the capacity to ensure their identity in a public space; they are not interested in interacting and acting in a public space. Instead they retreat into the social space of the family where they are secure against any interactions which could threaten their identity.

So we have a situation in which individuals and their families are excluded by their inability to act in a public space, by their incompetence in the context of a normal day, and by the fact that they need support but do not get it. They are not excluded by the space or the structure of a space, or by the reputation of a neighbourhood. Nevertheless, the structure of a social space and the lack of conditions for realising an urban life-style lead to an accumulation of social problems. These areas are peopled solely by those with individual difficulties, difficulties such as those caused by modernisation and by political decisions such as those referring to the local housing market.

In the Czech Republic the situation is similar to the development in western Europe. In the cities meanwhile we find processes of spatial segregation, and in the bigger cities we observe a division of neighbourhoods so that there are good residential areas and also deprived areas. But we cannot say that the city's capacity for social integration is already threatened – not yet! There is another problem: young people grow up and act under the conditions of a re-enforced modernisation and the social changes resulting from the shift from socialism to capitalism. The development of an urban youth is typically characterised by an alienation from the social and political processes, from the State and also from the local government. We can observe the typical developmental processes of individualism and consumer behaviour in response to an increasing consumer market. Young people in urban centres behave, and are conscious of themselves, in ways that are closer to our western lifestyles than to the traditions of their own country. Young people do not as yet see any relationship between their housing situation or their neighbourhood and any form of exclusion.

5.6
Consequences for Social Work with Young People

If the process of integration by traditional work loses its meaning, and if societal integration is no longer determined by integration into working processes, inclusion in the field of reproduction become more and more meaningful. But at the same time, if the integration in socio-ecological contexts as a central field of reproduction does not succeed, what are the consequences for young people and what are their alternatives? We have already recognised that young people are more or less forced to remain within their own neighbourhoods. This is the point at which social work must begin. The approach is one of initiating learning processes, and of developing competencies and consciousness alongside all objective chances, restrictions, subjective possibilities and deprivations. All of which are the conditions indicative of subjective interpretations of the world (Dubet, Lapeyronnie, 1994).

To do this, the social professions must first develop their own awareness of the increasing importance of social space, and of the spatial contexts for integration, the development of competencies and for the psycho-social conditions of identity. Community work must recognise the connection between developing individual capacities and competencies, and the improvement of social spaces, and the seizure of spaces by people acting in a specific area. And we must also find relationships between the structure, the arrangement and the equipment of an urban area, on the one hand, and the degree of the accumulation of social problems on the other hand. But that is not enough. Social work has to intervene in social-political decisions and in the processes of urban development (Alisch, 1998).

The French examples show us that it is not enough to work with children and young people, we must also use social policy to improve their living conditions. It is an illusion to believe that we can improve individual competencies and capacities, or that we can create change in the consciousness of young people without changing the circumstances of their life, namely their education, their housing, their health, and the economic conditions of their parents (Dubet, Lapeyronnie, 1994).

This subject still needs to be transferred into the theory and the methods of social work as community work, especially under the following aspects.

1. Social work must more and more discuss the question of how young people take possession of space, how they define an area as their own, and how they discover their environment under conditions of deprivation (Böhnisch, Münchmeier, 1993).
2. Social work must recognise that young people are only able to change their situations if they are accepted by others. And they only are able to accept others if no-one wounds their sense of identity and integrity. Young people are only able to act if they can articulate their interests and needs as reasonable demands. Therefore, what must social work change and improve to enable people as parents to act reasonably within the education process, and to communicate with their children and young people? Social work must support processes of self-definition and self-articulation. Young people must be supported in finding their identity and their competencies so as to articulate their interests. Social work must influence the social policy of the community with – and not

for – its young inhabitants. Social work needs to work with young people to represent their interests towards institutions and organisations, and this action must first and foremost be directed against the administration. Inhabitants must intervene in the processes of planning and decision-making regarding the improvement of their living conditions. Social work has to support this process and must help develop opportunities for participation (Herriger, 2002).

If social work has to develop concepts regarding the way in which young people can use their opportunities to acquire an area as their own space, several perspectives are required.

– Young people must possess an area in response to their own needs and wants, and not because of its objective structure.

– Young people, as inhabitants of deprived areas, must be aware that the objective structure of the area – the buildings, the quality of the flats or the environment of the flats – cannot always be changed by the inhabitants. They must learn that there is no realistic alternative to living in a particular area but they do have opportunities, and they do have the ability to change their situation.

– Young people are often forced to live in such areas, and in the main they are already deprived, usually by the economic poverty of their parents. One of the main goals of social work is to work with young people to develop strategies enabling them to accept the circumstances of their current lives, yet without losing their perspectives and their imaginations.

– Young people need measures which operate on a very low level of social integration. This is because they must become aware of themselves as actors in a process and they must make their own experiences. They must be aware that they can change their own situations by themselves, and our experience is that this can only be successful on a very low level.

– Social work must support all the processes which reinforce the individual's own capacity. All young people have capacities, even under conditions of deprivation. They quickly learn what it means to articulate their needs, and how to influence decisions. In such a context this is helpful for their identity and their status. If young people decide that they need a youth centre in which to meet each other, they must be enabled to represent their interests to the responsible institutions. Yet this representation should not take place through the social worker, they must do it by themselves. And they must develop thought processes which connect their abilities with their identity: "I am able to do something, therefore, I am somebody, no matter where I come from".

Social work has to support all these processes. The difficulty is that young people must be socially included under the conditions of their structural exclusion. That dilemma is a challenge for every social worker.

Bibliography

ALISCH M. (hrsg.) (1998), *Stadtteilmanagement, Voraussetzungen und Chancen für die soziale Stadt*, Leske + Budrich, Opladen.
BAHRDT H. P. (1971), *Die moderne Großstadt: soziologische Überlegungen zum Städtebau*, Wegner, München.
BAUM D. (1996a), *Can Integration Succeed? Research into Urban Childhood and Youth in a Deprived Area in Koblenz*, in "Social Work in Europe", III, 2, pp. 30-5.
ID. (1996b), *Wie kann Integration gelingen? Städtische Kindheit und Jugend im Sozialen Brennpunkt – Bedingungen und Folgen räumlicher und sozialer Segregation*, in "Kind Jugend Gesellschaft", 2, pp. 49-56.
ID. (1998), *Urbanisierung der Armut*, in J. Mansel, K.-P. Brinkhoff (hrsg.), *Armut im Jugendalter: soziale Ungleichheit, Gettoisierung und die psychosozialen Folgen*, Juventa, Weinheim, pp. 60-75.
ID. (1999), *Der Stadtteil als sozialer Raum – Sozialökologische Aspekte des strukturellen Kinder- und Jugendschutzes*, in Bundesministerium für Familie, Senioren, Frauen und Jugend, *"Bevor es zu spät ist..." Präventiver Kinder- und Jugendschutz in sozialen Brennpunkten. Fachtagung im Rahmen des Aktionsprogramms "Entwicklung und Chancen junger Menschen in sozialen Brennpunkten"*, DCM, Meckenheim, pp. 30-57.
BÖHNISCH L., MÜNCHMEIER R. (1993), *Pädagogik des Jugendraums: zur Begründung und Praxis einer sozialräumlichen Jugendpädagogik*, Juventa, Weinheim, II ed.
BREMER P. (2000), *Ausgrenzungsprozesse und die Spaltung der Städte: zur Lebenssituation von Migranten*, Leske + Budrich, Opladen.
BURGESS E. W., PARK R. E. (eds.) (1925), *The City*, University of Chicago Press, Chicago.
DANGSCHAT J. S. (hrsg.) (1999), *Modernisierte Stadt, gespaltene Gesellschaft: Ursachen von Armut und sozialer Ausgrenzung*, Leske + Budrich, Opladen.
ID. (2000), *Segregation*, in H. Häussermann (hrsg.), *Großstadt: soziologische Stichworte*, Leske + Budrich, Opladen, pp. 209-21.
DEINET U. (1993), *Raumaneignung in der sozialwissenschaftlichen Theorie*, in Böhnisch, Münchmeier (1993), pp. 57-68.
DUBET F., LAPEYRONNIE D. (1994), *Im Aus der Vorstädte. Der Zerfall der demokratischen Gesellschaft*, Klett-Cotta, Stuttgart.
FARWICK A. (2001), *Segregierte Armut in der Stadt: Ursachen und soziale Folgen der räumlichen Konzentration von Sozialhilfeempfängern*, Leske + Budrich, Opladen.
FRIEDRICHS J. (1995), *Stadtsoziologie*, Leske + Budrich, Opladen.
FRIEDRICHS J., BLASIUS J. (2000), *Leben in benachteiligten Wohngebieten*, Leske + Budrich, Opladen.
GOLENKOVA Z. (2004), *Soziale Integration und Desintegration der russischen Gesellschaft*, Institut für Soziologie, Russische Akademie der Wissenschaften, St. Petersburger.

GOLOD S., KLEZIN A. (2004), *21. Jahrhundert – Pluralisierungstendenzen der Familienformen in Rußland*, Institut für Soziologie, Russische Akademie der Wissenschaften, St. Petersburger.
HÄUSSERMANN H., KRONAUER M., SIEBEL W. (hrsg.) (2004), *An den Rändern der Städte: Armut und Ausgrenzung*, Suhrkamp, Frankfurt a.M.
HERRIGER N. (2002), *Empowerment in der sozialen Arbeit. Eine Einführung*, Kohlhammer, Stuttgart, II ed.
KRONAUER M. (2002), *Exklusion. Die Gefährdung des Sozialen im hoch entwickelten Kapitalismus*, Campus, Frankfurt a.M.-New York.
LEONT'EV A. N. (1973), *Probleme der Entwicklung des Psychischen*, Athenäum-Fischer-Taschenbuch-Verlag, Frankfurt a.M.
LÖW M. (2001), *Raumsoziologie*, Suhrkamp, Frankfurt a.M.
PAUGAM S. (1991), *La disqualification sociale. Essai sur la nouvelle pauvreté*, PUF, Paris.
SCHUBERT H. (2000), *Städtischer Raum und Verhalten. Zu einer integrierten Theorie des öffentlichen Raumes*, Leske + Budrich, Opladen.
SHUBKIN V. (2004), *Russische Jugend in der Transformationsgesellschaft an der Schwelle zum 21. Jahrhundert*, Institut für Soziologie, Russische Akademie der Wissenschaften, St. Petersburger.
VORTKAMP W. (2003), *Partizipation und soziale Integration in heterogenen Gesellschaften. Louis Wirths Konzeption sozialer Organisation in der Tradition der Chicagoer Schule*, Leske + Budrich, Opladen.
VOZMITEL A. (2004), *Transformation des Lebensstils und der Lebensweise im postsowjetischen Rußland*, Institut für Soziologie, Russische Akademie der Wissenschaften, St. Petersburger.
WACQUANT L. (2004), *Roter Gürtel, Schwarzer Gürtel: Rassentrennung, Klassenungleichheit und der Staat in der französischen städtischen Peripherie und im amerikanischen Ghetto*, in Häussermann, Kronauer, Siebel (2004), pp. 148-99.
WIRTH L. (1938), *Urbanism as a Way of Life*, in "The American Journal of Sociology", XLIV, pp. 1-24.

6

Single Mothers and the Effects of Intensive Aid on the Quality of Their Lives: The Examples of the Netherlands and Cyprus

by *Anne van den Berg* and *Maria P. Michailidis*

6.1
Introduction

The number of single-parent households has increased markedly over the past two decades in virtually every major industrialised nation, with the exception of Japan (Burns, Scott, 1994; Santrock, 1999). Although the specific reasons and consequences of this trend vary somewhat from nation to nation, according to Blankenhorn (1995), this family structure is being blamed for a wide spectrum of developmental problems in children, ranging from health problems to academic failure. Such condemnation, though, is often linked to a distorted stereotype, such as that of the single mother with limited education and limited social support. This mother neglects her children, has no ambition and spends her time collecting welfare cheques and watching hour upon hour of television. In some countries it is easy to demonstrate that this stereotype is false. However in other countries, studies on single-parent families, and in particular on single mothers, are limited although all the indications show that the number of these families will continue to rise. In examining the phenomenon of single parenthood, and single motherhood in particular, we expose the inadequacies of a "welfare system which assumes women's dependency, their responsibility for care, and a partial involvement in the labour market" (Williams, 1997, p. 272). In some European countries, single mothers are treated as prospective breadwinners, and in others they are treated "first and foremost as mothers". This is because they are not required to register for work until their youngest child is 16 years old; however, this also means that these mothers remain dependent on low State-benefits unless they can earn sufficient income. Recently, legislation in numerous European countries has been under attack by policy-makers and social scientists because of trends which are shifting the financial dependency of single mothers away from the State and on to the biological father.

6.2
Comparative Cases

This comparative cross-cultural essay set out to identify, analyse and explain similarities and differences between the situation of single mothers in the Netherlands and Cyprus. The research offers a deeper understanding of differences between the two societies, their structures, cultures, socio-economic settings and social service institution and, in particular, the intensive aid services for single mothers. The results of this chapter suggest a need for new ideas and new approaches regarding this type of aid in the home countries; the consequences for social work are also considered.

6.3
Models of Welfare

To compare the social policy and models of welfare, and their impact on the position of single mothers in the Netherlands and Cyprus it is necessary to clarify differences in their social and economic systems. In a joint publication on *Social Europe* from the Dutch Centraal Planbureau (CPB) and Sociaal en Cultureel Planbureau (SCP) the authors refer to Gøsta Esping-Andersen whose research distinguishes between different types of welfare States in Europe (Dekker *et al.*, 2003). In the EU, according to Esping-Andersen, a distinction can be made between the Scandinavian countries which have high levels of public provision for the entire population and which are directed towards securing greater equality; the Anglo-Saxon countries with limited public provision for citizens who are unable to secure adequate provisions via the market; central European countries which operate mainly via employee insurance and semi-public arrangements; and southern European countries which still have very limited provisions guaranteeing a basic income. The model used in Cyprus is a combination of the Anglo-Saxon and central European schemes; the Netherlands is positioned midway between Scandinavia and central Europe (for more details on this subject cf. *supra*, CHAP. 3).

6.4
Social Policy

All European Union member-States have developed National Action Plans (NAPs) in which they present their policies on the fight against poverty and social exclusion. The social inclusion of all citizens was a key objective of the Lisbon strategy (Lisbon European Council, 2002).

Everyone must be able to participate in society and one of the key points of the European Council in Nice 2000 was to "act on behalf of the most vulnerable".

The Netherlands continues the policy of promoting the combination of work and care tasks, and pays a good deal of attention to improving the availability, quality and affordability of childcare facilities. But new policy is increasingly showing signs of liberal characteristics. This is for instance illustrated by the privatisation of reintegration into the labour market, and the plans to abolish the distinction between private and compulsory State health-insurance with a view to reducing the burden on collective resources and leaving more to market forces.

In Cyprus the basic objectives of governmental social services have been aiming at securing a minimum acceptable standard of living for all citizens, especially for those who do not participate, or who only participate to a limited extent, in the production process. The aim is also to attain a more equitable distribution of the national income and the tax burden, both between different income groups as well as regions. Furthermore, social services aim to implement as well as to improve existing social programmes while preparing for the introduction of new institutions, new programmes and schemes which will effectively respond to the expectation of those in real need.

6.5
General Objective

The objective of this chapter is to illuminate the effects of intensive aid on the self-reliance and independence of single mothers, and to show what is and what can be done to improve the empowerment of this group. Firstly the chapter focuses on the effects of intensive social aid on the self-reliance and independence of single mothers, and how this affects the process of regaining social inclusion in each of the home countries. Then the results are compared with the second country, in respect of the socio-economic and cultural circumstances.

This chapter is based upon a comparative data collected from randomly selected single mothers in each country. In the Netherlands information was collected during in-depth interviews; in Cyprus semi-structured interviews and questionnaires were used. The aim is to shed light on the issues that impact on the lives and the well-being of these mothers and their children in their social context.

This chapter presents sections of two large research projects which attempted to investigate the single-mother families from the woman's perspective, and it aims to analyse the following:

- factors that hinder and improve the independent life of a single mother;
- choices that women make during the offered aid period and their motives;
- the results of this change.

6.5.1. Social Exclusion and Reintegration

Socially excluded people are those who are not allowed to belong, or are not able to belong, or are not willing to belong to society (Schuyt, 2002). Single mothers, as a group, are not excluded but they are at risk of becoming so when they have to face various sudden or unforeseen problems simultaneously. The situation can seriously compromise the balance between the woman's capacities and her daily responsibilities. A woman's competence to overcome this situation is influenced by protective factors (e.g. self-esteem, resilience, autonomy, relatives, social network) and stress factors (e.g. debt, homelessness, illness). Intensive aid intervention takes place so as to prevent further social exclusion. The reintegration into the labour market is also a means of preventing single mothers from isolation and exclusion. Their reintegration improves the chances of their children reaching their full potential too. Overall, the chapter is about the process of empowering single mothers and improving their level of independence, and asks whether intensive social aid empowers women enough to make their re-socialisation a success today and in the near future.

6.6
Single Mothers in the Netherlands

In Dutch research a one-parent family is identified as one in which one adult lives permanently with, and is responsible for, the upbringing of one or more young children. These families commonly result from the death of a partner, the collapse of a relationship or an extramarital birth (Plantinga, 1999). In 2001 there were 202,000 single-parent households in the Netherlands of which 88% was female. Out of these single parents 1% was between 16 and 24 years old, 90% was between 25 and 49 years, and the other 9% was 50 years or older (Lehmann, Wirtz, 2004).

It used to be that a single parent living on social benefits could remain at home with their children until the youngest child reached the age of 12. However the Dutch government has introduced a new law (*Work Social Assistance Act* or *WSAA*, 2004) which has changed this situation. The current starting point is that every Dutch citizen is responsible for earning his own living and thus participates in the labour market. The *WSSA* makes an exception for single parents until the youngest child is 5 years old; single parents can stay on benefits until that point. To decrease the number of people on social security benefits, local governments have been authorised to create customised care. According to Buseman (2003), 20% of one-parent families obtains an income from paid employment. Another 20% gets by with a combination of alimony payments and social security benefits. The rest barely manages with social security benefits. As well as having to face a crisis in her own marriage, the single mother is also confronted with a network crisis. Generally 40% of her contacts is broken.

Examples of the kind of intensive aid offered to single parents in the Netherlands and Cyprus are described below.

6.6.1. Intensive Social Aid by Xonar

In 2001 the Dutch umbrella organisation Federatie Opvang calculated the capacity for all residential services for homeless women – and their children – as 1,853 places (Trimbos-instituut, 2004). One of these services is Xonar vrouwenopvang en hulpverlening (Xonar) in Maastricht. It is a unique residential service which women with or without children can call upon for aid. The interrelated and often reinforcing problems of these women include physical abuse, sexual abuse, psychiatric problems, child rearing problems, limited independence and unwanted pregnancy. Only women with a serious drug or alcohol addiction, psychiatric illness or a severe mental handicap are ineligible for this aid. Together, the social work professional and the single mother set targets and develop an individual plan. They focus on the future, i.e. social integration and independence, and carry out what is realistic under the circumstances.

They aim to increase competencies by:
- learning new skills;
- reducing or extending tasks;
- reducing stress;
- activating or increasing protective factors.

Part of Xonar's method involves a housing strategy, which is divided into three phases. Although there are certain house rules, the women can move about freely whilst caring for their children. Depending on the woman's developments (e.g. demonstrations of responsibility, education skills) she can move on to the next phase and finally to one of Xonar's equipped apartments. There the woman is fully responsible for herself and her child, her expenses, free time, the child's school or kindergarten etc. Through the local housing corporation she can apply for a suitable house. The intensive aid programme ends here although a follow up programme is available if required.

6.7
Single Mothers in Cyprus

The *Public Assistance and Services Law 8/91* (1975) defines single parents as individuals who are unwed mothers, widows or widowers, or whose spouse is in prison for over five years, is missing or who has been deported and has dependent children. However, the 2004 modification of the existing law has extended the category of single parent to include individuals who are divorced or separated.

In Cyprus, the Department of Social Welfare Services of the Ministry of Labour and Social Insurance provides family support programmes which aim to alleviate/prevent the risks associated with social exclusion and poverty. Literature on women has demonstrated that female-headed households run a high risk of falling into poverty, and this is what needs to be avoided in Cyprus. Statistical information from recently conducted surveys in Cyprus (Varnavidou, Roussou, 2004) revealed that female households bear an unequal share of the burden of poverty compared with households headed by a man. Where households are headed by single mothers, the family will fall down to the poverty line if the mother becomes unemployed. It appears that a large number of women in this situation come from refugee backgrounds (due to the 1974 events in Cyprus), and so have little support from their extended families.

In terms of aid to single parents, the *Public Assistance and Services Law 8/91* in Cyprus includes special provisions to support single-parent families headed by single mothers. These provisions aim to promote human dignity and to help the family become independent of public funds. This includes public assistance in the form of money and/or services may be granted to these women even when they are fully employed. The main criterion for eligibility is that this type of family has inadequate resources for meeting its basic and special needs as determined by law.

Also, other measures to benefit women of this category include:
- improvement and expansion of childcare facilities;
- provision of special allowances for working people who keep dependent elderly parents at home;
- improvement of the vocational guidance and training system;
- increase of the minimum untaxed income.

According to the statistical services of Cyprus, 378 single parents – as defined by the existing *Public Assistance and Services Law 8/91* (1975) –, and 437 divorced and separated parents received public assistance in 2003. This indicates that the percentage of single-parent families is, at 4%, relatively low in Cyprus when compared with the rest of the European

Union. 97% of these families is headed by women; the proportion of single unwed mothers is a mere 1% whereas single motherhood resulting from divorce adds up to 3%, (*Loxandra Project*, 2000). As previously stated the Cypriot welfare system's provisions are limited to the support of unmarried mothers and widows. Currently the legislation does not consider divorced parents as single parents and thus any contribution is left to the discretion of the director of the Welfare Office.

6.7.1. Intensive Social Aid

As far as the Cypriot situation is concerned, the absence of formal structured intensive aid programmes has resulted in the growth of a number of private programmes. These programmes have attempted to fill the gap in an effort to assist single parents, and in this case single mothers, in their struggle to become independent. The *Loxandra Project* (2000) identified needs connected with further education, vocational training and home-based businesses, and attempted to meet these needs with an intensive social aid project.

The *Project* was developed in order to improve the quality of vocational training for individuals who had been "disadvantaged" by socio-economic factors, and had the ultimate goal of increasing the women's readiness to reintegrate into the community. These women were either unskilled or semi-skilled, and they had been striving to acquire necessary skills in order to become part of the productive labour market to combat their social and economic exclusion. Lastly, the project was aiming to support single women during this transitional period of reintegration by providing them with continuous psychological support. The *Project*'s expectations of this training programme were used as a foundation for future independent services, as well as those to be developed in collaboration with job centres, prospective employers and training teams.

A group of twelve Cypriot single mothers was identified as being interested in the *Project*, and these women were trained for three months. A number of them were able to find jobs during the training period, and some immediately after the training period had ended. The *Project* helped these women reintegrate successfully and smoothly by giving them social and psychological support as well as by meeting their financial needs.

In the above sections, the position of single parents in the Netherlands and Cyprus has been outlined and an example of an aid project in each country has been considered. Now the chapter will examine the effects of such assistance.

6.8
Interviews: The Key Research Instruments

The use of interviews (in-depth or semi-structured) has been very valuable for gathering the woman's experiences and personal reflections. A semi-chronological order was used to describe life stories: the present, the problematic past, the intensive aid period, and the future. The women were invited to tell their stories in their own way. The interview approach also provided the possibility of exploring additional research issues and, maybe more importantly, issues that moved the women during the interview.

Throughout the interviews, the interviewer's attitude was one of "active listening" so as to show understanding. ("Active listening" is a method of listening whereby you reflect back your understanding of what a person says to you. This is meant to confirm to them that you have understood their message, and to give them a chance to correct you if you have not. More importantly, however, this communicates your acceptance of the person's thoughts and emotions.) The repetition of valuable story parts was also used to summarise and to review issues. During the entire interview process, it was important to show faith in the woman "telling the truth" and to accept her story unconditionally. This created a climate in which she could speak freely about behaviour, experiences and opinions.

6.9
The Indicators

The main research questions in the interviews were about whether intensive social aid empowers women to make integration a success, today and in the near future. Because the improvement of competencies have a direct impact on the ability to succeed at social integration, the interview questions and the subsequent presentation of results centre around the specific indicators used for determining social integration and competence-building, namely:
- creating and maintaining living conditions;
- handling and maintaining changes in family relationships;
- creating a stable and stimulating education environment;
- handling health and caring issues;
- participating in networks (through labour, clubs);
- filling up free time;
- building social networks (friends) and participating in them and handling new intimate relationships;
- individual qualities (social skills, flexibility, education level, self-esteem);

- the individual's environment (relatives, friends, social network);
- stress factors (what is experienced as stressful).

6.10
The Dutch Case

In order to draw up the effects of intensive aid on single mothers' self-reliance and independence, the experiences of single mothers had to be collected and analysed. Therefore it was decided to conduct qualitative research and to collect individual life stories by in-depth interviews. A life story is one's description of what one perceives to be the meaningful parts of one's life (Oplatka, 2001). In the present study, the woman is asked to deliver her personal experience while the interviewer takes on the role of a potential listener. The story focuses on the problems faced at the moment when the woman decided to look for aid, and how that aid was located. It looks at the problem-diagnosis, the aid offered, the processes and outcomes; the final results, the life changes problem resolution, and the potential for independent living. The outcome of the interviews is not intended to be representative of single mothers in general.

6.10.1. Results of the Dutch Interviews

The women that participated in the Dutch interviews ranged from 17 to 38 years of age; they all had one child aged between 1 and 6 years. They all lived in rented accommodation and they all had different ethnic backgrounds. Most had fled from domestic violence or homelessness. Their first need was to find rest before rebuilding their lives, and in all cases the discovery of other women in similar forms of distress was an important comforting factor. The women did not have formal employment nor did they receive financial support from their former partners. They received social benefits (WWB-Wet Werken Bijstand) and family allowance. A private reintegration office was available to them, and offered them supervised workplace experiences in local companies.

6.10.2. Creating Living Conditions

During the stay at Xonar, the women were satisfied with the personal mentor who supervised their development process. They were particularly pleased about being responsible for the execution of their own plan. It was an important form of empowerment. The older women were strongly motivated to become independent; they made quicker progress and had clearer perspectives for the future. The younger women struggled with this and were more reserved about the future. Having moved on from Xonar, the women are now able to create their own living conditions. They are satisfied with their new houses and with the move towards independent living. They are less satisfied with the uncertainties of the job training programme. Paradoxically, the women are hesitant about starting work yet they complain about the boredom of being at home.

6.10.3. Handling and Maintaining Changing Family Situations

Women who had their own family lives prior to entering Xonar were able to care for their children from the start. Those who had a child right before or during the intervention period had to learn to do this. The provision of specific training on assertiveness, budget planning, mobility, hygiene, family law etc. helped most women gain some independence. Some women also required trauma or behaviour therapy provided by an external professional institution. At the time of the interviews, the women's family situations were stable.

6.10.4. Creating a Stable and Stimulating Education Environment

Over time, the women learned to become responsible for their own apartments, budgets and appointments. The organisation of sessions on relevant issues contributed to this learning. For example, "good morning" sessions involved each woman informing the group of her plans and appointments for the day. The session taught the women how to structure a day, e.g. how to manage the baby's feeding schedule and arrangements with the lawyer or doctor. Another very useful type of session was the "thematic" session on subjects such as communication with the baby, child rearing issues, healthy eating habits, first aid etc. Learning occurred as a result of the contents of the session as well as from the exchanges amongst the women/mothers themselves. Currently, the children's education is led by the mother and in some cases supported by day care or primary school.

6.10.5. Handling Health Care Issues

All the women follow the Dutch national child health protection plan. At this stage, the women and their children appear to be in good health even though some have a history with drugs.

6.10.6. Filling up Free Time

Given the lack of formal employment, the women have a lot of free time and most of them find it hard to fill it. They lack friends with whom to socialise and to plan activities. Again, paradoxically they find being alone boring yet they hesitate to make new contacts. Much of their free time used to be spent with other Xonar women and their children; some even became close friends. However, after Xonar, many of these women moved and this led to the loss of their contacts and increased their isolation.

6.10.7. Building up and Participating in Social Networks (Friends, Relatives...)

Most women find it very hard to build a new social network after losing the greater part of their old networks through divorce or as the result of moving to another city (for Xonar). Even more problematic is the situation of the ethnic minority women who have few friends and whose relatives are too far away to provide any support. These women find it particularly hard to trust life outside Xonar. Upon completion of Xonar's programme, the women are left to develop their new social networks independently.

6.10.8. Individual Qualities and Skills

Motivation is a key quality when it comes to developing independence, and Xonar bases its work upon the women's individual qualities. The more mature women were quicker to realise the importance of becoming independent than were the younger women. In the group session on domestic violence, the older women were able to process past experiences and use these to develop new skills. In contrast, some of the younger women are still struggling today to combine their child rearing tasks and their own individual needs. In some cases, women had to learn to speak Dutch during their stay at Xonar and this proved to be an indispensable condition for independent living. Most of the women still lack the necessary skills to equip their new houses and they have no networks to call upon for assistance.

6.10.9. The Individual's Environment

Entering the intensive aid period in Xonar was described as both a safe haven and a frightening step to take. Meeting single mothers with similar experiences was very encouraging for all. After Xonar, several of the women lost this supportive environment and they still hope to recuperate this loss through employment.

6.10.10. Stress Factors

By taking the step towards the intensive aid programme, the women left most of their stress behind them. Some are still involved in juridical procedures for gaining custody of their children and creating visiting arrangements for the father. For others, ex-partners are still a distant threat. Once these arrangements have been made some women still fear the quality of the implementation of the agreements made, and ask for official child protection.

6.11
The Cypriot Case

In order to gain a clearer understanding of the impact and the effects of intensive aid on single mothers' self-reliance and independence, the experiences of single mothers needed to be examined. The information depicted below is based on primary data collected during and after the training through questionnaires administered to all twelve women, and semi-structured interviews conducted with three of these women after the completion of the programme. Thus, quantitative and qualitative research was conducted. As with the Dutch case, this case looked at the problem, the aid offered, the process and its outcome (changes in lives, the resolution of certain problems, and the potential for independent living). However, as in the Dutch study, the outcomes of these interviews are not intended to be representative of single mothers in general.

6.11.1. Results of the Cypriot Programme

The *Loxandra Project* seemed to be the first structured effort in Cyprus to deal with the needs of unemployed single parents, especially women. This was a structured attempt to support the population under study to enter the labour market and ultimately to improve their quality of life. The specific problem of unemployment amongst single parents who are mainly unskilled women highlights the inequalities that appear to exist between men and women. In Cyprus, as in most European countries, a large percentage of women are housewives, they are less educated and more financially dependent than men. As a result, women generally have fewer opportunities in life than men. In all, 500 single parents – not as defined by the existing law because the sample included divorced and separated parents as well – were selected by the snowball design (Aaker, Day, 1990). Of these, twelve single mothers agreed to participate, and they all completed the *Project*. These were single mothers, that is women who were either divorced, separated, widows, or unmarried mothers, who responded to the needs assessment survey and who participated in the interview process. The survey was examining to what degree these families had financial, educational, social and psychological needs which had to be met before they could reintegrate successfully.

Findings from the reported data conclude that the predominant portrait of the single mother in Cyprus was that of a working mother with children and a low income. She was generally a high school graduate living in adequate housing, and she usually had custody of the children whilst nearing the heaviest financial burden for them. As reported, most of the single-parent's income was spent on rent, and groceries, and less was spent on medical expenses, recreation and personal expenses. In line with findings from other European countries, and given the limited services and shortcomings of the legislation provided by the Cypriot State, the mother is the one who bears most of the financial burden for child rearing. A number of these women reported receiving financial support from their former partners; however they also added that they were very frequently in the courts due to long delays in alimony payments. Interestingly, most women also reported some type of financial help from their parents.

The participants were trained for a period of three months, and the curriculum included communication strategies, self-development, assertiveness, hygiene, cooking, budgeting, marketing, and computer skills. The trainers were trained in advance in order to be aware of the needs of the specific group. Among them was a psychologist who not only served as a trainer but who also responded to the numerous psychological needs of these women during and after the training process.

6.11.2. Living Conditions of the Participants

Considering the general life-style of the Cypriot population, the satisfactory responses of the sample regarding their living conditions were not a surprise. The majority of the sample reported living in a house or an apartment of a satisfactory condition. However, some reported that heating was insufficient and this could be problematic because heating is of primary importance considering the very low winter temperatures in Cyprus, especially at night. These women felt that having their own space was a form of empowerment in that they could develop and live their lives with their children, independently. Taking into consideration the closeness of the Cypriot families and the fact that traditional extended families have not disappeared, it could be stated that some of these women had family members in close proximity, and this facilitated their living conditions.

6.11.3. Handling and Maintaining Changing Family Situations

The main difficulties or reservations that the women expressed during and after the training process concerned the feeling that they had less time with their children, and occasionally they feared that they were neglecting them. However, in general they were very optimistic and believed that the training would ultimately help them increase their incomes, and consequently their quality of life, independence and social facilitation. A small percentage of the women expressed the fear that they might not succeed in the programme, and some feared losing their allowance from the Department of Social Welfare Services of the Ministry of Labour and Social Insurance. However, the women generally felt that they were helped and motivated by the psychologist who provided psychological support and counselling during the transitional period.

6.11.4. Creating a Stable and Stimulating Education Environment

The educational training programme was intended to open new horizons for single parents who were in urgent need of becoming financially independent with new employment possibilities. These women had multiple needs, and the programme attempted to help gratify them through a designated curriculum. The programme was adjusted to reflect some of the constraints which affected the women's lives, such as the need for babysitters or for transport arrangements. There were flexible teaching hours, and overall the *Project* was composed of courses which were more practical in nature with the emphasis on group activities, role-play and hands-on-experiences.

6.11.5. Handling Health Care Issues

Most of these women did not express any major health problems, although from the questionnaires it could be concluded that due to their financial difficulties, any health issues were given a low priority. Nevertheless most of these women and their children used the subsidized medical services offered by the Ministry of Health.

6.II.6. Participation in Networks (through Labour, Club, or School)

The women in the *Loxandra Project* did not participate in any formal type of network; however, they did express the need to belong to a group composed of people facing similar problems.

6.II.7. Filling up Free Time

The responses indicate that the single women mainly felt deprived of money and time for themselves. These women did not express any need to fill in free time. They had all the responsibilities of raising children alone, they were committed to financial, welfare and psychological support programmes, and consequently they had no time for themselves.

6.II.8. Building up and Participating in Social Networks (Friends, Relatives...)

When the women of this study joined the *Project* they did not report any significant changes in the behaviour of the people in their immediate environment. However, they did emphasise that after their divorce many of them experienced a decline in living standards, in terms of both financial status and their social lives as a family. Yet most of them had good friends who supported both the mother and her children. In some cases, where the mother was of a low socio-economic and educational background, there were reports that the children felt some type of discrimination at school, and that they were generally socially excluded.

As far as the social conditions they experienced during and after the training, the greater majority of the sample felt that they had close friends who supported them and treated them with sympathy, love and understanding or at least they maintained the same attitude as before the training. It must be emphasised that in small communities such as those in Cyprus, families live in close proximity to each other. As a result, the immediate family such as parents and other close relatives support each other, at least financially, and in such a way they form the most common of social networks. This creates a dependency upon the people in the immediate environment. In our case the parents of the single mother helped as much as possible, however in some cases this kind of support can lead to parents exerting strong control over needy members of the family.

6.11.9. Individual Qualities and Skills

Most women who expressed an interest in the *Project* wanted reintegration alongside professional assurance and an increase in income. Their ulterior motive was to ensure a better standard of living for their children. So these women were motivated enough to start and complete the *Project*. Some felt that due to their family circumstances, which did not allow them to be properly employed, they did not possess the skills and capabilities required for a career and successful reintegration. This could imply a sense of low self-image, mainly as a result of the conditions they had to face. However they did express the need to belong to a group facing similar problems, worries and challenges.

6.11.10. The Individual's Environment

The *Loxandra Project* attempted to promote equality of access to initial training for single mothers, and it also aimed to promote the acquisition of skills necessary to combat social exclusion. Being part of the *Project* made these women feel that they were given a special opportunity to develop as mothers and as women. They were also able to place a greater emphasis on the value of education and training. As these women developed close relationships with each other in the group, they felt safe and intrinsically motivated to continue. They felt more self-confident, and as a result of constant support from the trainers, the psychologist and their peers they progressed successfully, each at their own pace, towards the completion of the programme.

6.11.11. Stress Factors

One finding which concurs with the current research on single mothers is that the participants felt that their role as single mothers deprived them of certain "rights" in life. For example, having no time for themselves due to too many responsibilities, and having no social life. These are some of the stresses that impact on the social and psychological development of these women. These were worked on during the *Project*. Other stresses concerned the relationship with the other parent. It was reported that although the relationship with the other parent was mostly average, the issue of alimony was causing them numerous problems. Also the absence or loss of a partner from the household produced a type of grief along with a range of feelings such as anger, fear, sadness and anxiety. These needed to be explored, managed and addressed during the *Project*. Other issues pertinent to single mothers included the presence, in very small percentages, of prejudice, sexual harassment, and avoidance by relatives. These are some of the additional stresses which needed to be considered and managed.

6.12
Conclusions: The Dutch Case and the Cypriot Case

Some conclusions can be drawn about the effects of intensive social aid on the self-reliance and independence of single mothers as a way towards social inclusion. Examples of good practice have been identified in the aid provided by both the Xonar programme and the *Loxandra Project*. They appeared to have had a relatively strong impact on the women's lives, although the aid was of temporary duration and so the women had to go on to manage independently. Overall, three key elements that appeared to "make or break" the journey towards successful social inclusion considered: self-empowerment, labour market reintegration, and the rebuilding of social networks.

A significant contribution to the women's social inclusion was the development of self-empowerment, a regained responsibility for their own situations, increased self-esteem, increased awareness in terms of dealing with finances, application forms, government agencies, courts of lay etc. Although the participants' ideas for the future were rather vague and they hesitated to make concrete plans, these women were more accepting of their new situations and had tried to make the best of them. In the Dutch case the ethnic minority women, in particular, were actually more integrated into society after the intensive aid period. Learning to speak the Dutch language was a critical success factor.

Additionally, in the case of the Dutch women, the lack of a (strong) social network affected all but one single mother. The availability of a single friend or a family member was too small a basis from which to rebuild a new life, especially in a new city or environment. Some women were "locked up" at home with their children for years, without friends to introduce them into the new environment, or a babysitter to allow them to socialise or work. However, unlike the Dutch case, the majority of the Cypriot women, due to the smallness of their communities, and their traditionally strong family ties, were rarely deprived of social support or social networks. Also, although the search for work could have lead to employment and important (new) contacts for rebuilding a social network, few of these women, especially the Dutch ones, considered the search for a new job as a current option.

Reintegration into the labour market was necessary in order to gain independence and to play an active role in society. However, the women demonstrate little effort to find employment that would have released them from the social security system. In both cases, the small but reliable social benefit income was quite satisfactory. Their lack of initiative had them waiting for the private reintegration office to look for a job placement that could lead to employment. The Dutch mothers with very young children had not even considered contact with the reintegration office. In fact, most were reluctant to use childcare. It was striking that the element of time was of little relevance for these women and yet they felt burdened by boredom and loneliness. The effect of this in both countries was that they lost and wasted time which could have been used to educate themselves through schooling or labour market experiences. This loss weakened their future position on the labour market. A more creative use of the women's regained self-esteem, energy and motivation towards independence could have been used to fill the gap between the moment of departure from Xonar or Loxandra, and the moment of entry into the labour market.

The departure from Xonar (including the social workers and the other single women), the lack of a strong social network and the lack of immediate employment opportunities ensured that the single mothers were still vulnerable even though their overall situation has improved. The vacuum created after the departure from Xonar brought about the potential for new threats like frustration, isolation, or even of developing "wrong" new friends. For these reasons alone, some follow-up on the more vulnerable cases could prove very valuable for the women and for the investment made by Xonar.

In the Cypriot case, the completion of the intensive aid programme had made a significant contribution to the participants both psychologically, physically and cognitively. As these single mothers acquired skills and knowledge, they felt more educated and capable. As their self-esteem and their concepts of themselves increased, so did their self-reliance, self-confidence, and thus their independence. The degree of readiness for reintegration into the community was increasing being built up at a slow but steady pace. The programme helped them develop a social identity within a group, and this considerably helped them towards gratifying some of their needs for belonging. The issue of gaining the necessary independence to become active participants in society was a factor that contributed a great deal towards reintegration into the different strata of society.

It is interesting to note that in Cyprus, due to the small (albeit increasing) number of single mothers and the greater homogeneity of the population, intensive aid programmes are limited. In addition, they are mainly concentrated in the private sector. In terms of the public sector, the Department of Social Welfare Services of the Ministry of Labour and Social Insurance limits aid as far as financial, social and psychological support is concerned. However we hope that there will be more developments in the future because Cyprus is now part of the European family.

The present chapter aimed to explore the circumstances surrounding the reintegration of single mothers who, according to the literature, urgently need to become financially independent and to create new employment opportunities. This chapter attempted to highlight that, despite the multiple cultural, religious, political and social differences between the two countries, single mothers faced comparable situations in each country. In both Cyprus and the Netherlands, single mothers coped with similar worries, anxieties, skills, and basic stresses.

To conclude, it is clear that the particular problems and the circumstances of single mothers are similar in the Netherlands and Cyprus. As some of the needs were clearly addressed in this chapter such as emotional support, proper safe housing, affordable quality childcare, and further educational and job skills training, the topic of single mothers is a major one. With the rapid changes in the family structures of many societies in recent years the issue of single parents needs further examination. Further social policies need to be introduced so as to focus on the creation of networks and the development of creative approaches in dealing with single mothers. Broadening the spectrum of services will give a voice to these women who often live in poverty and isolation, and will ultimately result in improving their quality of life.

Bibliography

AAKER D. A., DAY G. S. (1990), *Marketing Research*, Wiley, New York, IV ed.
BLANKENHORN D. (1995), *Fatherless America: Confronting Our most Urgent Social Problem*, Basic Books, New York.
BRANNON L. (1999), *Gender: Psychological Perspectives*, Allyn and Bacon, Boston, II ed.
BURNS A., SCOTT C. (1994), *Mother-Headed Families and why They Have Increased*, Erlbaum, Hillsdale (NJ).
BUSEMAN E. (2003), *Sterker dan ooit: drie vrouwen over hun leven na de scheiding*. Opzij, Weekbladpers Tijdschriften, Amsterdam.
COUNCIL OF EUROPE (2002), *Cyprus 2001*, www.coe.int/T/e/social_cohesion/population/Demographic_Year_Book/2001_Edition/Cyprus%202001.asp.
DEKKER P., EDERVEEN S., JEHOEL-GIJSBERS G., MOOIJ R. DE (2003), *European Outlook 1: Social Europe – Single European Social Policy still a Bridge too Far. Annex to the State of the European Union 2004*, CPB-SCP, The Hague.
DOWIT T. (1991), *Meisjes begeleiden naar een zelfstandige toekomst*, NIZW, Utrecht.

FÄRBER F. (2001), *Reactie van EAPN Nederland op het Nationaal Actieplan ter bestrijding van armoede en sociale uitsluiting*, European Anti-Poverty Network/Nederland, Utrecht.

FEDERAL RESEARCH DIVISION – LIBRARY OF CONGRESS (1993a), *Family and Marriage*, in Id., *Cyprus: A Country Study*, countrystudies.us/cyprus/24.htm.

ID. (1993b), *Status of Women*, in Id., *Cyprus: A Country Study*, countrystudies.us/cyprus/25.htm.

HEEL A. VAN, WARMER S. (1997), *Gericht op de toekomst; toekomstgericht begeleiden van cliënten van opvangvoorzieningen bij sociale integratie*, NIZW, Utrecht.

HENDRIKS A., WILLEMS M. (1999), *Zelfstandig wonende jonge moeders: en ze leefden nog lang en gelukkig*, Hogeschool, Maastricht.

HOLSTEIN J. A., GUBRIUM J. F. (1995), *The Active Interview*, Sage, Thousand Oaks (CA).

KUIPER W. (2001), *Sociaal op maat: onderzoek naar de rol van de provincies in de strijd tegen armoede en sociale uitsluiting*, Stichting Sjakuus, Utrecht.

LEHMANN P., WIRTZ C. (2004), *Household Formation in the EU – Lone Parents*, in "Statistics in Focus", III, 5 (http://www.eustatistics.gov.uk/statistics_in_focus/downloads/KS-NK-04-005-__-N-EN.pdf).

LISBON EUROPEAN COUNCIL (2002), *Presidency Conclusions*, http://ue.eu.int/ueDocs/cms_Data/docs/pressData/en/ec/00100-r1.enO.htm.

Loxandra Project (2000), Leonardo da Vinci SPFs, Intercollege, Nicosia, Unpublished Report.

MACIONIS J. J. (1999), *Sociology*, Prentice-Hall, Upper Saddle River (NJ), VII ed.

MEER K. VAN, NEIJENHOF J. VAN (1997), *Exploreren van probleemsituaties*, Bohn, Stafleu, van Loghum, Houten.

MEINEMA T. (2002), *Nationaal Actieplan Social Inclusion 2003*, in "Intermezzo", 6, pp. 6-9.

MENGER R., JHINKOE-RAI S. (eds.) (1997), *Tienermoeders – preventie, opvang en begeleiding*, SWP, Utrecht.

OLSON D. H., DEFRAIN J. D. (1996), *Marriage and the Family: Diversity and Strengths*, Mayfield, Mountain View (CA).

OPLATKA I. (2001), *Building a Typology of Self-Renewal: Reflection upon Life Story Research*, in "The Qualitative Report", VI, 4, www.nova.edu/ssss/QR/QR6-4/oplatka.html.

PLANTINGA J. (1999), *Alleenstaande moeders en de systematiek van de verzorgingsstaat. Een vergelijkend onderzoek naar de sociaal economische positie van alleenstaande moeders in Nederland, Denemarken, Duitsland, het Verenigd Koninkrijk en Italië*, Onderzoekschool Arbeid, Welzijn en Sociaaleconomisch Bestuur, Utrecht.

PRUD'HOMME N. (2003), *Single-Parent Families*, ISSA Conference, http://www.issa.int/pdf/sanjose03/2prudhomme.pdf.

RAIJER P. (2001), *Zij aan zij: een onderzoek naar de behoeften van gevluchte jonge moeders*, Hogeschool, Maastricht.

REPUBLIC OF CYPRUS (2004), *Social and Labour Policy*, http://www.cyprus.gov.cy/cyphome/govhome.nsf/LookupIDs/65E78C2D007A54D9C2256A7100399744?OpenDocument&languageNo=1.

SALEMANS F. (2003), *Projecthandleiding SPH*, Nelissen, Soest.
SANTROCK J. W. (1999), *Life-Span Development*, McGraw-Hill College, Boston, VII ed.
SCHUYT K. (2002), *Social Exclusion: The Least, the Last, the Lost and the Latest*. International Conference on Social Welfare, NIZW, Rotterdam.
TRIMBOS-INSTITUUT (2004), *Maatschappelijke zorg – Maatschappelijke opvang inclusief vrouwenopvang*, www.trinbos.nl.
Van tienermoeder tot carrièrepil; uitkomsten van een conferentie op 12 juni 2002 te Amsterdam (2002), in "Op gelijke voet", XXIII, 3.
VARNAVIDOU M., ROUSSOU M. (2004), *Replies to Questionnaire on the Implementation of the Beijing Platform for Action (A/52/231)*, http://www.un.org/womenwatch/daw/followup/responses/Cyprus.html.
WEL F. VAN, KNIJN T. (2002), *Alleenstaande ouders over zorgen en werken*, Elzevier, Den Haag.
WILLIAMS F. (1997), *Feminism and Social Policy*, in V. Robinson, D. Richardson (eds.), *Introducing Women's Studies: Feminist Theory and Practice*, Macmillan, Houndmills.

7
Current Trends in Supporting Children, Youth and Their Families in Two European Urban Regions: Amsterdam and Madrid

by *Wilfred Diekmann* and *Agustín Moñivas*

7.1
Introduction

About fifty years ago youth care was understood to be the sum of youth protection (legal intervention with parental authority) and youth care (mainly residential and some foster care). However this system often led to results that were unsatisfactory, unproductive or both. While in some cases removing a child from its parent(s) and bringing up the child in long- or short-term residential care might be inevitable, it is most undesirable. The removal is often ineffective and even harmful for a child and, accordingly, it should be avoided wherever possible (Hermanns, 2001).

More and more, a common view on youth care or, more broadly speaking, care for youth is taking shape; one where the measures of social work intervention are in the young person's living environment, and where the assistance extends to the parents by supporting and enabling them to raise their children in a more productive manner. Whilst this new vision on youth care is still developing, the youth care services in Amsterdam and Madrid are making real attempts to implement it to meet the challenges of current youth care issues in practice.

This chapter will briefly describe youth and youth care in Amsterdam and Madrid and then go on to present and characterise a new view on youth care. This is followed by a brief case study in each city to illustrate the youth care services in practice. Some of the interesting differences between the two cases may have to do with the different types of (welfare) States represented. However, an initial conclusion would appear to be that "outreach" methods in youth care require specific competencies for the social workers involved regardless of the type of (welfare) State.

It is also worth clarifying that the term "youth care" is understood as the translation of the Dutch term *jeugdhulpverlening* and the Spanish *atención a los menores*. It comprises many forms of service provision for children, young people and parents. The youth care does not encompass, for example, the (child) psychiatric services that belong to the health care system as these services are quite different in terms of culture, views, working methods, finances etc.

7.2
Youth in Amsterdam and Madrid

Amsterdam is a much smaller city than Madrid but similarly it is part of a region consisting of significantly larger communities. Both cities have a similar percentage of young people, and the cultural make-up of the population is very diverse. Furthermore, there is an increasing number of ethnic minorities within the parameters of both cities. TABS. 7.1-7.2 identify basic information on the population composition (TAB. 7.1); and on the breakdown of age groups the under-19s (TAB. 7.2) in both cities.

TABLE 7.1
Inhabitants of the cities of Amsterdam and Madrid (2003)

City	Population	Regional population	Ethnic groups (%)
Amsterdam	736,000	1,500,000	38.5
Madrid	3,000,000	5,600,000	12.3

Sources: www.onstat.amsterdam.nl; www.comadrid.es/iestadis.

TABLE 7.2
Population under 19 years in the cities of Amsterdam and Madrid (2003)

Amsterdam		Madrid	
Age	Population	Age	Population
0-4	46,400	0-6	312,150
5-9	37,000	7-11	264,065
10-14	36,000	12-18	349,754
15-19	35,000		
Total	154,400		925,969

Sources: www.onstat.amsterdam.nl; www.comadrid.es/iestadis.

7.3
Youth Care in the Netherlands and in Amsterdam

In the Netherlands there is a distinction between youth care and youth protection, although the border is diminishing. Youth protection in the first place is a legal system constructed to stop and prevent problems like child abuse, neglect and juvenile delinquency. It is possible to override the parents' authority and to order the supervision of parents. Family supervision agencies are important in the Dutch youth care system. The social workers involved are responsible for the contact with children, youngsters and their families and they have the authority to take important decisions in regard to, for example, compulsory placements in (semi)-residential facilities. The family supervisors are the so-called case-managers of mandatory youth care.

The care itself is done by the youth care services (*jeugdhulpverlening*), via residential or non-residential services, as well as by other services like youth psychiatry. Foster care is part of the youth care system. Furthermore, youth treatment is not necessarily compulsory. As a whole, there are often significant problems with young people in Amsterdam City, and the rate of supervision orders is relatively high (14 per 1,000 youngsters every year: Slot, Braak, Theunissen, 2004).

The last decade has seen the development of regional youth care services (Bureaus Jeugdzorg). These services provide for one entrance for every child, youngster or parent with child/youth rearing problems. The core tasks of the regional youth service are the diagnosis and assessment of youth care needs. Each of the five districts in Amsterdam City has a regional youth care service as well as other large youth care organisations (currently decentralizing their services to reach clients). The youth care organisation SAC-Amstelstad Jeugdzorg is an example of one that recently reduced its youth residential care to a minimum by concentrating on supporting parents, children and youth at home.

These reconstructions are part of the endeavour to create a system of providing help which is as near to the natural living environment as possible. A new *Act on Child and Youth Care* (2004) tries to fix and legitimise these developments. However, some problems persist, and these are characteristic of a bureaucratically organised welfare State, namely a lack of co-ordination between different service areas – youth care, health care, housing, work and income etc.

7.4
Youth Care in Spain and in Madrid

Spain has a public social security system for all citizens, and sufficient social assistance and services for those in situations of need. The social services system consists of provisions and services of the State administration (national level), the administration of the Autonomous Communities (regional level) and the local corporations (local level). All of Spain's 17 Autonomous Communities have authority on matters of social services. The 1990 Sectorial Conference of Social Affairs created the framework for the

shared planning of social welfare and launched the following activities to protect children and their families and to prevent harmful social situations:
- interministerial and regional co-operation: to develop and apply the *Penal Responsibility of Minors' Law* (2000) and to develop procedures in the Minors' Court;
- grants for youth support programmes;
- promotion of a family support policy.

The Childhood Observatory was also created in 1999 to gather information on children and their quality of life and the changes they experience. Furthermore it proposes social policies for improvement in the different spheres of childhood (Francisco, 2002).

The general framework is quite well developed in Madrid given that the same political party governed during three administrations for eight years (until 14 March 2004). The basic services are delivered by the municipal social services, and constitute the primary level for general social services. The Social Services Centres (SSC) offer social services to individuals and families, and they also develop social programmes for the larger community, i.e. the *Prevention and Family Programme*, the *Minors' and Families' Care Programme*.

7.5
Changing Views on Youth Care

Whether in the Netherlands or in Spain, youth care is increasingly seen as supporting children, youngsters and their parents in their natural living environments. In fact this is comparable to the changing attitudes in psychiatric care (Bommel, 2003). This does not mean that there is no need for intensive residential care but that families should be supported in every way possible. This may span from short-term, non-intensive care to long-term intensive care.

Many factors influence this process including the perception of the role of citizens in society and the limitations of (welfare) States. Care provided in the natural living environment places citizens in a central position and encourages them to use their own competencies to solve their own problems. Its emphasis is on people and how they should be able to count on each other, live and work together, and help each other. This is, of course, directly linked to social exclusion. In fact this is one of the most important issues in European social policy today (Dekker *et al.*, 2003). Unfortunately, however, it becomes increasingly clear how difficult it is to develop a new approach to youth care services in European countries, not least of all because of the level of existing bureaucracy which often turns out to be counter-productive (Gilbert, 2002).

For the last five decades discussions on the youth care system have been constant and are inspired by the lack of achievement in the current system which removes people's responsibilities (e.g. parents), isolates them from their social environment (e.g. residential care) and neglects their strengths and their natural social environment. This is why the ecological system approach, as supported by Germain (1979), can be described as a more effective paradigm towards care. Many other authors support the theoretical foundation of this "alternative" approach. Some of the Dutch authors include Hermanns and Leu (1998), Hermanns, Mordang and Mulders (2002), and Spanish authors include Paul Ochotorena (1988), López (1995), Casas (1998), Gaitán (1999), and Roldán et al. (2003).

For the purpose of this chapter, the Hermanns, Mordang and Mulders' (2002) perspective is specifically identified as the main source for the following statements which characterise the theoretical foundation of the ecological system theory.

1. *Upbringing and growing up are characterised by self-regulation and adaptation.* In most cases upbringing succeeds and, even in problem situations, parents are able to meet the needs of their child. There is no "best way" to raise a child. There are different (family) systems, different environments and circumstances with different people. There is no single way to successfully raise a child. Mechanisms of self-regulation and adaptation play an important role in this process. There may be limited information on how the two work, but they are reliable (re)sources.

2. *Self-regulation is threatened by an accumulation of risk factors.* The risks and stresses of daily life rarely have a dominant or long-term harmful effect. Still, research demonstrates that an accumulation of risks and problems is potentially harmful for the development of (young) people. They can be linked to the person, e.g. an illness, ill temperament, and disability; to family concerns, e.g. inadequate housing, a parent with mental illness, mistreatment; and to social problems, e.g. poverty, war.

3. *If self-regulation is interfered with, there is a severe change and complex problems arise.* Multiple risk factors tend to lead to developmental problems. This is particularly true when the self-regulation of the system is affected. The (family) system breaks down.

4. *In general these problems are multiple: the type of problem is determined by the specific traits of the child, the parents and the social and cultural context.* Problems in the functioning of the (family) system lead to new problems and affect the development of the members of the system through e.g. behavioural problems, learning disabilities, depres-

sion etc., according to circumstances. The problems are thus complex and multidimensional. This jeopardises further development although it is difficult to predict in what way (especially from a diagnostic point of view).

5. *The protective traits of the child, the parents and the context can compensate for the effects of accumulated risks.* Problems are often tackled by focusing on problem resolution or by compensating for deficiencies. People's protective factors have specific mitigating effects upon risk factors. These apply to the child (temperament, intelligence, sense of humour), the family (strong personalities, good relationships) and the context (rewarding employment, financial means, pleasant neighbourhood, good school and friends).

6. *Social support is a very strong protective factor.* Good relations within and outside the family are important. It is critical to have support available when it is needed. It can be informational, practical, emotional etc. People living in a situation with social support are able to bear more than those without.

The characteristics of the theory discussed lead to the view that youth care should be based on the restoration and/or strengthening of the social support for youth and parents in the natural living environment. The ultimate goal is the restoration of self-regulation and adaptation! Youth care should "compensate" only when and where it is strictly necessary and should mainly promote and facilitate the possibilities and competencies of the (members of the) system whenever and wherever possible.

More specifically, then, youth care provided by an ecological system theory approach should be a professional way of promoting social support work in the client's natural living environment, work on concrete needs, demands and problems and, finally, work in (and with) the client's networks. These characteristics are those of a demand-oriented approach to youth care service provision. They cover features that are different to those of a social worker following the more traditional approach to youth care, namely a diagnostic-oriented approach. The differences between the two approaches are reflected in TAB. 7.3.

The demand-oriented model uses an ecological system approach. This approach is particularly important in relation to the increasing diversity in societies (ethnic groups, cultures, life-styles, problems, sociocultural contexts) and the growing complexity of metropolitan societies. There is no single way to live a family life or to raise a child. Societies will only be able to meet the needs of diversity by having an eye for differences and by using the strengths therein.

TABLE 7.3
Diagnostic- and demand-oriented approaches to youth care

Diagnostic-oriented approach	Demand-oriented approach
Professional defines problem.	Client (system) defines problem.
Professional thinks of solutions.	Client (system) thinks of solutions.
Professional is responsible.	Client (system) is responsible.
Professional thinks in terms of (fixed) traits.	Professional thinks in terms of processes.
Emphasis is on problems.	Stress is placed on strengths and possibilities of client (system).
Specialisation plays an important role.	Generalist approach.
Support and/or care is delivered by (and in) institutions.	Support and/or care is delivered at home.

Source: Hermanns, Mordang, Mulders (2002).

The following sections describe two cases based on life situations: one in Amsterdam and one in Madrid. The purpose of these cases is to demonstrate how professionals in both cities attempt to use the ecological system theory in their work within different youth care contexts and systems. We will conclude by reflecting on these cases, and refer to the similarities and differences between the two systems. This is not meant to be an exhaustive comparison but to reflect the impressions and ideas of the authors.

7.6
Dutch Case

Johnny is a 7-year-old boy who was placed in residential youth care at the early age of 18 months. Since that age he has lived in several institutions including a child psychiatric placement. Johnny has a mother, a father and a 13-year-old brother. The mother and father live together in a very small house. She has a bi-polar psychiatric disorder and has psychotic tendencies, while he suffers from phobias and hyperventilation. Much like Johnny, the older brother has settled in several types of residential care over the years. Johnny's behaviour has always been difficult. His own diagnosis implies reactive attachment disorder and oppositional defiant disorder. His increased behavioural problems are leading to his placement in yet another institution (as soon as there is a place available).

Johnny's case was taken to a meeting composed of different partners within the youth care system, namely, the family supervisor, representatives of the regional youth care services and those of the child psychiatric services. An official of the regional youth care services inquired about the history of the case and wondered why the parents have played such a minor role. In the past, Johnny's parents rarely attended scheduled meetings. One of the youth care workers then offered to talk with Johnny's parents at home and proposed video-home-training (VHT) to improve parent-child communication. The parents accepted the offer and VHT was attempted.

An individual plan was set up for Johnny in which he could stay at home for three weeks with the support of the youth care services and with VHT. The arrangement was a success as Johnny's behaviour improved after having been reunited with his parents. After this, a second plan was proposed to organise a family group-conference whereby members of Johnny's social network searched for solutions to the problem. The participants included Johnny's parents, maternal grandmother, maternal aunt and her husband. Together, they decided that Johnny would try to stay at home, go to a special school and visit some after-school youth clubs. He would be able to stay part of the time with his aunt and the rest with his parents. The mother would lower the dosage of her medication in order to decrease the (invalidating) side effects. Lastly, a larger house would be sought for the family. In spite of some problems (e.g. housing policy) the arrangement was a success and, half a year later, Johnny is doing well. The communication with his parents has improved and his mother's psychiatric problems have decreased.

Although this is but a single case, the youth care worker feels that it has demonstrated the value of ecological system theory, by applying a demand-oriented approach in youth care. On the other hand, the case also demonstrates the consequences and the force of an embedded diagnostic-oriented system that is also institution-oriented, and in which the client (Johnny and his family) is torn apart from the professionals providing support. Authors like Hermanns (2001) actually state this system can even be said to violate the *Convention on the Rights of the Child*, especially the article on the right to grow up at home with your parents.

7.7
Spanish Case

Antonio is a 46-year-old man married to María (37), and father to Roberto (15), Antonio (12) and Carolina (5). This family has limited financial resources. Antonio is long-term unemployed but gets some income from occasional odd jobs and the help of the extended families from both sides. María stays home due to schizophrenia but receives no regular treatment from the mental health services. Antonio is left to care for his wife and the younger children, and to take responsibility for the household tasks. The parents find themselves overwhelmed with the situation of raising the children, and lack the skills to do so. Antonio's mother helps care for the children and the household. María's family occasionally helps, but the relationship is strained because her parents cannot accept their daughter's mental illness.

At a certain point, the children's schools sent the social services a report detecting "socio-familial problems". It stated that Roberto had difficulties getting along with others due to excessively passive behaviour. Pedro's behaviour was excessively aggressive and Carolina had no obvious difficulties. The report went on to state that the children lacked the attention of an adult at home and that they frequently went to school without having bathed and/or wearing inappropriate dress for the season. The children appeared to have inadequate eating habits and a deficient diet and, lastly, they showed a high level of absenteeism.

The report was processed by the social work units' programme, which led to a visit to the family's home to assess the risk situation as outlined in the report. The assessment led to the family's placement in a programme called *Family and Co-Living* which offered them a treatment plan. The process starts with an in-depth study of the family, home visits and meetings with other professionals, and the results lead to the development of the treatment plan, which is worked out by the social worker and the family. The plan aims to provide parents with the skills and abilities required to tend to the needs of their children so that they can remain at home. Antonio's family's plan included the following steps:
– submission of an application for "income maintenance" to provide the family with a stable, minimum income;
– Antonio is referred to an employment search workshop and to an employment foundation to prepare and train him to search for employment;
– María is referred to the Mental Health Unit to monitor her mental illness;
– a home assistance service is provided to help the family with household tasks, food preparation, and cleanliness;
– a volunteer is assigned to help María carry out certain tasks and to accompany her to the Mental Health Unit when necessary;
– Antonio and María are referred to a social skills' workshop to improve their relationship and to socialize with people in similar situations;
– Roberto and Antonio are referred to a youth programme for workshops two afternoons per week; street educators will also begin to work with them and to help them integrate in recreational groups;
– Carolina is included in one of the workshops which target children under 6 years of age.

The family treatment plan is followed-up by a social worker from the *Family and Co-Living Programme*. This professional is responsible for both internal and external resources including the schools and the Mental Health Unit. The second professional in the *Family and Co-Living* team helps carry out the plan of action, namely, organising the domestic life, budgeting, nutrition and hygiene. The additional home assistance programme and the family's participation in educational groups re-enforces this task. In addition, parenting skills are taught with a focus on setting limits, administering awards and consequences, and establishing a regular routine. At the same time, the extended family is addressed, especially Antonio's family, to co-ordinate help and to provide support.

Real progress is evident in relation to the enabling and empowering of Antonio and his family. María receives care and her condition has improved steadily. Antonio has a permanent job and the children attend school regularly. There is order in both child and domestic care.

7.8
Reflection on the Dutch and Spanish Cases

These cases may appear to be different but they both implement a fresh view on child, youth and family care. In the Dutch case, it was an individual youth care worker that chose to apply a demand-orientated approach, which turned out to be a success. In the Spanish case, the care system itself seems to support this approach altogether.

Some reflections on the utility of the two cases:
– in both cases we can see how risk factors in families are detected by working very closely with them, and by meeting them in their own environment;
– we can see the importance of connecting different sectors, programmes and projects (schools, health centres, mental health units, employment foundations etc.): this demonstrates that youth care in itself is not enough;
– the cases permit us to visualise the importance of the ecological system approach: they provide an idea of the competencies required for working with children, youth and their families.

Lastly, it is apparent that in the case of the Netherlands it is very difficult to organise demand- or client-centred support due to the highly developed welfare State. Services are organised in several separate columns of highly organised bureaucracies, often with old-fashioned tendencies and with dissimilar objectives, procedures and money supplies. It is thus extremely difficult to co-operate in specific client-centred arrangements. On the other hand, Spain appears to work quite well from a client-centred approach and in an integrated manner, which may be largely accredited to new operational legal arrangements.

7.9
Consequences for the Competencies of Social Care Workers

This comparative study shows that services for children, young people and their families form a very specific field of practice with different methods of intervention. In addition to case management, administration and community organisation, there are specific approaches for practice with individuals, nuclear and extended families, and groups. This contextual awareness is of the utmost importance in today's complex multicultural, multidimensional societies.

The ecological system theory helps the social worker maintain a focus on the interaction between systems (e.g. individual, family, neighbourhood, school), and continually look for ways to intervene in more than one relevant system (Bronfenbrenner, 1986, 1995; Belsky, 1980, 1984, 1993). The social worker is then required to have a broad knowledge and a skill base from which to serve clients, and to have the ability to select appropriately from that base to meet client needs (Sheafor, Horejsi, 2003). Furthermore, as children and adolescents are not adults, the techniques and approaches effective with adult clients may not work with children (Coles, 1997). Thus, social workers wishing to work with youth need specific, additional competencies in, for example, risk assessment and transition processes (Moñivas, 2002, 2004).

However we have to realise that even when "techniques" and know-how are sufficient, we have no guarantee that the situation will resolve itself in a really empowering way with the maximum use of the social system's resources (Roede *et al.*, 2003). More and more, we are coming to the conclusion that it is very important for social work students and professionals to learn to watch and listen with openness, simply to see and experience what happens, and to establish a functional working relationship with the client. To this end, the social work profession will always be a mix of knowledge, skills and attitude or, this maybe better stated as, head, hands and heart.

Bibliography

AYUNTAMIENTO DE MADRID (2000), *Programa de atención a menores y familias*, Ayuntamiento de Madrid, Madrid.
BELSKY J. (1980), *Child Maltreatment: An Ecological Integration*, in "American Psychologist", XXXV, 4, pp. 320-35.
ID. (1984), *The Determinants of Parenting: A Process Model*, in "Child Development", LV, 1, pp. 83-96.
ID. (1993), *Etiology of Child Maltreatment: A Developmental-Ecological Analysis*, in "Psychological Bulletin", CXIV, 3, pp. 413-34.

BOMMEL M. VAN (2003), *Hulp in eigen omgeving. Amulantisering in de hulpverlening*, Bohn, Stafleu, van Loghum, Houten.
BRONFENBRENNER U. (1986), *Ecology of the Family as a Context for Human Development*, in "American Psychologist", XXXII, pp. 513-31.
ID. (1995), *Development Ecology through Space and Time: A Future Perspective*, in P. Moen, G. H. Elder Jr., K. Lüscher (eds.), *Examining Lives in Context: Perspectives on the Ecology of Human Development*, American Psychological Association, Washington, pp. 619-47.
CASAS F. (1998), *Infancia. Perspectivas psicosociales*, Paidós, Barcelona.
COLES B. (1997), *Welfare Services for Young People*, in J. Roche, S. Tucker (eds.), *Youth in Society: Contemporary Theory, Policy and Practice*, Sage, London, pp. 98-106.
DEKKER P., EDERVEEN S., JEHOEL-GIJSBERS G., MOOIJ R. DE (2003), *European Outlook 1: Social Europe – Single European Social Policy still a Bridge too Far. Annex to the State of the European Union 2004*, CPB-SCP, The Hague.
FRANCISCO C. DE (ed.) (2002), *Spain Today*, Oficina del Portavoz del Gobierno, Madrid.
GAITÁN L. (1999), *El espacio social de la infancia. Los niños en el Estado de bienestar*, Comunidad de Madrid, Madrid.
GERMAIN C. B. (ed.) (1979), *Social Work Practice: People and Environments, an Ecological Perspective*, Columbia University Press, New York.
GILBERT N. (2002), *Transformation of the Welfare State: The Silent Surrender of Public Responsibility*, Oxford University Press, Oxford.
HERMANNS J. (2001), *Kijken naar opvoeding. Opstellen over jeugd, jeugdbeleid en jeugdzorg*, SWP, Amsterdam (esp. chap. 13, *Jeugdzorg en de rechten van kinderen*).
HERMANNS J., LEU H. R. (eds.) (1998), *Family Risks and Family Support: Theory, Research and Practice in Germany and the Netherlands*, Eburon, Delft.
HERMANNS J., MORDANG H., MULDERS L. (2002), *Jeugdhulp thuis. Een alternatief voor uithuisplaatsing*, SWP, Amsterdam.
INSTITUTO DE ESTADÍSTICAS DE LA COMUNIDAD DE MADRID (2003), *Anuario de estadísticas*, Comunidad de Madrid, Madrid.
INSTITUTO MADRILEÑO DEL MENOR Y LA FAMILIA – CONSEJERÍA DE SERVICIOS SOCIALES (2002), II *Plan de atención a la infancia y la adolescencia*, Comunidad de Madrid, Madrid.
JANSSENS M., TALMA M., MANUHUWA D. (2002), *Competentieprofiel intensief pedagogisch thuishulpverlener*, NIZW, Utrecht.
LÓPEZ F. (1995), *Necesidad de la infancia y protección infantil*, MAS, Madrid.
MOÑIVAS A. (2002), *The Competencies Required for Working with Families*, paper presented at the 2nd ASIPS Conference *Family Network Support and Youth Care*, Hogeschool, Amsterdam.
ID. (2004), *The Competences Required for Social Work Practices*, paper presented at the Spanish Social Work School Congress, Huelva, April.
PAGÉE R. VAN (ed.) (2003), *Eigen Kracht: Family Group Conference in Nederland*, SWP, Amsterdam.

PAUL OCHOTORENA J. DE (coord. de) (1988), *Maltrato y abandono infantil. Identificación de factores de riesgo*, Servicio central de Publicaciones del Gobierno Vasco, Vitoria-Gasteiz.

ROEDE E., AS J. VAN, DIEKMANN W., HERMANNS J. (2003), *Helpen bij opvoeden; jeugdzorg vanuit een pedagogische paradigma*, HUS, Amsterdam.

ROLDÁN E., RODRÍGUEZ A., BARAHONA M. J., CASTILLO A., MOÑIVAS A., SANTOS C. (2003), *Trabajo social en el área de menores y la familia. Supuesto teórico-práctico*, Universidad Complutense, Madrid.

SHEAFOR B. W.; HOREJSI C. R. (2003), *Techniques and Guidelines for Social Work Practice*, Allyn and Bacon, Boston, VI ed.

SLOT N. W., BRAAK J. J. VAN DEN, THEUNISSEN A. (2004), *Slechter af in de stad. Waarom worden er in de stad Amsterdam meer ots'en uitgesproken dan elders?*, BV, Diuvendrecht.

YPEREN T. A., BOOY Y., VELDT M. VAN DER (2003), *Vraaggerichte hulp, motivatie en effectiviteit van jeugdzorg*, NIZW, Utrecht.

Websites

Netherlands

www.amsterdam.nl.
www.bjaa.nl (Bureau Jeugdzorg Amsterdam).
www.jeugdzorg.nl (about youth care).
www.justitie.nl (Ministry of Justice).
www.minvws.nl (Ministry of Health, Welfare and Sports).
www.nizw.nl (Netherlands Institute of Care and Welfare – NIZW).
www.onstat.amsterdam.nl.
www.sac-amstelstad.nl (SAC-Amstelstad Jeugdzorg).

Spain

http://www.madrid.org/comun/serviciosSociales/0,3153,52810701_0_53490529_,00.html (Madrid Community).
http://www.madrid.org/inforjoven/ (Madrid Community).
www.munimadrid.es/ (Madrid City Council).
http://www.orientared.com/arc/menor.pdf (Ministry of Justice).
www.map.es/gobierno/muface/vi75/repor.htm.
www.socialeurope.com/english.
http://www8.madrid.org/iestadis/fijas/basicas/dguide.htm (statistic institute).
www.savethechildren.es/organizacion/abusconclus.htm.
www.unaf.org/Organizaciones/maci.htm.

8
Sexual Abuse and Child Protection in England, France and Germany

by *Rolf H. Piquardt*

8.1
Introduction

For about the last twenty years, the sexual abuse of children has been a topic of interest throughout Europe, not just in the public media but also in the research environment of the social sciences. In the early 1980s women's liberation movements were the first to point out a problem which was not new to social workers, teachers, doctors or lawyers, although publications on the subject seemed to be taboo then. One of the political demands surrounding the "sexual revolution" of the late 1960s was that people should break the habit of keeping unpleasant truths secret, and so it is surprising that this movement did not contribute towards an open discussion of sexual manipulation and discrimination.

The growing public interest of the last decade is reflected in the number of publications: the German data bank PSYNDEX has increased from 15 in 1987 to 113 in 1995; at the same time the English data bank, PSYCHLIT, has increased from 72 to 723 (Amann, Wipplinger, 1997). However, there is still a tendency among some practitioners to see the victim as a seducer or to devalue the abuse as a fantasy, as Freud did it in his "seduction theory". A further problem is that many social workers and pedagogues in voluntary and statutory youth help-institutions lack experience. They feel insecure when it comes to identifying sexual abuse and intervening in the right way. Moreover, Hartwig and Hensen (2003) point out that sexually abused children and young people seldom get the kind of educational help they need in Germany. One case indicates that a 17-year-old girl had been placed in 14 different foster and residential homes within two and a half years, during which time 30 "experts" tried to work with her (file from the Youth Service Department).

In this context one needs to ask which aid systems are offered by a country like Germany, and how effectively they work. Another question is: how do other countries handle the problem of child abuse, and do their aid systems influence the strategies of their users? To answer these questions, an understanding of the judicial and administrative framework is as important as a consideration of the feelings and attitudes of the "helpers" themselves, i.e. the social workers and pedagogues in their respective countries.

By comparing the different systems, by looking at the similarities and differences, we can take the first step towards understanding another culture, and towards an understanding of the individuals who form society with all its peculiarities and oddities. Andre and Walz (2003) refer to this as the "intercultural orientation as a fundamental principle of social work". The second step involves a correction, and perhaps a change of attitudes and an updating in problem-solving activities. The third step can then be a common education programme, leading finally to common work in various fields, e.g. child protection in Europe. Williams (2003) has made concrete suggestions on how to internationalise the curriculum for social work students in an essay on the international perspective in social work education.

One way of learning more about differences and similarities in different countries is through "cross-cultural research", which is understood as a process of generating dialogue between cultures that were previously ignorant of one another in particular respects. Thus, the research both flows from, and contributes to, the process of globalization or "Europeanization", which produces the conditions of life with "reflexive modernity" (Hetherington *et al.*, 1997).

The present chapter is based upon two cross-cultural studies in which I was part of the German team. The first study focuses upon practitioners and a fictional case of possible child abuse. It also takes into account the views of the child protection system in one of the participating countries. The second study compares the experiences of parents with their country's aid system.

8.2
Terminology and Statistics

One difficulty in cross-national studies in the social field lies in the comparability of the research objects and social institutions because words carry different connotations within each system. The French *inspecteur* is a central figure in the administrative of French child protection but he/she cannot be compared with the German *Inspektor*. In English publications, the German Jugendamt (Youth Office) is often referred to as a Social Services Department, probably because it delivers social services to young people and their families. "Child protection", when translated into German, carries the connotation of a special service. Yet in Germany the Kinderschutzdienst (KSD), which is concerned with child protection, is only a voluntary agency. Another terminological problem lies in choosing the correct word for the research object. Amann and Wipplinger (1997) refer to 23 different German terms for "sexual abuse"; as early as 1979, Finkelhor found 9 such terms in the Anglo-American literature, ranging from "child rape" to "victimisation". The next problem is how to define "sexual abuse", *abus sexuel* or *sexueller Missbrauch*, an important condition for the statistical registration. As with definitions of aggression there are close and wide definitions of sexual abuse. The first definition emphasises the bodily contact between abuser and the victim, the second includes verbal attacks, the production and consumption of child pornography, the pressure to prostitute etc.

The importance of definitions becomes clear when looking at the statistical distribution of sexual abuse. This applies to studies identifying the incidence, i.e. the number of new "cases" each year, as well as to those studying the prevalence, i.e. the absolute number or percentage of abused persons within a population. Ernst (1997) points to three possible sources of error concerning "case definition":
– the age limit for childhood and youth;
– the age difference between abuser and victim;
– the definition of sexual actions.

Further errors relate to the sample (who is ready to speak about their own experience with sexual abuse?), the questioning instruments and the "research section". Finally, one has to consider where the "cases" come from: the police, the Office of Criminal Investigation, Youth Offices, hospitals, the Department of Health, or the National or Regional Bureau of Statistics.

Bange compared studies in Europe and the US and found corresponding numbers with respect to the occurrence of sex abuse when comparable definitions were used. According to these findings, 10-15% of women and 5-10% of men up to the age of 16 have suffered from unwanted and enforced sexual attacks (Hartwig, Hensen, 2003).

8.3
The Research Methodology

The simplest way to compare different national systems – political, economic, educational, and social ones – is to look at their structure, their historical background, their typical processes, their functioning and efficiency etc. An easy general overview is often presented in a diagram which is then used to discuss similarities and differences. Another way is to look at a system from the view of those involved, i.e. the practitioners in the case of help-systems (first study); and the clients, that is the parents and the children (second study).

8.4
First Study

The aim of this study was twofold: to learn about the child protection system of the other country in terms of how it worked for those directly involved in making it work; and to discover social workers' views on another country's practice and system. It was also necessary to work with practitioners in order to understand the systems they worked with. A description of a social work system is almost impossible to understand unless it is attached to case material; equally, it is difficult to get a proper understanding of social workers' actions and decisions without any knowledge of the surrounding system.

In each country, about ten interested social workers were identified, and they then agreed to come together in two meetings. At the first meeting, they were presented with a written case involving a 3-generation family with problems. The problems were presented in four stages (cf. BOX 8.1). Three questions for each stage were designed in order to find out what the practitioners would do, why they would do it, what the local constraints and possibilities were, and the theoretical and conceptual basis of their thinking. After having answered the questions, the group came together to discuss the case and to consider what they might plan to do, what were the rights and responsibilities of the characters, and what roles and tasks the professionals should adopt. These were all further factors which could influence interventions.

At the second meeting, after a short information about the child protection system in the country concerned, the social workers saw a dubbed video in which their foreign colleagues were discussing the same case. The subsequent discussion about what they felt regarding interventions, procedures, and organisational and institutional frameworks in both their own and the other country was also video-recorded for later analysis.

BOX 8.1
The problem case presented to practitioners

STAGE 1

Mrs Smith contacts the Social Services Department (SSD). She says that she is worried about her daughter's marital problems. She is not specific about the nature of the marital problems. She also conveys anxieties about the nature of the relationship between her son-in-law and her granddaughter, her daughter's child by a previous marriage. Her daughter's family comprises:
- father: Jack, age 40;
- mother: Valerie, age 33 (Mrs Smith's daughter);

- daughter: Frances, age 13 (Mrs Smith's granddaughter; Jack's stepdaughter);
- son: Andrew, age 4 (Mrs Smith's grandson).

The family is not known to the SSD.

STAGE 2

Valerie and Jack have refused to see the social worker so there is no further contact until one month later, when the worker at Andrew's playgroup contacts the SSD because she is concerned about him. She says that his attendance at the playgroup is irregular, that he is excessively violent towards the other children and that his mother seems depressed.

STAGE 3

Two weeks later, the social worker has seen Valerie once, but did not get much information from her. Frances' teacher contacts the SSD. Frances has asked her teacher if she can talk with a social worker. She has run away from home for three days and has just returned. She complains of violence between her parents. She also expresses a concern that her relationship with her stepfather is more intimate than she would like it to be, but she will not say anything else about it.

STAGE 4

In the course of discussions with the social worker, Frances decides that she wishes to stay at home but that she wishes to continue receiving help from the social worker. Eight days later, the playgroup worker contacts the SSD again. She says that Andrew is increasingly violent and distressed. The worker has suggested that Valerie should take him to the doctor but she has refused. The worker is worried about Andrew. Frances says that the marital violence is continuing, but her mother does not wish to leave home. Frances says no more about her relationship with her stepfather.

Source: Cooper *et al.* (1996).

8.5
Second Study

An interesting aspect of comparing help-systems in different countries can be found in the kind of strategy community care consumers use in order to get help. Are there different ways of approaching services that are more or less likely to be effective depending on the service systems that you face? To answer this question, we used semi-structured open-ended interviews to explore the personal stories of thirteen mothers in England, France and Germany, and their involvement with child welfare services (BOX 8.2).

BOX 8.2
Interviewer's checklist

Have they told me about:
- family structure; do I have enough information to construct a genogram?
- how they were referred to the SSD?
- the family's perception of the problem and of the solution?
- the family's perception of the social worker's perception of the problem and of the solution?
- the resources offered and resources wanted?
- the people involved (social worker from social services, family help, probation officer, someone from the family guidance clinic, counsellor, health visitor, general practitioner, teacher, police etc.)?
- meetings attended?
- the experience of court proceedings?
- the experience of being represented by a solicitor?
- post-court experience?
- feelings about contact with child(ren), parents and siblings?
- where the child was placed and how that decision was reached?
- how disagreements were handled?
- any changes of social worker or other professionals?
- the family's expectations, hopes and fears about the future?
- their views on rights, responsibilities and best interests?

This study represented pilot research, i.e. the results have no relevance in a statistical or quantitative sense; the stories are personal and subjective and cannot be taken for objective and accurate descriptions of how the systems function. The information is of a different nature, it is about how it feels to be a user of these systems. Cooper *et al.* (1996) point out that cross-country comparisons are particularly powerful in "identifying blind spots", and a comparison of service users' stories thus heightens awareness and makes visible expectations about the behaviour of institutions and of the individuals who use them.

8.6
The Child Protection Systems

8.6.1. Germany

Laws specifically enacted for the benefit of young people are the *Child and Youth Service Act* of 1990 – *Kinder- und Jugendhilfegesetz* (KJHG) –, the *Protection of Young People in Public Act*, the *Federal Educational Grants Act*, the *Protection of Young Persons at Work Act*, and the *Fed-*

eral Social Assistance Act. Emphasis in the KJHG is on prevention, help and counselling, not on control. Help has to be appropriate and to be determined individually, i.e. dependent on the specific case. It gives young people the right to approach services without parental knowledge or permission, and to receive counselling in their own right if they so wish. The Youth Office (Jugendamt – JA) represents the administrative institution that is responsible for applying the KJHG for its users. It offers a vast range of help fostering and adoption to support payments and social work in school.

In case of sexual abuse, the subsection Generic Social Services (Allgemeiner Sozialdienst – ASD) is generally involved in offering help in critical and emergency situations, and in providing educational help (open and residential field support). Co-operation with voluntary welfare organisations is necessary, because they deliver the services which the JA itself is not able to offer. In case of sexual abuse children can be removed without an order but with the judge's knowledge and agreement, and parents or caretakers need to be informed immediately and heard within 24 hours.

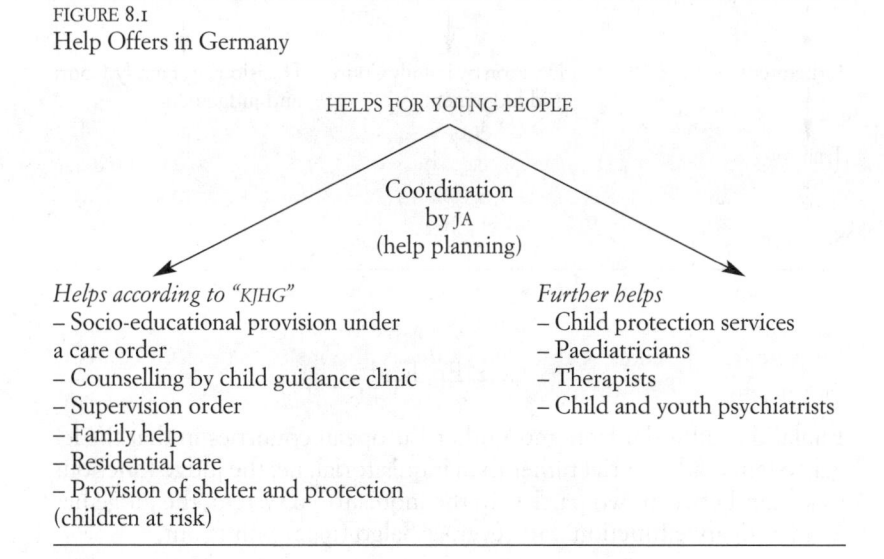

FIGURE 8.1
Help Offers in Germany

HELPS FOR YOUNG PEOPLE

Coordination
by JA
(help planning)

Helps according to "KJHG"
– Socio-educational provision under a care order
– Counselling by child guidance clinic
– Supervision order
– Family help
– Residential care
– Provision of shelter and protection (children at risk)

Further helps
– Child protection services
– Paediatricians
– Therapists
– Child and youth psychiatrists

Moreover, social workers in the JA have a duty to assist the Family and Guardianship Courts in gathering information and providing assessments, however they are not obliged to give evidence. If the child's welfare is in danger, the Family Court can decide to withdraw of parental care.

FIGURE 8.2
Judicial possibilities in cases of child abuse in Germany

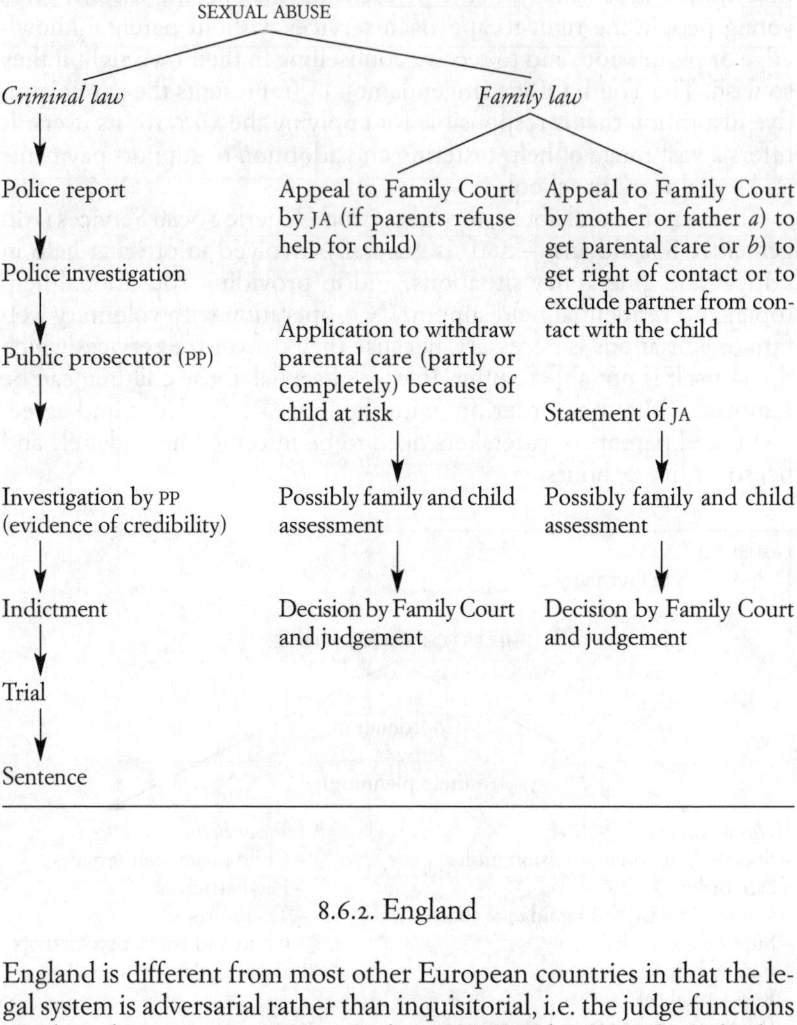

```
                              SEXUAL ABUSE
                    ╱                          ╲
         Criminal law                              Family law
              │                       ╱                          ╲
              ▼                       ▼                           ▼
       Police report          Appeal to Family Court      Appeal to Family Court
              │               by JA (if parents refuse    by mother or father a) to
              ▼               help for child)             get parental care or b) to
       Police investigation                               get right of contact or to
              │                                           exclude partner from con-
              ▼               Application to withdraw     tact with the child
       Public prosecutor (PP) parental care (partly or
              │               completely) because of
              │               child at risk               Statement of JA
              ▼                       ▼                           ▼
       Investigation by PP    Possibly family and child   Possibly family and child
       (evidence of credibility) assessment               assessment
              │                       ▼                           ▼
              ▼               Decision by Family Court    Decision by Family Court
       Indictment             and judgement               and judgement
              │
              ▼
       Trial
              │
              ▼
       Sentence
```

8.6.2. England

England is different from most other European countries in that the legal system is adversarial rather than inquisitorial, i.e. the judge functions as arbiter between two parties. In the inquisitorial system, the judge has an investigative function. However, as Salgo (1992) points out,

> the general trend I have observed is, on the one hand, the introduction of some inquisitorial elements into adversarial proceedings in systems with Anglo-American traditions, and on the other the implementation of some adversarial elements into inquisitorial proceedings in countries with the continental European tradition.

FIGURE 8.3
The English child protection system

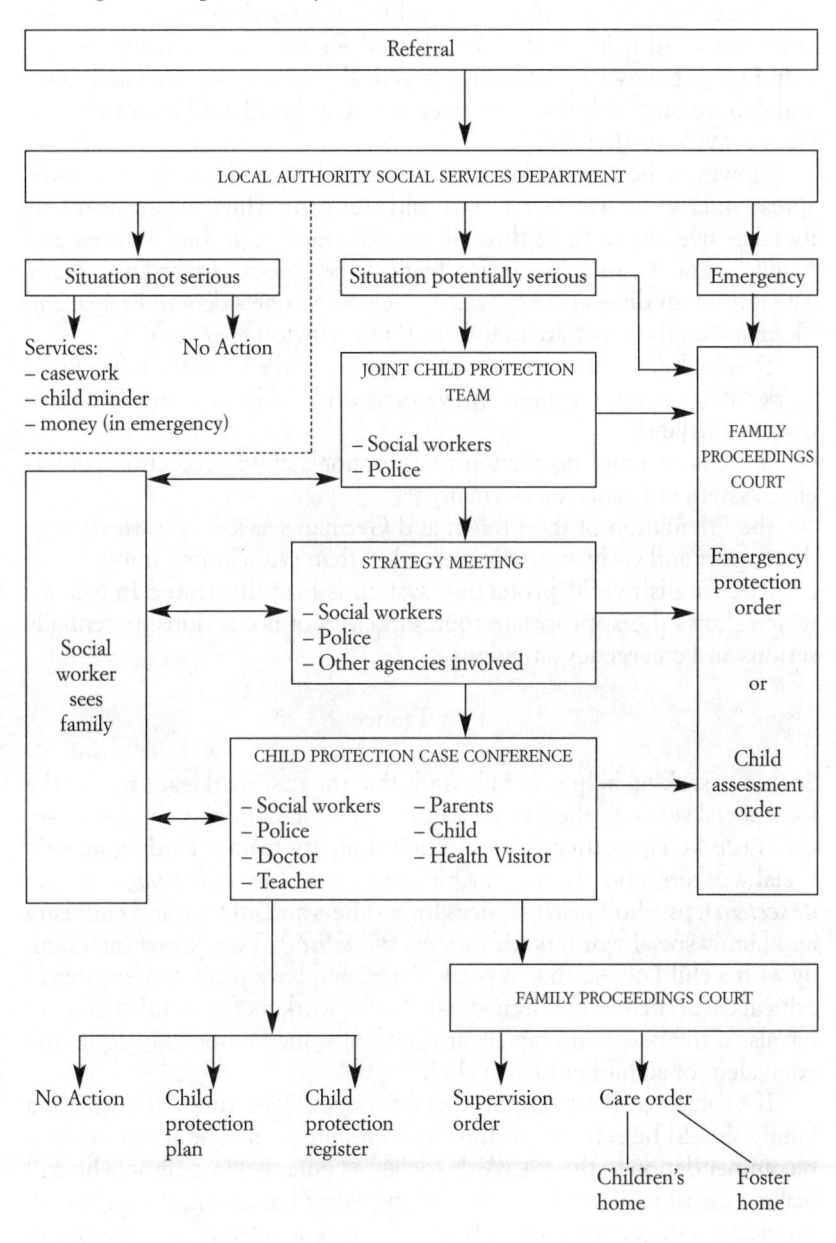

```
                                    Referral
                                       │
                                       ▼
               LOCAL AUTHORITY SOCIAL SERVICES DEPARTMENT
        │                              │                        │
        ▼                              ▼                        ▼
  Situation not serious      Situation potentially serious    Emergency
        │                              │                        │
   ┌────┴────┐                         ▼                        │
   ▼         ▼              JOINT CHILD PROTECTION              │
Services:  No Action               TEAM                         │
- casework                    - Social workers ─────────►  FAMILY
- child minder                - Police                     PROCEEDINGS
- money (in emergency)             │                         COURT
                                   ▼
                           STRATEGY MEETING              Emergency
  Social      ◄──►         - Social workers   ─────►    protection
  worker                   - Police                        order
  sees                     - Other agencies involved
  family                        │                             or
                                ▼
                    CHILD PROTECTION CASE CONFERENCE      Child
              ◄──►   - Social workers  - Parents  ─────► assessment
                     - Police          - Child            order
                     - Doctor          - Health Visitor
                     - Teacher
                                │
                                ▼
                        FAMILY PROCEEDINGS COURT
   │         │            │            │            │
   ▼         ▼            ▼            ▼            ▼
No Action  Child        Child      Supervision   Care order
         protection   protection      order       ╱      ╲
            plan       register                Children's  Foster
                                                home       home
```

Source: Cooper *et al.* (1996).

The local authority also has a duty to investigate where it has "reasonable cause to expect that a child is suffering or is likely to suffer significant harm" (*Children's Act 1989*) and is authorised to provide services when the child is in need. A local Children and Family Team delivers help in urgent cases by providing practical support, financial assistance and counselling. Voluntary agencies as well as health and education services provide further aid.

However, the system of non-governmental organisation is not as widespread in England as it is in France and Germany. Thus, the local authority takes over some tasks through special teams, e.g. the Children and Family Team, the Juvenile Justice Team or the Out-of-Hours-Duty-Team. The important differences between England on one side and France and Germany on the other are as follows (Hetherington *et al.*, 1997):
– the eligibility criteria are drawn far wider and encourage more social work intervention and more preventive work in France and Germany than in England;
– there is no child protection register, nor a child protection conference system in France or Germany;
– the orientation of the French and German services is towards family support and early intervention, rather than crisis intervention.

The English child protection system is best illustrated in FIG. 8.3 which shows the appropriate routes in cases of not serious, potentially serious and emergency situations.

8.6.3. France

Someone seeking help generally finds that the first road leads him to the local social services, the Circonscription d'interventions sanitaires et sociales (CISS). This office has a multidisciplinary team including generic social workers who are responsible for a certain area (*assistants sociaux de secteur*), psychologists, services for mothers and infants, and childcare and family social workers (*éducateurs spécialisés*). They know each family with a child of less than 6 years of age, and have team conferences in critical cases such as children at risk. Social workers frequently make referrals to the psychotherapists at the Centre médico-pédagogique, the equivalent of a child guidance clinic.

If a social worker from the Social Services Department thinks that a family should be referred to the children's judge, he/she has to make a recommendation to the ASE (Aide sociale à l'enfance) inspector, who will make a decision. Therefore, the ASE inspector has an important role in providing a negotiating space before the case is referred to a children's judge (*juge des enfants*), who often, and not only in the case of children

FIGURE 8.4
The French child protection system

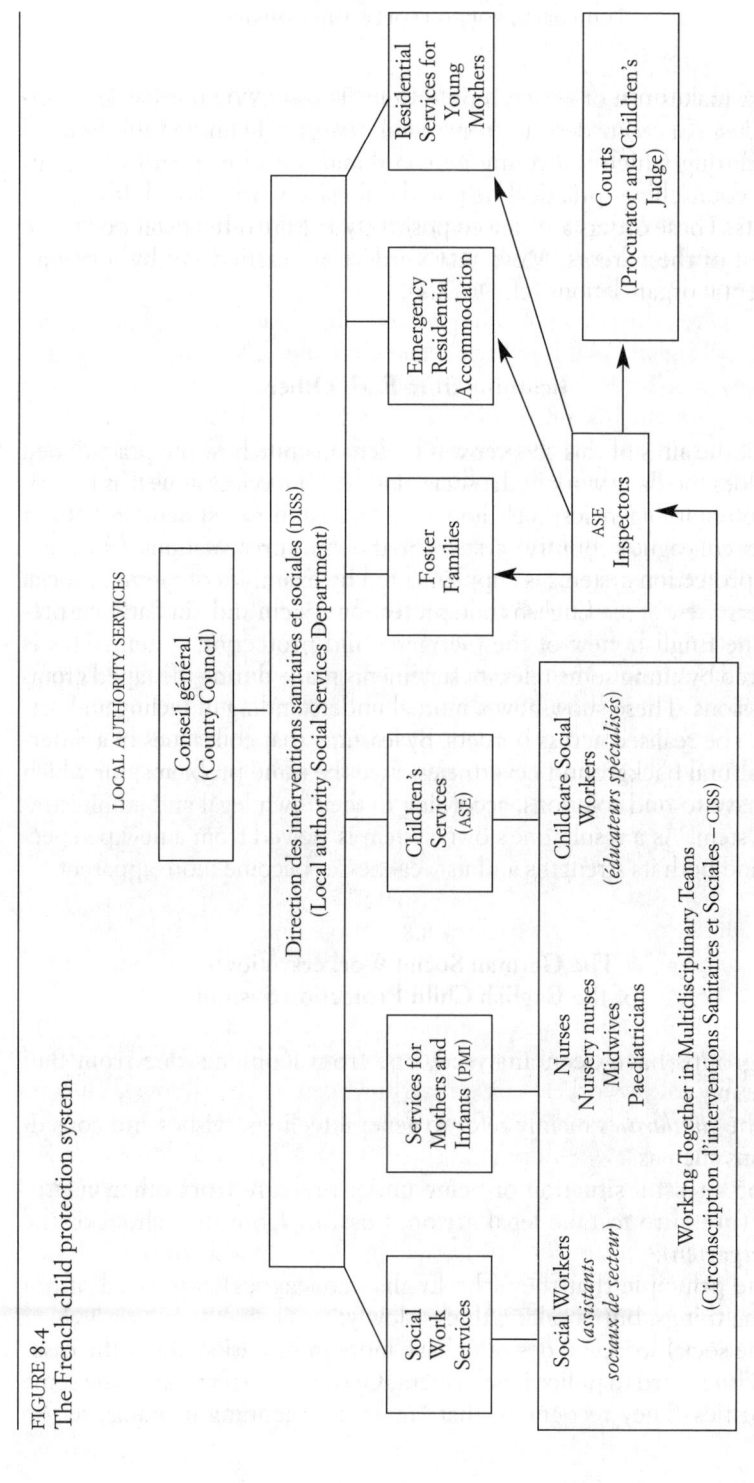

```
LOCAL AUTHORITY SERVICES

                    Conseil général
                    (County Council)
                          |
        Direction des interventions sanitaires et sociales (DISS)
                (Local authority Social Services Department)
    ┌──────────┬──────────────┬──────────────┬──────────────┬──────────────────┬─────────────────┐
 Social      Services for   Children's     Foster         Emergency           Residential
 Work        Mothers and    Services       Families       Residential         Services for
 Services    Infants (PMI)  (ASE)                         Accommodation       Young Mothers

 Social      Nurses         Childcare Social Workers                ASE
 Workers     Nursery nurses (éducateurs spécialisés)                Inspectors
 (assistants Midwives                                                                Courts
 sociaux de  Paediatricians                                                          (Procurator and Children's
 secteur)                                                                            Judge)

         Working Together in Multidisciplinary Teams
         (Circonscription d'interventions Sanitaires et Sociales – CISS)
```

Source: Coopet *et al.* (1995).

at risk, makes use of supervision orders. These AEMO (*action éducative en milieu ouvert*) orders are controlled, temporally limited educational aids, during which the young person remains at home, and which include counselling, practical help and intensive work with children and parents. These orders are viewed positively and are often extended at the request of the parents. Most AEMO orders are carried out by non-governmental organisations (cf. FIG. 8.4).

8.7
Learning from Each Other

One of the aims of this chapter was to demonstrate how the practitioner, who does the daily work in the social and youth services as well as in various voluntary agencies, feels about his/her country's system and about his/her colleague's country's system. So the short presentation of the three child protection systems is supplemented by examples of German social workers' view of the English child protection system and, similarly, we present the English view of the German child protection system. This is achieved by citing some relevant statements made during the taped group discussions. These show how a mutual understanding of feeling and acting can be realised across borders: by learning that colleagues of a different cultural background nevertheless face the same problems, for which they have to find solutions, according to their own legal and administrative system. As a result, one's own system is viewed from a new perspective, and both its strengths and its weaknesses become more apparent.

8.8
The German Social Workers' View of the English Child Protection System

Two groups have been analysed, one from Koblenz, one from Bad Doberan.

The *similarities* mainly refer to general feelings, wishes and considerations such as:
– the stressful situation of being under pressure from other institutions (pressure to take legal action, possibly from the school or the kindergarten);
– the principle that they (the English colleagues) expressed of not rushing things, but of taking things slowly;
– the social workers' desire to have more information about the case.

With regard to police involvement, German social workers saw some similarities. They recognised that "there are planning meetings set up which initially exclude the police" but that on the other hand (from the same participant) "children or young people who voluntarily go somewhere for help must understand that the police may become involved".

A further similarity was seen in the "consideration of the consequences of a court appearance". This presented problems for the social worker who had to consider whether it might be harmful for the child if the case was unsuccessful in court, i.e. if the perpetrator was acquitted: "If he is acquitted, it is a carte blanche for the perpetrator just to carry on" and "What would it mean for the others if the perpetrator was acquitted?". The situation is exactly the same in England as in Germany. Finally, the situation whereby the Social Services Department or the JA can, in an emergency, take a child into residential care is very similar in both countries.

The first *difference* that was noted was the much earlier stage at which the English colleagues involve other agencies such as the health visitor. That procedure created a danger that the perpetrator might get wind of the fact that he is suspected of ill treatment and could "put enormous pressure on the child to keep quiet". Also, there is no system of health visiting in Germany. In any case, German social workers do not seem to have high expectations of the value of medical examinations because most doctors "don't have enough experience" to make a correct diagnosis. Moreover, "many doctors are too hesitant about becoming involved in cases of sexual abuse to make a diagnosis of it".

The fact that in England young people "who voluntarily go somewhere for help must understand that the police may become involved" was also seen as being different from the German experience. One participant emphasised that in such cases in Germany the child is free to decide whether "He/she will go to the JA or to the police". The child is told that "we won't go behind your back if you come to us for help". Yet once the police are involved or once the case becomes part of the legal system, the "possibility of working in a child-centred way" is gone, as the worker from the JA put it.

All German social workers agree that a child-centred approach is much better for the children, if necessary, this work can take place without the parents' knowledge. The two following statements illustrate this view.

In cases of abuse or ill treatment we are able to spend a long time working with a child without her parents' knowledge. We have sufficient time to build up a relationship and trust and can work together with the child to see how things can best go forward (KSD).

Here, despite the differences and uncertainties concerning the different areas of responsibility between the KSD and the JA, it is possible to work in a child-centred way (JA).

In the English system this seemed to be less possible: "the social workers and helpers have to think very carefully about how to proceed and how to include the child".

One participant comments on "this practice in England of interviewing a child in front of a camera". In her experience this would be extremely difficult for children, especially where feelings of shame and guilt are involved. "And what – she asked – is done with smaller children, who often tell you things in an indirect way?". (In England, the disclosure interview with the social worker is recorded on video for possible use in a Family Proceedings Court.)

Having seen the video of the English discussion, the Bad Doberan social workers were struck by the legal and procedural factors that characterised the work of their English counterparts. One participant commented on the way that the issue of "proof" frequently cropped up in the English discussion, adding:

I think perhaps there is a significant difference in that in England there are these procedures, whereas we have greater scope for working in a flexible way. That makes it somewhat easier when there is a greater range of options between, on the one hand, taking no action in the case, and on the other, taking it to court.

The English system "seemed more like law enforcement, which we are no longer so keen on here. Our system places greater emphasis on a period in which trust can be built up, with a view to convincing the parents that it is possible for us to help protect their children".

"We are not bound by these procedures, so we have the opportunity of going back again, without having to take any action that would close down the options".

8.9
The English View of the German Child Protection System

After having seen the video of the German social workers' discussion, an English social worker commented: "It was remarkably reminiscent of many case conferences that I've attended". English social workers identified *differences* between their system and the German one, but these differences were relative rather than absolute.

1. The greater range and variety of social work services that are available in Germany:

there are more practitioners who can get involved and try to do things. We don't have that. OK we can refer people to a child guidance clinic or hospital department, but it's very hit and miss.

I found myself thinking that having so many agencies. The plus side of it is that you get more choices, but the minus of it is that there was clearly conflict in their points of view... Different agencies have different value systems... How much would they really all work together?

2. The greater autonomy of social workers in Germany:

I actually liked their system... Ours seemed so rigid after that.

They certainly seemed to speak with a lot of confidence... That did strike me as I was watching the video. They seemed to be talking as if, 'I am a professional and this is what my agency does'. That is OK.

I'd like to think how a group of English social workers would be; whether they would have the same confidence or whether they would say (especially the local authority workers), 'people shout at me because I don't get it right all the time'.

3. Relative independence from the legal arena in Germany:

The power not to act, not to involve the legal process. That's something that is missing in our system I think. Child protection procedures are streamlined the moment there is an allegation. It feels that the whole statutory thing takes over. I feel that's a loss in our system.

The non-statutory status of the two groups of people gave them the flexibility to try and engage in different ways without the overriding fear that statutory ones have, that they have got to get it right. I think one of the difficulties of our procedures (and we have got stacks of them in child protection) is the underlying assumption that there is a right way of carrying out child protection measures; not that there are right *ways*.

4. Child-centred orientation:

Our system is too much focused on investigation and immediate action. A long-term view, a more child-centred view, would be more helpful.

I found that more honest... There are times, as one German colleague commented, when we, as adults, actually have to do things to protect the child... That may look a bit severe and may curtail the rights of the parents... but you're investigating situations in which the child may have been abused by the parents... I actually think that there are times when I should be able to talk to the child away from the parents... What worries me is that there seems to be an assumption that if I am allowed to do that, I will somehow abuse or misuse that information. I think their approach is more honest: that there are times when professional people should take the gloves off.

8.10
Child Protection – Viewed from the User's Perspective

As mentioned above, a second study tried to look at the relationship between help-systems and the help-seeker, with the underlying hypothesis that a certain system might favour certain people, but might have more disadvantages for others because of different "coping styles" or strategies. Thus, by comparing the subjective experience of parents who have been involved with child welfare services in different countries it might be possible to detect differences in successful strategies.

In each of the three countries two types of mother could be identified: the proactive, critical and assertive ones, and those who had difficulty in asserting themselves and who rather arranged themselves within a given situation. Their stories demonstrate how the different national systems can appear from the receiving end, i.e. the effectiveness of coping strategies seems to depend on the available help-system. These strategies can be systematized as part of the personality according to a concept proposed by Baldock and Ungerson (1994) in relation to models of participation in the care market. In a study of community care consumers they suggested four categories characterising the behaviour of service seekers:
1. *consumerism*: clients with this attitude trust in their own abilities and resources and would even pay for the necessary help by themselves; they actively seek opportunities for help, and they often have a very individualistic approach: in the main, they find what they want in the social market, whether from statutory or voluntary services;
2. *privatism*: in this category one finds people with a tendency to solve problems without seeking help from others; they are proud of their independence and refuse support even in cases of emergency;
3. *welfarism*: this attitude is represented by people who are convinced that it is their right to get support, and thus use all of the possibilities which the State offers free of charge;
4. *clientalism*: this is the traditional way of claiming support characterised by the "passive hope" of receiving help; if official authorities reject claims for help or ignore justified requests, this type of person will accept it, just as they will accept any proposed help.

All English, French or German mothers could be classified according to the above categories but their success in finding optimal help for themselves and their families was to a high degree dependent upon the welfare system they lived in. Active individualists, representing a consumerist mode of participation, have better chances in a system with many alternatives like the German one. In this case they fare better than people who accept all offers of help. These individuals are more in accordance with clientalism, an attitude that fits better in the English system, where, particularly in emergency cases, procedures are clearly outlined. As Piquardt and Hetherington (2003) point out, the English system

demonstrates a rationing of resources with attention paid to clarity, openness and a hierarchy of need. But in engaging with the English system, being pro-active is not necessarily helpful as it suggests an ability to manage without help and therefore a lesser need.

The French system, on the contrary, appears to be appropriate for users who may be quite demanding, but who accept the offered services and who know how to take advantage of them (welfarism).

This way of looking at young people and their parents in the welfare system might help the practitioner to understand that "difficult clients" are not only difficult because of specific personal features, but also because they have become "victims" of a help-system with its rules, which determines success and failure when searching for and using support. The challenge for child welfare services is to identify parents whose participation in the care market makes co-operation difficult, and to find a way of ensuring that their families get the help they need. This applies in a special sense to persons who, as migrants, have been socialized in cultures with different norms, structures and rules for effective strategies.

8.11
Outlook

Television and the Internet are increasingly changing our world; the accompanying processes of globalization and internationalisation generate new challenges for social work. Education and training at universities and schools of social work have to take this into account, as do further education courses and programmes.

Amongst other problems, there are those arising from the increasing migration of people from the former eastern bloc countries, from war areas and from Third World countries. In most cases, the cultural backgrounds of these people mean that it is difficult for them to achieve a life free of conflict in the first two generations. Other problems result from the contrary tendencies of growing nationalism, often as reaction to a "many-cultures-society", and changes in the job market. On the other hand, however, internationalisation brings many new opportunities for social work through easier exchange of information with regard to relevant problem fields, methods and procedures, law systems, administrative structures and education. This exchange of information is also achieved through feedback from colleagues in other countries and from other cultures.

"Learning from difference" means "to expose to foreign practice as a means of stimulating critical reflection on one's own domestic practice" (Hetherington *et al.*, 1997). The comments of German and English practitioners concerning the child protection system of their counterparts from the other side of the Channel demonstrated how, by becoming aware of the similarities and differences of their practice and the underlying concepts, this might work.

Curriculum contents at relevant institutions should be internationalised, foreign exchange placements for students should be institutionalised, and teacher and researcher exchange programmes should be promoted. All of this is already taking place to some degree. However more is required. Of equal importance would be a special exchange programme for practitioners in the social field in order to let them experience differences in culture, in values and in practical work "on the spot". Personal experience needs to supplement the comparisons made through written descriptions and videotapes.

Bibliography

AMANN G., WIPPLINGER R. (hrsg.) (1997), *Sexueller Missbrauch*, DGVT, Tübingen.
ANDRE G., WALZ H. (2003), *The Concept of "Human Rights-Orientated Sustainable Development" in Social Work Education*, in "Social Work in Europe", X, 2, pp. 3-10.
BALDOCK J., UNGERSON C. (1994), *Becoming Consumers of Community Care: Households within the Mixed Economy of Welfare*, Joseph Rowntree Foundation, York.
COOPER A., HETHERINGTON R., BAISTOW K., PITTS J., SPRIGGS A. (1995), *Positive Child Protection: A View from Abroad*, Russell House, Lyme Regis.
COOPER A., HETHERINGTON R., PIQUARDT R. H., SMITH P., SPRIGGS A., WILFORD G. (1996), *Eight European Child Protection Systems: A Preliminary Report*, Brunel University, Uxbridge.
ERNST C. (1997), *Zu den Problemen der Epidemiologischen Erforschung des Sexuellen Missbrauchs*, in Amann, Wipplinger (1997), pp. 55-71.
FINKELHOR D. (1979), *Sexually Victimized Children*, Free Press, New York.
HARTWIG L., HENSEN G. (2003), *Sexueller Missbrauch und Jugendhilfe*, Juventa, Weinheim.
HETHERINGTON R., COOPER A., SMITH P., WILFORD G. (1997), *Protecting Children*, Russell House, Lyme Regis.
PIQUARDT R. H., HETHERINGTON R. (2003), *Erfahrungen von Müttern mit Angeboten der Jugendhilfe in 3 Europäischen Ländern*, in "Kind, Jugend und Gesellschaft", 2, pp. 56-61.
SALGO L. (1992), *Child Protection in Germany*, in M. Freeman, P. Veerman (eds.), *The Ideologies of Children's Rights*, Kluwer, Boston, pp. 265-88.
WILLIAMS J. (2003), *Is Inclusion of an International Perspective Relevant or Feasible in Social Work Education?*, in "Social Work in Europe", X, 2, pp. 31-6.

9
Interdisciplinary Teams and Transdisciplinary Networks for Child and Family Inclusion: The Relevance of European Theory to Lithuanian Practice

by *Nijolė Večkienė* and *Julija Eidukevičiūtė*

9.1
Introduction

Social exclusion is a multidimensional issue which has an impact across Europe. It can of course be defined from a number of perspectives and assumptions. Later in this chapter we will discuss definitional issues, but for introductory purposes a UK definition from Pierson (2002) will suffice. He suggests that social exclusion can be defined as a process that deprives individuals and families, and groups and neighbourhoods, of resources required for participation in social, economic and political activity as whole.

Such social exclusion in practice has been the focus of research across much of Europe. One example is VET *against Social Exclusion* (Večkienė *et al.*, 2000), a study funded by the European Training Foundation and undertaken in Lithuania. Its findings indicate that women and children are demonstrably one of the biggest excluded groups in Lithuanian society. Other research comprehensively demonstrates the profound and complex nature of the situation of children (Kanišauskaitė, 2003).

This chapter will suggest that the complexity of the social situation in post-Soviet countries, and social exclusion in itself, require multidimensional solutions possible only through interdisciplinary and transdisciplinary participation. Otherwise, as research shows (Eidukevičiūtė, 2002; Cijunskaite, 2004), a low level of accessibility to social services can create situations in which children are outcasts.

Social work traditions are still underdeveloped in post-Soviet societies, and there is no history of interdisciplinary and transdisciplinary collaboration with which to address child welfare issues. Co-operation and collaboration within professional groups become a burden. That creates contradictions between expectations of, and capacities within, social work. This in turn affects interventions and social work processes, and these then impact on the outcomes of intervention in family life. Research and theory from other European countries – and the US – can in part contribute transferable experience and skills to improve the situation in areas of central and eastern Europe.

The *aim* of this chapter is to investigate some models for examining different experiences in child inclusion through interdisciplinary teams and transdisciplinary networks within social work. Initially the chapter reiterates the (albeit sometimes contradictory) need for a more globalized thinking in social welfare. Then it examines some contextual issues of social exclusion in Lithuania. Theory from France (Bourdieu) is drawn on to offer a framework for understanding the service user in his/her social context, and the characteristics of the social exclusion of children and families will be discussed. The chapter then considers theoretical aspects of interdisciplinary teams and transdisciplinary networks for social inclusion in social work, drawing on the knowledge and experience available from the UK and from some US texts against which to compare and evaluate Lithuanian's relatively new experience of such working systems. Original primary research, undertaken in Lithuania by us, considers attitudes in work with children and families. This is drawn on to underline the need for multidisciplinary strategies to increase the community's role in preventing the social exclusion of children.

9.2
Globalization and Social Inclusion as a Challenge for Social Work

Arguably, the question of social inclusion should be part of the national policy context in which social work practice should also be embedded. According to Dominelli (2004), although international globalization forces shape social inclusion, local governments must offer and implement appropriate localized responses to global issues.

It has now been established that globalization is one of the important trends which have an impact on the identity of social work as a profession. Lorenz (1998) demonstrates that identity as a concept can never be simple or fixed, and that the references which helped establish "packages" of identity, such as nationality, gender or education, are becoming more fluid and can change character rapidly. He also points out that social professions are implicated in this process of complex identification. As social work is a profession engaged in changeable and multiple self-definitions, openness and clarity, for example, have become particularly important. In facing those issues social workers should not "reject attempts to make them more accountable, and try to declare openly what their 'products' are and how they account for interventions" (Lorenz, 1998, p. 15).

Globalization has facilitated the internationalisation of social problems. Social issues have become important from one part of the globe to another. Governments have seriously to consider transnational social trends like migration, unemployment, terrorism, prostitution and other social issues. Lorenz (1998) argues that the effects of globalization lead to a greater range and complexity of social issues, and that the social professions must respond accordingly.

Lorenz also emphasises that globalization, like European integration, can be both a source of new opportunities, and a severe threat. Dominelli (2004) notes that globalization trends have enabled social workers to appreciate the independent nature of the world. Globalization has also made social workers aware of the problems that mark the world's social landscape, problems that require cross-border solutions and bring social workers into the political arena in the national and international domain. "The internationalization of social problems involves the globalization of the local, and the localization of the global" (Dominelli, 2004, p. 33). According to the author, there is a challenge to the locality-based nature of social work that encourages practitioners to think about *international dimensions* in a *more systematic and organised manner*. In this context it is especially important to share experience between western, central and eastern European countries. On the one hand, the consequences of globalization mean that countries cannot cope with their social issues alone. On the other hand, Lorenz and Scibel (1998) emphasise the international dimension, because only through international comparisons can universal principles be established and be distinguished from nationally-bonded habits and conventions.

9.3
Lithuanian Identities, Bourdieu and Social Exclusion

Social work in Lithuania is fifteen years old, as it is in other post-Soviet countries. Social work as a profession is known, but most people are uncertain about the actual aims of social work and the goals of social workers. It is an important specificity of Lithuanian social work that it is a social profession which has *never* had a clear identity because it is just developing. Commonly it is understood as "help" (mostly material) and care. And there are many uncertainties about social work as a tool for empowerment, and about issues such as the extent to which clients are able to participate in decision-making.

Social exclusion existed in Lithuania during Soviet times but it was not officially recognised or discussed. Most social services were institutionalised and structured according to communist ideology. After Lithuania became an independent country in 1991, social work as a profession appeared, and attempted to identify the existence of social problems and to limit their major consequences, primarily social exclusion.

The theoretical ideas of Bourdieu (1990), writing in France in the late 20th century, can be usefully applied to identify and analyse some specificities of, for example, "identity" issues in different European countries. Within the Lithuanian context, Bourdieu's work facilitates an understanding of how the Soviet period and the changes of the recent years have influenced social exclusion. Using his notion of social spheres (fields), for example, it can be argued that rapid and radical changes determined not only transformations of separate social fields, but also changed the whole Lithuanian social space remarkably (Grigas, 1998).

Where Bourdieu is particularly useful is in his complex analysis of the person as constituted within social space. The position of an individual in the social space, his/her behaviour and applied strategies depend on his/her *habitus* which include culturally specific *internalised* social structures. This allows us to claim that *habitus* are inevitably the product of the particular historical and social context.

What happens with the structures of social space when they are suddenly and radically transformed? Bourdieu (1990) acknowledges that *habitus* do not form a static structure; they can be corrected by adjusting to the new social space. However, mental structures, which have been formed by predominating moral norms and value systems during socialisation, do not necessarily change rapidly enough to be in parallel with new, still forming social structures. According to Bourdieu, *habitus* are prone to save their stability and defend themselves from changes by rejecting new information, which can then lead to a denial of newly created *habitus*. Then the old *habitus* are out of synchronisation with new circumstances and so are inadequate.

People's dispositions have not adjusted to the objective chances existing in the social system. Their actions and practices are not suitable for present conditions because their *habitus* were created by conditions which no longer exist. In such cases, people cannot adapt to new social structures, they cannot take advantage of all the possibilities on offer and they suffer from so-called *hysteresis* (Bourdieu, 1990). This, then, connects with social exclusion.

Kuzmickas is a Lithuanian philosopher, a politician and also a signatory of Lithuanian independence. He has talked about the impact of the Soviet years on individual consciousness and has noticed the process outlined by Bourdieu taking place in the Lithuanian nation (Kuzmickas, Astra, 1996). He remarked upon the following changes: features such as independence, individuality and a feeling of responsibility disappeared; obedience, passiveness, a tendency to wait for instructions, collective irresponsibility appeared. Post-Soviet societies now need new ways of being, but the *habitus*, as discussed above, carry history, and there is a mismatch between who people have become under communism and who the new situation demands that they be. This, then, is Bourdieu's thesis in practice. Both Bourdieu and Kuzmickas emphasise the meaning of interaction between individuals and their environment within contextual specificities. This perspective will be the standing point for further analysis of social exclusion as a social phenomenon.

9.4
Definitions of Social Exclusion

As well as being a product of the complex relationship between people and their (internalised) culturally specific location, the process of social exclusion can also be viewed as primarily a consequence of poverty and low income. Other factors such as discrimination, low educational attainment and depleted living environments also underpin it. Within this process people are, through a significant period in their lives, cut off from institutions and services, and from the social networks and developmental opportunities enjoyed by the great majority of society. However there are debates about the whole notion of social exclusion, a phenomenon which can be seen variously as a fact, a state or a process.

Within a European context, Barnes *et al.* (2002) explain that Graham Room was the person who in 1994 recommended that EUROSTAT should change its concept of poverty from a financial one to a multidimensional one. They emphasise that much of what is claimed as new in the analysis of social exclusion can also be found in poverty studies. Multidimensionality of social exclusion extends the actuality of interdisciplinary teams and transdisciplinary networks in social work. Barnes *et al.* (2002) apply Room's (1999) description of social exclusion and present five key factors defining social exclusion as a *process*:
1. social exclusion is multidimensional – it is not about income alone but about a wide range of indicators of living standards;
2. social exclusion is dynamic – analysing social exclusion means understanding a process and identifying the factors which can trigger entry or exit;
3. social exclusion has a neighbourhood dimension – deprivation is caused not only by a lack of personal resources but also by insufficient or unsatisfactory community facilities;
4. social exclusion is relational – the notion of poverty is primarily focused upon distributional issues, namely the lack of resources at the dis-

posal of an individual or a household; in contrast, social exclusion focuses more on relational issues: inadequate social participation, lack of social integration and lack of power;
5. social exclusion implies a major discontinuity in relationships with the rest of society.

Moreover Barnes *et al.* (2002) imply that the notion of social exclusion has the potential not only to highlight differences in resources between individuals and groups of individuals, but also to explore the key issues of autonomy and dependency, communication and collaboration between individual and society. This largely UK-based analysis is useful for understanding the multifactorial nature of social exclusion, and can usefully be applied to the Lithuanian context.

Shinman (2003), writing specifically within a transnational perspective, has a different emphasis. She argues that social exclusion can usefully be interpreted through the dimensions of "risk factors" and "disadvantage". She defines some core elements of social exclusion in families with young children; these can also be seen as indicators and/or measures of social exclusion, for example low participation in society, inadequate financial resources, feelings of isolation and powerlessness and deficient social networks. In her study she distinguishes the following elements of this conception, which identifies social exclusion as a *state*:
1. multidimensionality: personal, psychological, social, legal, physical, ecological, cultural, political etc.;
2. the accumulation of disadvantage (material and non-material);
3. an obstruction imposed on access to goods, services, opportunities or rights that are recognised by society as necessary;
4. lack of financial resources (an important but not indispensable condition);
5. a denial of the political and social rights that democratic societies accord to all citizens;
6. stigmatisation, reinforced by labelling and stereotyping;
7. powerlessness, hopelessness and loss of dignity on the part of those experiencing social exclusion.

Shinman (2003) adds ways in which those main elements can be evidenced:
a) social manifestations: poor social networks, insufficient social support, lack of a social life and a feeling of being ostracised;
b) financial manifestations: cannot make ends meet or afford basic necessities, obliged to live in substandard housing;
c) psychological manifestations: lack of confidence, self-respect, feelings of hopelessness, lack of control, mental health problems;

d) physical problems: poor health, poor physical development, poor parenting, neglect, failure to develop positive identity.

The author concludes from these models that it is not useful to emphasise the "causes" of social exclusion since no single factor or combination of factors could be seen to predict or determine it. A better approximation was to think in terms of risk factors, since the complex interplay of such factors appears to define the path into or out of social exclusion for each individual and family (Shinman, 2003).

As illustrated below, the situation in Lithuania demands a thorough analysis so as to facilitate intervention with the socially excluded. Given the relatively newly forming context of social work, models of exclusion from Europe and the US, such as those above, can be drawn upon to "fill the gap". Also, given the contemporary research context in the country itself, these models can be combined with research to become a useful stage in the development of local models. The globalization of social work knowledge, both acting on and being acted on by local specificities, is increasingly affecting social work here in Lithuania and across the rest of Europe. This process can, for example, help social workers recognise and address social exclusion in different contexts.

9.5
Tackling the Social Exclusion of Children and Families: The Lithuanian Case

As was suggested in SECTION 9.1, the social exclusion of children and families can become a seriously negative issue in itself, and it can result in lasting consequences for the future of individuals, families and groups.

For many years, providing support for families in complex situations was understood as being merely the maintenance of basic physiological needs: shelter, food, basic clothes. Social, economic, cultural and political causes were not taken into consideration. During Soviet times, the understanding of child welfare in Lithuania emphasised education. Parents had both an obligation and right to take care of their children. Indeed, parental care and upbringing had a defined direction – "according to the principles of communistic morality" (*Matrimonial Law*, 1963). The main goal was to overcome physical and educational neglect. At the same time there was no notion of psychological, sexual, or physical abuse, or any other kind of child abuse.

This attitude towards social issues is still the underpinning ethos of innovative social policy. But more recent understandings of the profession, including its skills and knowledge, are provoking permanent changes. In child and family policy there is a continuous process of development in the creation of new structures, and in looking for new ways to approach contemporary social issues. For example in the process of preparing for the project on Lithuanian demographic strategy, which was supervised by professor Vlada Stankūnienė, workers were provided with data characterising the problems faced by children and families in Lithuania.

One of the issues in Lithuania is the increasing number of families which are understood as problematic. According to the Department of Statistics of the Republic of Lithuania, during the last decade the number of families at social risk increased twofold (TAB. 9.1).

TABLE 9.1
Families at social risk in Lithuania (1995-2002, thousands)

	1995	1996	1997	1998	1999	2000	2001	2002
Families	9.7	12.6	14.9	15.1	16.0	18.1	18.7	18.5
Children in them	25.6	29.9	34.3	34.4	36.9	40.3	42.8	40.0

Source: Lietuvos Vaikai (2003).

The growing number of families and children at risk is the theme of much discussion and there are two particularly important but differing aspects. On the one hand, many families face diverse economic and political changes: difficulties in adapting to permanently changing economic, political and social situations. Of course, the most challenging of these changes, and the one involving the greatest demands, was the change from a planned economy to a market economy. As theorised by Bourdieu earlier in this chapter, lots of families could not adapt. The situation was both complex and difficult and required families quickly to find a new and balanced way of being in society. Those families who are considered to be at risk are those whose "strategies" could not provide a means of adapting to these societal changes.

On the other hand, after Lithuania ratified the *Children's Rights Act* (1995), there was an increased intensity of social services. The majority of children at social risk are mainly dependent on the work of child protection agencies. It is important to emphasise that during the last decade, documents which legislate for child protection were formulated and accepted, and formed the basis and the main preconditions for development and change within the child protection system.

Even in the biggest towns, there is still a lack of professional services which could provide help and support for the whole family, and in rural districts this process is just at the initial phase. Some children are separated from their families and enter the childcare system. The State decides whether parents have neglected their parental roles and obligations and have failed to create safe environments for the child, and the State can then take over the parental rights and obligations. However unlike in many parts of Europe the family still plays the most significant role in parenting, and a large percentage of children in foster care are fostered by their relatives. Nevertheless even for those children there is a lack of the social services (interventions and resources) which would empower them to become a significant part of society, and therefore that particular group of children always faces the risk of exclusion.

TABLE 9.2
Children who have lost parental care in Lithuania (2000-2002)

	2000	2001	2002
Total of children	2,597	2,863	3,003
Children under 7 years of age	897	1,080	1,220
Children directed to private persons or families	1,287	1,274	1,359

Source: Lietuvos Vaikai (2003).

The activities of the child protection system are also challenged by the fact that there are many more children and young people in poverty than, for example, older citizens. Trends appear to indicate that household containing children up to the age of 18 years form one of the biggest social groups living in poverty. Child poverty in central and eastern Europe is widespread and in Lithuania it is high. In 2000, 26% of all citizens were children under 18 years of age, and 31% of them was living in poverty. 20% of children are under 7 years of age is living in poverty.

TABLE 9.3
Level of poverty in different households in Lithuania (1998-2000, %)

Type of household	1998	1999	2000
One adult with child of up to 18 years	22.0	25.7	14.9
Married couple with children	13.9	15.5	15.3
Other households with children	24.8	21.9	24.1

Source: Lithuanian Human Development Report 2001 (2002).

Kanišauskaitė (2003) investigated the needs of adolescents living in poor families, particularly in relation to the way in which social and financial factors manifested themselves in social exclusion. Young people's social needs are always limited to those places/activities which have no cost. During the research Kanišauskaitė points out that day care centres for children are needed not only because of the food they provide, but also because of the activities which are delivered. Children cannot take part in other out-of-school activities because of the costs involved. The research also demonstrates that because of this and other associated difficulties, social inequality has an impact on children's relationships with their peers.

Drawing mainly on the UK context, Dominelli (2004) examines social work with children and families to question the idea that children should have fewer rights than adults. It is a "rights perspective" which is gaining ground in Europe generally (cf. *supra*, CHAP. 1). Dominelli also argues against rooting views of children within adult power relations, and suggests that children need to be thought of as autonomous beings living within collective contexts where their health and safety should be the concern of all members of society, not just their biological parents. Dominelli critiques current developments in social work with children and families to show that defining children as private possessions has deleterious implications for both children and adults, especially mothers who are solely responsible for their children's care. She contends that the development of social and community networks which can safeguard children's interests and rights is more likely to produce an environment conducive to promoting children's growth to maturity as full citizens, and this development is an essential element of any child welfare service that focuses on child and parent well-being (Dominelli, 2004).

This debate is also important in Lithuania, where it is becoming recognised that the social aspects of social exclusion are the most important. Conditions like social isolation and powerlessness impact on definitions of the role of social workers in relation to social inclusion and empowerment. Deficient social networks, another issue on exclusion which was discussed above, demand a whole range of services and expertise from different professions. This suggests the need for and the potential importance of interdisciplinary teams and transdisciplinary networks.

9.6
Theoretical Aspects for Child Inclusion: Interdisciplinary Teams and Transdisciplinary Networks

A social work which aims to address exclusion needs primarily to focus on groups, families and individuals with weak social networks. If a family is strong enough to create an environment suitable for supporting a child's development, then the family unit is unlikely to need formal help from social services. Pierson (2002) discusses *network poverty* in the UK context, a situation which deprives people (users of social support and informal help) of what that person needs to participate in community life

and to enjoy the standards of living shared by the majority of people. Mastering what networks are and how they thrive is an essential element when tackling the social exclusion of users. Pierson (2002) describes two kinds of network:
– networks for getting *by*: they are close, supportive networks embedded in the everyday relationships of friends, neighbourhoods and family; these can supply gaps in childcare;
– networks for getting *ahead*: these networks provide crucial information on jobs, education, training, and on a range of options for advancing individual interests; in many ways they are the opposite of networks for getting by but they can achieve so much more.

Once again we have a model devised within the western European context which can be useful for understanding the situation of Lithuanian families and their social needs. It is evident that in both contexts, until the networks are self-sufficient and seem "natural", and communities themselves have resources for support and maintenance of families as an ordinary part of community life, intervention will be required.

Changes in the structure of familial, political, social and economic life challenge not only the family but also the community. The complexity of social exclusion requires multidimensionality within which individual issues also require individualised approaches to social inclusion. Collaboration and communication play an important role within teams and networks. Here we are more interested in the collaborative aspect. The process of collaboration can, for example, lend itself well to addressing issues resulting from the complexity and multidisciplinarity of social exclusion.

Multidisciplinary collaboration is a core concept in this chapter. As pointed out earlier, this is a relatively new field in Lithuania, and the experience and literature of multidisciplinary work, as they have developed across much of Europe and the US, are proving helpful for an analysis of the national (actual and potential) picture. Multidisciplinary collaboration is, then, usually described as work with scientific and/or professional groups whose activity is interdependent and whose members have diverse skills and disciplinary or professional backgrounds that are applied to their programmes (Goodwin, 1996). International experience would suggest that these collaborations can range from dyads or partnerships to teams, to large projects, and transdisciplinary networks. In many countries, the development of shared knowledge is a major goal of multidisciplinary collaborations (Leidner, Jarvenpaa, 1995). This process requires collaborators to participate in the construction and organisation of information and ideas, and to use what they learn to create innovative work products. The development of shared knowledge includes not just the exchange of task information, but coming to agreement on goals and practices for collaboration. The development of shared knowledge is influenced by the "mindset" participants bring to the collaboration and the social structure of the group (Kiesler, Hinds, Weisband, 1999).

Interdisciplinary teams and transdisciplinary networks can usefully be conceptualised as different cases of multidisciplinary collaboration at different social levels. Interdisciplinary teams, in this chapter, are seen as ones which act at the *micro* level (collaboration between professionals) and transdisciplinary networks as acting in *meso* and *macro* level (co-operation between organisations, politicians and departments within the State). Also international collaboration between countries provides a broader significance for macro level collaboration.

According to Walter and Petr (2000), transdisciplinary networks, co-operation, co-ordination and collaboration between agencies form a "key strategy" in efforts to change fragmented human services into an infrastructure that addresses the multiple needs and issues of children and families in a more comprehensive and efficient way (FIG. 9.1).

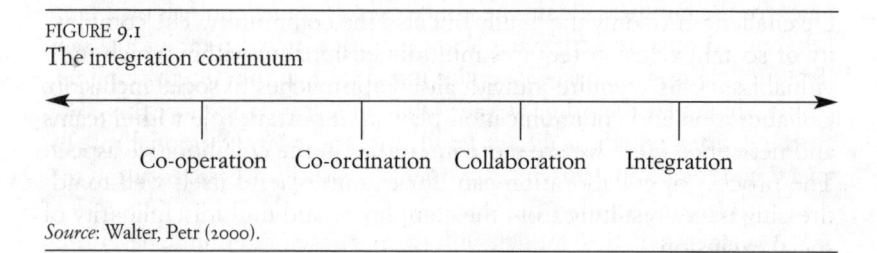

FIGURE 9.1
The integration continuum

⟵―――|―――――|―――――|―――――|―――⟶
    Co-operation Co-ordination Collaboration Integration

Source: Walter, Petr (2000).

Walter and Petr (2000) emphasise the role of co-ordination and co-operation between agencies which are working as networks. Co-operation, co-ordination, and collaboration between agencies form a continuum or a hierarchy of increasingly shared decision-making, processes and structures.

In talking about transdisciplinary networks it is important to distinguish between co-operation and co-ordination. Co-operation is, according to Bruner (1991), an *informal* exchange between agencies, with more or less frequent communication and a form of friendly co-existence. Co-ordination however involves some *formal* relations between agencies, whose staff will meet regularly to share their own ideas and plans, and discuss joint activities, while each agency maintains its own set of goals, structures, and responsibilities. In that way agencies are responsible to each other (Walter, Petr, 2000).

Abramson and Rosenthal (1995) define interagency collaboration as a smooth process through which a group of diverse, autonomous actors, each representing different professionals, undertakes joint initiatives, addresses shared problems, or otherwise achieves common goals. One of the important factors in such arrangements is formal commitments, within transdisciplinary network arrangements, to work together for specific and agreed purposes and outcomes. Collaboration can be described as a partnership that implies a durable and persistent relationship. It is possible when the tasks and goals of interdisciplinary teams are shared and closely connected to each other. As a result, mutual benefits and interdependence can be important aspects for interdisciplinary teams.

Social workers will have differing roles and functions in interdisciplinary teams, depending on which agency they are representing. In Lithuania, during the process of supporting and developing interdisciplinary teams, agencies could have different roles in the community. For example, municipality (State/statutory/local authority) social workers who protect children's rights are essentially administrators of the whole municipality; social workers in NGOs provide various professional services for the family as a unit; the police exercise State controls over families, and co-operate with other services in dealing with individual family issues. This is the basis of service integration within interdisciplinary teams which play the primary role with families, and therefore this could be the process which facilitates family inclusion. An additional role for social workers in interdisciplinary teams is to address issues of interaction and dynamics within the team.

A further analytical model, with the purpose of defining, describing and analysing co-operation, co-ordination and collaboration between interdisciplinary or transdisciplinary teams, is provided by Walter and Petr (2000). They formulate nine main dimensions, which have to be taken into account so as to construct useful and purposeful teams. They highlight "sharing" as the key issue, and suggest that as well as stakeholder involvement and common goals and tasks, teams must share responsibilities, rewards, resources, authority or decision-making, evaluations, structures and, importantly, teams must subscribe to shared visions and values (cf. FIG. 9.2).

As you can see from FIG. 9.2, shared visions and values have been highlighted as being essential to successful initiatives, and to support and reinforce interdisciplinary and transdisciplinary collaboration. A consensus of values has been identified as one essential precondition for successful collaboration whereas disagreement or dissonance in values, or in the motivation to integrate services, causes unsuccessful attempts at collaboration that fail to include staff and communities.

FIGURE 9.2
Shared values as the core dimension of interagency collaboration

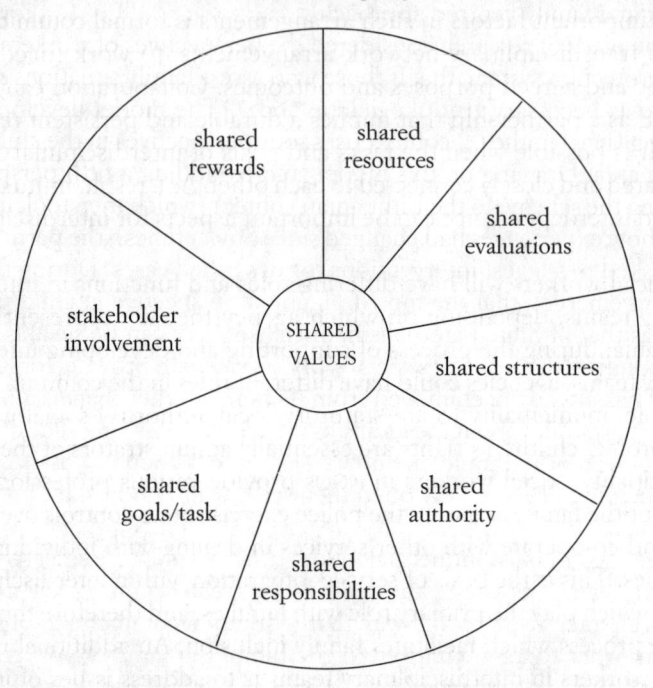

Diagram: A circle divided into eight segments around a central "SHARED VALUES" hub. The segments are labelled: shared rewards, shared resources, shared evaluations, shared structures, shared authority, shared responsibilities, shared goals/task, stakeholder involvement.

Source: Walter, Petr (2000).

In relation to family work in Lithuania, it seems that one of the main aspects of shared values, which are the key concept for collaboration, is the integration of a family-centred approach. One of the paternalistic characteristics in services for family and child protection is to separate the family into two parts: the first and the most important part is the child, and the other, which sometimes seems to be taken as just an "appendage of the first", is the parents. The notion prevails that the parents' task lies in creating an environment for the child's development. Devising social services for the whole family – taking into account that child inclusion is not possible without the inclusion of the whole family as a unit – without separating the family into different parts is one possibility for implementing the idea of empowering support and avoiding the fragmentation of social services for the family.

Research projects undertaken by Večkienė, Eidukevičiūtė, and Cijunskaite, in Vytautas Magnus University in Lithuania, will now be considered in more detail. They demonstrate that although officially there are networks and teams providing social services for the family, in reality they are just in the creation stage, and as yet there seems to be little by way of a family-centred approach.

One piece of research considered the perspectives of workers in the child protection system, that is those who assess family situations and intervene as necessary (Eidukevičiūtė, 2002). The model developed by Harding (1995) in the UK context uses four perspectives in the child protection area. Drawing on this model, and by adding a fifth perspective adapting the scheme to the Lithuanian context (which then took into account how experiences had changed since Soviet times), the participants were asked to suggest interventions for described cases. During that research it emerged that the most influential perspective in child protection was that of State paternalism. Social services can be seen as somewhat punitive: in most cases social work services are provided only when a child has already been moved from its family rather than as a preventive strategy. Ideas about the family as inviolable are strong. The children – and indeed other family members – are understood as passive agents in the helping process; very often their wishes and understanding of the situation are rejected.

The second most influential model discovered in the research is the modern defence of the birth family and parents' rights. This model is mainly characterised by the way that workers recommend a lot of services in order to keep children in the biological family. Workers were planning support and services for every member of family, and for the family as whole. The service users were given active roles in deciding what kind of social services the family would need. One of the aspects which emerged during the research was that there was collaboration between different agencies providing different kinds of specified services. Workers were taking empowerment perspectives, by which they were strengthening the family. It is important to add that the empowering interventions were usually suggested by professional social workers mainly working in non-governmental organisations. These social workers also acted in agencies for the protection of children's rights, in schools and as social pedagogues, even though the participants of the research were a multidisciplinary collection of police officers for child delinquency.

There was also a child protection model from Soviet times which has many similarities with State paternalism. The helping process is provided by using power and threats, and as in State paternalism models the child is taken from the biological family to childcare institutions. This main task and its requirement have an ideological emphasis, based on the assumption that if the family is creating an environment which is understood as damaging, then the alternative to the biological family should be institutional care. In the research only a few child protection workers suggested interventions which could be described as being orientated by children rights and child liberation. Workers were listening to children but not necessarily acting on their voices.

Cijunskaite (2004) investigated interdisciplinary collaboration in the prevention of juvenile delinquency. In the research she notes that interdisciplinary collaboration is still in its early developmental stage. The main principles of collaboration are only partially realised, team members do not always find that the necessary conditions for collaboration are accessible or comprehensible. During this qualitative research it emerged that no participant in the interdisciplinary team conceived of the family as partners. Interdisciplinary communication cannot be successful where the family is understood as the object rather than the subject of interdisciplinary intervention. This denies the family their own strengths and coping mechanisms during the process. Within social services, divergent understandings of the family's role can overburden the helping process in individual cases, and a clear value system cannot be shared if values are not agreed, harmonised and habitualised. The family-centred approach is one feature of successful interdisciplinary teams and transdisciplinary networks.

It can be argued that improving social inclusion cannot just be the responsibility of interdisciplinarity in social work interventions, but that in the construction of social policies, there must be more attention paid in to address social inclusivity in post-Soviet countries. In policies and laws which relate to the role of family, the emphasis is on obligations, and there is not enough attention given to support and help families or the communities within which they function.

Social policy, realised by and facilitative of the work of interdisciplinary teams and transdisciplinary networks, is at the heart of family and child social inclusion. Coote, Harman and Hewitt (1998) suggest some general guidelines for family policy in the UK which the authors would like to see applied to the Lithuanian context. These could be important for strategic planning and as possible ways of looking for common goals:

1. families are *social*, not natural phenomena: families change over time; they are susceptible to and shaped by economic and political developments;
2. the most important thing is the *process*, not the label: the family is changing, there are reasons for and consequences of that change; in the main, social policy is sensitive to what happens in families, rather than to the label or the status attached to different living arrangements: there is an emphasis on the importance of the process and the relationships;
3. children come *first*: children are the most important resources and

everyone has an obligation to them, whether they are parents themselves or not; family policy should be primarily concerned with the process of bringing up and caring for children;

4. policy must work *with*, not against, the grain of change: the aim of public policy-makers should be to understand the nature of change and make the best of it;

5. *encouragement*, not coercion: policy can encourage some kinds of behaviour and discourage others;

6. a *long-term* perspective: it is important to recognise that significant changes in the nature of family life develop slowly over a long period of time; there is a lag between cause and effect: policy-makers must take into account the effect of change;

7. a *European* perspective: the close integration of the EU means that individual countries can no longer devise social policy in isolation from each other.

These core concepts could provide the conditions for a shared commitment at different levels in the context of Lithuania's emerging interdisciplinary teams and transdisciplinary networks which are implementing individual inclusion within the community. This could help create a notion of what these teams and networks could mutually espouse, including notions of what divides and links different sources within individual environments.

9.7
Conclusions

As this chapter has argued, then, a complex understanding of the individuals in their social environment is needed so as to develop an inclusive practice with children and families. Theory and practice models from Europe – for example from France and the UK – can provide frameworks for understanding and development in the Lithuanian context. Local research provides the additional knowledge-base for the understanding of the direction practice must take. The chapter has also argued that both social exclusion and social inclusion are multidimensional, and intervention needs a complex understanding, knowledge and skills. The exclusion of families and children is (painfully) experienced in the community and is also a community issue. Thus, we conclude, interdisciplinary collaboration is crucial to enable social workers to act as partners within whole communities as well as within families. Social policy needs to underpin and support this.

As this chapter shows, co-operation between different European countries opens up new possibilities for the transference of knowledge and experience. Perhaps this co-operation can also contribute to international interdisciplinary and transdisciplinary collaborations, although this adds even greater levels of complexity. Through multidisciplinarity it is possible to add international and global elements to understanding and to practice, though local variations and conditions remain as crucial dimensions. Greater understanding, developed from a whole range of European sources, when added to local research must invariably increase the sum of knowledge which can be accessed to improve practice with families, children and communities in multidisciplinary contexts.

Bibliography

ABRAMSON J., ROSENTHAL B. (1995), *Interdisciplinary and Interorganizational Collaboration*, in *Encyclopedia of Social Work*, vol. II, NASW Press, Washington.
BARNES M. et al. (2002), *Poverty and Social Exclusion in Europe*, Edward Elgar, Cheltenham.
BOURDIEU P. (1990), *The Logic of Practice*, Polity Press, Cambridge.
BRUNER C. (1991), *Thinking Collaboratively: Ten Questions and Answers to Help Policy Makers Improve Children's Services*, Education and Human Services Consortium, Washington.
CIJUNSKAITE M. (2004), *Interdisciplininis bendradarbiavimas – nepilnamečių nusikalstamumo prevencijos veiksnys*, bakalauro darbas, VDU, Kaunas.
COOTE A., HARMAN H., HEWITT P. (1998), *Family Policy: Guidelines and Goals*, in J. Franklin (ed.), *Social Policy and Social Justice: The IPPR Reader*, Polity Press, Cambridge, pp. 105-13.
DOMINELLI L. (2004), *Social Work: Theory and Practice for a Changing Profession*, Polity Press, Cambridge.
EIDUKEVIČIŪTĖ J. (2002), *Vaiko apsauga Kaune*, magistro diplominis darbas, VDU, Kaunas.
GOODWIN C. (1996), *Transparent Vision*, in E. Ochs, E. A. Schegloff, S. A. Thompson (eds.), *Interaction and Grammar*, Cambridge University Press, Cambridge, pp. 370-404.
GRIGAS R. (1998), *Socialinių įtampų Lietuvoje laukai*, VPU, Vilnius.
HARDING L. (1995), *Perspectives in Child Care Policy*, Longman, London.
KANIŠAUSKAITĖ V. (2003), *Paaglių, gyvenančių skurstančiose šeimose, socialiniai poreikiai*, bakalauro darbas, VDU, Kaunas.
KIESLER S., HINDS P., WEISBAND S. (1999), *Multidisciplinary Collaboration*, http://www.idc.nit.edu/multicollab.
KUZMICKAS B., ASTRA L. (1996), *Šiuolaikinė lietuvių tautin? savimonė*, FSI, Vilnius.
LEIDNER D. E., JARVENPAA S. L. (1995), *The Use of Information Technology to Enhance Management School Education: A Theoretical View*, in "MIS Quarterly", XIX, 3, pp. 265-91.
LIETUVOS VAIKAI (2003), *Statistikos departamentas prie Lietuvos Respublikos Vyriausybės*, Vilnius.

Lithuanian Human Development Report 2001 (2002), Socialinės apsaugos ir darbo ministerija, Vilnius.
LORENZ W., SCIBEL F. W. (hrsg.) (1998), *Soziale Professionen für ein soziales Europa*, IKO, Frankfurt a.M.
PIERSON J. (2002), *Tackling Social Exclusion*, Routledge, London.
ROOM G. (1999), *Social Exclusion, Solidarity and the Challenge of Globalization*, in "International Journal of Social Welfare", VIII, 3, pp. 166-74.
SHINMAN S. (2003), *Tackling Social Exclusion in Families with Young Children: A Trans-National Enquiry*, in "Social Work in Europe", X, 3, pp. 4-13.
VEČKIENĖ N. et al. (2000), *VET against Social Exclusion*, Vytautas Magnus University, Kaunas.
VEČKIENĖ N., VEČKYS V. (2003), *Social Exclusion in the Process of Transition: The Lithuanian Case*, in M. Bochenska-Seweryn, J. Grotowska-Leder (eds.), *Old and New Poverty in Post-Communist Europe: Challenges for Social Work*, Jagiellonian University, Krakow, pp. 71-85.
WALTER U. M., PETR C. G. (2000), *A Template for Family-Centered Interagency Collaboration*, in "Families in Society", LXXXI, 5, pp. 494-503.

Section C
The Profession

10

Professionalization and Status for Child Welfare Workers: A Way of Mapping a Working Area in Social Work

by *Peter Dellgran* and *Staffan Höjer*

10.1
Introduction

In social work literature from all over the world, one recurrent characteristic is its dependence on the local context. However, another frequent attribute is an obvious heterogeneity in each country and cultural setting. In any given context various kinds of social work appear, with different organisational settings, histories, traditions, tasks, functions, regulations, jurisdictions, methods and techniques.

Nevertheless, in all European countries child welfare, with a connection to social work, can be detected. Sometimes other concepts are used, in the US it is often referred to as "family service" and in the UK "children in need" or "family support". Child protection is a notion that only covers part of the activities and as an alternative "childcare" is often used. In most European countries the term "child welfare" is used as an overarching concept (Spratt, Callan, 2004). In a general sense child welfare can be described as programmes and policies which are oriented towards the protection, care and healthy development of children (Barker, 1999). This way the State takes an interest in the welfare and well-being of children and families, where children's needs, both physically and mentally, should be satisfied. If this is not the case the State expects local authorities to intervene by working with parents and children to improve the situation or, if not possible, to remove the child from the parents (Hessle, Vinnerljung, 1999). Of course this child welfare has its unique traits in different nations, with relations between different professional and non-professional actors involved – cf. for instance Lorenz (1994) on different welfare models or Campanini and Frost (2004) on the development of the profession in different countries in Europe.

Not all (perhaps not even most) child welfare is handled within social work or by professionals called social workers. Foster care is one part of child welfare where this is an obvious thing. In Sweden about 18,500 children (8.5 of 1,000 children 0-17 years old) were in care with placement outside their own home at some time during 2001. Of these, over 70% was placed in foster families, supposed to take on the task of supporting and comforting a needy child, and also to help the child maintain relations with the natural family (Höjer, 2001, 2004). These foster families are not educated social workers but ordinary families doing a kind of voluntary work, albeit with professional features. However, looking at social work, child welfare and child protection are core activities for a great number of European social workers.

Another point of departure that we want to consider concerns the standard of professionalization in social work. This strive for professionalization has been a constant companion of social work ever since Abraham Flexner (1915) made his famous speech at a conference for charity workers in Baltimore about the professional status for social work, indicating that at that time it could not be considered as a true profession. Since then many attempts have been made to further professionalize social work with the help of research and scientific knowledge. Of course the level of professionalization differs not only between countries, but also within countries, as this chapter will show. Ambivalence towards a maximised professionalization in social work has over the years also been a reoccurring theme in the debate, where some debaters have pointed out the risk of creating a gap between the interests of social workers and those of the service users.

We have found several studies describing the situation for children or families at risk and also studies comparing different kinds of child welfare interventions in European countries. There are comparisons concerning: child poverty and child policies (Vleminckx, Smeeding, 2000); the use of institutional care for children in Europe (Sellick, 1998); public childcare in Germany and England (Janze, 1999); child adoption policies (Garrett, Sinkkonen, 2003); foster care (Colton, Williams, 1997). Also some data about child abuse and child neglect in the US compared with Canada, Australia and Britain can be found in Waldfogel (1998). However, there are few descriptions or analyses of the professional standings or indicators of professionalization for child welfare social workers. This chapter is an attempt to present some information about the latter.

The aim of this essay is to present a way of mapping professionalization in social work by introducing a system of professionalization indicators. The target group is social workers acting with children, youth and families. Depending on the content of and conditions for their work, their degree of professionalization will be compared to other groups of

professional social workers. Of interest is also the understood internal status, trajectories and career patterns. To be more specific the following questions will be treated.
1. What differences regarding professionalization can be found between a number of different working areas in relation to child welfare in Swedish social work?
2. What internal status is given to these working areas?
3. What kinds of trajectories and career patterns can be found among the social workers working in child welfare?

In all we want to discuss what these career patterns imply for child welfare workers and for the future professionalization of social work. Another question of interest is whether or not these professionalization indicators can be used to describe and compare working areas in European social work.

10.2
Theorising Professionalization

Let us first of all illuminate different meanings of professionalization in order to focus on individual and collective strategies for professional development. A common view is that professionalization can be described as a *collective* process. We are in this sense talking about a specific occupational group (in this case social workers working within child welfare, but it could be teachers, medical doctors or engineers) and its different ways of reaching and improving status, authority, discretion and control over, for example, education and working conditions. In fact, this means strategies on an institutional level to create and regulate legitimate and effective relations to the State, other professions and the general public. Throughout history different occupational groups have strived for legitimacy, authority and power in relation to the State and society to clearly define and monopolize a certain occupational field through its exclusive formal knowledge. In this collective process, research, education and the production of scientific knowledge are important components (Abbott, 1988; Macdonald, 1995).

Professionalization can also be described as an *individual* process, explaining how the individual social worker becomes more professional in his/her daily work. When this side of professionalization is being described focus generally stays on competence and skills and how these traits are developed through experiences in practice, different forms of advanced education, specialisation and supervision. When it comes to the individual's relation to scientific knowledge, focus is on the ability to integrate, use and transform this knowledge in daily action (Eraut, 1994; Yelloly, Henkel, 1995).

The third way to discuss professionalization is to understand it as a *socialisation* process – the process of actually becoming a professional of a certain kind. This identity building, as a part of a social and cultural process, normally starts during the stage of undergraduate education and differs between professions (Camilleri, 1996). A fourth understanding of professionalization is focusing on it as a *societal* process, underlining structural changes, for example the expansion of the welfare States, that results in a quantitative growth of occupational groups defined as professions and in an increased reliance on professional knowledge and expertise. Last but not least a fifth perspective on professionalization reminds us that no profession can have anything other than a relative autonomy towards the State. The dependency towards the State has as one of its consequences that its conditions may be altered, any occupational field is continuously exposed to changes, challenging the knowledge domain it may have previously annexed. New knowledge, new vocational groups inside or outside the profession, the development of information technology, new legislation, changed economic conditions, new organisational forms, internationalisation, quality demands and social needs are all examples that may influence the position of professional groups. Any profession must in other words develop and maintain its ability to meet and handle change, uncertainty and risk that may weaken its competence and position (Becher, 1999).

Welfare professionals are often described as highly educated social groups who, thanks to hard-won and assigned scientific authority and expertise, manage to limit and monopolize certain fields of practice and knowledge. They have reached this position legitimated by university education and their claim to be the most competent to carry out specific services. They have thus reached a relative discretion in relation to the State and society as a whole when it comes to determining the content and conditions for its education and practice. In the sociology literature, professions can be described according to an ideal-typical Anglo-Saxon professional model as free entrepreneurs competing on the market or to a European professional model, as experts employed within the private, public or civic sector. In North America, professions are often presented as antitheses to bureaucratic organised work (Larson, 1977). These models do not necessarily cover the conditions in socialist countries, post-communist countries, or in many countries in Asia, Africa and Latin America. Here the sociology of the professions, as we see it, has a lacuna which needs to be filled.

10.3
The Professional Project:
Strategies on Collective and Individual Levels

As outlined above the first collective perspective on professionalization is often labelled as a professional project, described as a process, where the occupational group strives for different goals in order to improve its autonomy, reputation and status. Freidson (1994) and Larson (1977) conceive the profession as a social group that creates itself and develops strategies to keep and to improve its own position. Macdonald (1995) shows how the professional project is accomplished within both an economic and a social order. In a central position for both stands the claim for a monopoly on knowledge and competence and also on trust. Within the *economic* order the tasks for the profession are set in relation to the needs of the local and national State of getting certain tasks performed. In the *social* order the theme is rather the development of a certain culture with certain values and norms and how this will affect status and respectability. The professional project has as its concern to, as far as possible, get a societal sanction to be responsible and best suited for the treatment of certain duties. In this respect the professional project is also a political one since it contains an ingredient of boundary work with respect to other professions (Gieryn, 1999).

In the case of professional social workers in Sweden it is quite easy to name a number of more or less conventional activities in order to strengthen the profession, as a part of their professional project. For instance the birth of the concept of social work, the denomination of the occupational exam (in Sweden *socionom*), the struggle for professional supervision (and later specific education for supervision in social work), the continual reform of social work education, the formation of unions for social workers, the attempts to draw up a specific theory for social work, the establishment of codes of ethics for social work, the development of a master's degree in social work and the establishment of the authorisation system. A continuous process is the strive for academicalisation of social work, and the institutionalisation of the academic discipline in 1977 with professorships and research education in social work – for more on this history of the professional project for social work in Sweden cf. Wingfors (2004); Dellgran, Höjer (2003d). In each and every one of these examples we can find claims-making and boundary work in order to shut out certain groups or activities, or at times to incorporate some new areas or actors. As a whole, social work in Sweden can still be described as heterogenic and pluralistic with, in many cases, unclear borders with respect to other professions. This means there are many boundary objects, in terms of activities or tasks in which the profession is competing with other professionals. For instance, there is the question of which professionals are best suited to undertake family therapy (Rigné, 2002)?

We can also talk about a professional project from an individual perspective, meaning how individuals choose career patterns for increased autonomy and status. Very often different kinds of university education are used as a way of rising within the professional hierarchy, getting more prestigious jobs, with a higher degree of discretion and sometimes with a better salary. However strategies that involve professional expertise gained through other sources of knowledge, such as work experience, are also counted for in the private professional project – for more about relevant sources of knowledge for social work cf. Dellgran, Höjer (2005c).

10.4
Methods and Materials

In this chapter, material is presented from a survey that was sent to a random selection of Swedish social workers in the largest social work union in the autumn 2001. Exactly 1,000 professionals with at least a bachelor of social work (BSW) degree are included in the study. The approximated response rate is 72%. More information about the methodology can be found in Dellgran and Höjer (2003a, 2003d).

10.5
Six Working Areas in Child Welfare in Sweden

First of all, work within child welfare is a core activity in the daily life of many social workers in Sweden as in many other European countries. In many countries it is also a fairly popular area of social work. When social work students in Israel, the US and England were asked what client group they would prefer to work with, children and adolescents were given the highest overall preferences (Weiss *et al.*, 2002). Summing up all the following working areas in child welfare, they represent 35% of Swedish social workers. (The share working with, for example, substance abuse, social assistance or criminal offenders is much lower: Dellgran, Höjer, 2003d.) Before we take a closer look at differences and similarities among social workers involved in child welfare in Sweden, just a few words about their working tasks. The biggest group (17.8% of all Swedish social workers) has its practice at the local welfare office (cf. TAB. 10.1). Here social workers are responsible for investigating, assessing and acting in matters concerning child abuse, neglect, juvenile crime or other child or youth related issues. The local welfare office is involved in treatment and social support as well as with the exercise of formal authority. For the most part the activities of local welfare offices are regulated by the law.

TABLE 10.1
Professionalization indicators within different working areas for child welfare social workers in Sweden (2002, n = 1,000)

Working area	Social workers (%)	(a)	(b)	(c)	(d)	(e)	(f)	(g)	(h)	(i)	(j)
Child and youth psychiatric team	2.9	21.6	93.0	10.3	31.0	20.7	125.0	95.0	87.0	82.9	101.0
Specialised open care	3.6	13.2	86.0	11.1	0.0	16.7	101.0	119.0	131.0	50.3	97.0
Institutional care	1.9	11.2	84.0	10.5	0.0	10.5	100.0	110.0	101.0	34.0	100.0
School social work	7.3	15.9	75.0	4.2	2.8	16.7	94.0	101.0	112.0	37.5	90.0
Outreach work	1.5	9.2	79.0	20.0	0.0	0.0	122.0	109.0	125.0	29.6	92.0
Local welfare offices	17.8	10.9	91.0	8.5	1.1	9.0	97.0	90.0	89.0	47.6	96.0
Total child welfare	35.0	–	–	–	–	–	–	–	–	–	–
All social work	100.0	14.9	78.0	6.8	4.8	12.8	100.0	100.0	100.0	–	100.0

(a) Average number of occupational years as professional social worker (anova test $p < .001$) (analysis of variance).
(b) % with supervision (chi square test $p < .001$) (test of significance).
(c) % with master of social work (MSW) degree.
(d) % with degree in advanced therapy (step 2) (chi square test $p < .001$).
(e) % with authorisation (chi square test $p < .001$).
(f) % with high degree of research orientation defined as the summation of 5 variables according to individual self-declared valuation of 1. research as a source of competence, 2. up-to-date with research, 3. contacts with researchers, 4. beliefs in research as a means for improvement of future social work, 5. interest of applying for research education. Indexation where *total mean* = 100 (anova test $p < .001$).
(g) Overall satisfaction with working conditions by individual self-declared valuations of 15 separate aspects, among which: wage, working tasks, work results, organisation, local politicians, development of methods and competence, supervision, options for autonomy and creativity, responsibility. Indexation where *total mean* = 100 (anova test $p < .001$).
(h) Satisfaction with autonomy. As (g) but only according to 4 specific variables: creativity, autonomy, responsibility and possibilities for planning work time. Indexation where *total mean* = 100 (anova test $p < .001$).
(i) Degree of internal status measured by social workers opinions. For each working area the respondents were asked to evaluate status within social work according to a scale ranging from 1 (very high) to 5 (very low). % with very high or high status.
(j) Average monthly income (respondents with management tasks excluded). Indexation where *total mean* = 100 (anova test $p < .001$).

A little more than 7% of the social workers acts within school social work. In most cases there is only one social worker at each school and often the social worker is responsible for social work with students in more than one school. This educational welfare officer is to a varying degree co-operating with other professionals – i.e. special teachers, nurses, sometimes medical doctors, and psychologists – in a team responsible for the social support of students.

There is normally at least one child and youth psychiatric team in every Swedish municipality. To this team families can turn when they are facing problems with their child. School social workers or social workers at local welfare offices can also recommend that families go there. This psychiatric team does not exercise any formal authority but is working on a consultative basis predominately with counselling and therapy. The team is always headed by a psychiatric medical doctor and beside social workers it also consists of psychologists. A little less than 3% of social workers acts here.

Outreach work in Sweden is in most cases directed towards youth in the local community. (In other countries this is often defined as youth work.) It is community-based and is in most cases doing group work and structural work besides individual orientation. Another side of outreach work is community work directed towards all residents in a neighbourhood. This latter kind of social work was much more common in the 1970s and 1980s and has decreased a lot in the last decade. Today only 1.5% of social workers is involved in outreach work. Specialised open-care work is a category that holds many other different forms of open-care treatment. For instance different kinds of open treatment teams like MST (multisystemic therapy), family counselling, and youth advisory centres are some examples from this category, with in all a little more than 3.5% of the social workers dealing with this.

Within the institutional care system for children and youth in Sweden, social workers do not hold any dominant position. Barely 1.9% of all social workers acts within this area. Psychologists, social pedagogues and other welfare professionals also work within the institutional care system to only a small degree. Instead, most of the work is carried out by employees without a university education, making it a professional area without professionals.

10.6
Professionalization Indicators

Neither the choice nor the operationalisation of professional indicators is self-evident since there are obvious theoretical and empirical problems with deciding and comparing the level of professionalization. This is a fact whether we choose an individual or collective understanding of professionalization, and want to comment on complex aspects like level of competence, status, autonomy and discretion, or control over social work practice. Our more modest approach in this chapter aims to present what we call professionalization indicators (PI). These indicators describe certain advances – in terms of further education, orientation towards research and scientific knowledge etc. – among social workers in different working areas and organisational contexts. All of this implies professionalism but is not the same thing as assuming that some social workers are more competent and skilful in their job performance than others. Most of our indicators are relatively uncomplicated and it goes without saying for a study of professionalization, in any occupational field, that a number of indicators like the share of social workers with different kinds of prior education or authorisation deals primarily with the formal level of competence. At the same time supervision and advanced education are presumed to raise the actual competence and different occupational skills. Other indicators, as for instance the number of occupational years within a working area, are intellectually underpinned by the belief that professionalization can be seen as a continual process whereby learning and accumulated work experiences are important sources of knowledge.

10.7
Mapping Child Welfare

Using the professionalization indicators described earlier, the field of child welfare seems very heterogenic and unbalanced in many respects. The first indicator is *occupational years* (a). On average, social workers in Sweden have been occupied with professional, paid social work for 15 years. This can be held to be quite long in the European context. For instance in many of the eastern and central European countries social work had a new start after the changes initiated after 1989. In Hungary social work is still a very young profession in which all qualified social workers are newly graduated and usually in their thirties (Göncz, 2004). In England however two thirds of social service employees are over-40-year-olds (Harlow, 2004).

The most experienced child welfare workers in Sweden are the ones working in child and youth psychiatric teams (over 21 years), while the least experienced are outreach workers (9 years) and the ones at local welfare offices (11 years). In the larger cities the averages are much lower than in Sweden as a whole. These latter fields are commonly held to be "entrance areas", which means that a majority of newly examined social workers find their first jobs here.

The second indicator measures how many social workers have *supervision* (b). In Sweden, since the 1980s there has been a call for independent supervision (both on methods and on processes) from an experienced specifically educated social worker, not the manager of the organisation. This kind of supervision is not the same kind that is given to newly employed social workers by senior colleagues. Instead it is held to be a tool for further education, using experiences from practice as a curriculum for learning. This call has been quite successful, looking at the profession as a whole, 78% has supervision. In child welfare, child and youth psychiatric teams rank highest while school social workers rank the lowest. In all, child welfare ranks high when compared to the mean for other kinds of social work.

Different kinds of advanced education can, as mentioned earlier, be considered as reasonable indicators of professionalization. This study examined the frequency of seven types of advanced education, although only two are shown in TAB. 10.1. Nearly 7% of all Swedish social workers has a *master's degree in social work (MSW)* (c), although the figures are higher in all child welfare areas except for school social work. A total of 20% of outreach workers has a master's degree in social work. This may be explained by the fact that a couple of universities has a specialised master's education in community work. Another explanation could of course be the low number of outreach workers in the study.

A little less than 5% of Swedish social workers has an advanced *psychotherapy education* (d). In the field of child welfare the distribution is very unbalanced. More than 31% of the social workers in the child and youth psychiatric teams has such a degree. Often it is a prerequisite for getting a job in this area to have at least a basic therapy education. The only group of social workers with a comparatively high figure are the self-employed social workers (for more about privatisation in social work and a comparative analysis of public and private social workers cf. Dellgran, Höjer, 2005c).

The introduction of *authorisation* (e) by the largest union in the 1990s is considered an important step towards professionalization. For many years the union of social workers encouraged the State to introduce some form of certification for social workers. The State declined, however, due to the fact that social work does not have the same clear professional boundaries of liability as medical doctors and nurses, for instance. Delegation rules for social workers are set by local politicians, with little leeway for social workers' professional discretion and ethical codes. When the attempts to introduce certification failed, the union offered its own authorisation system in 1998. The requirements for an authorised social worker are a social work degree (BSW), at least three years of social work experience, supervision for two years (at least 100 hours), and two separate evaluations of the applicant's suitability from a management representative, supervisor and/or colleague. In addition, the social worker must commit to the above-mentioned ethical code. Of course, authorisation and certification are not totally compatible. A certification system would have entailed a set of rules on the consequences of infractions, and defined the relationship between the State, the public and the profession. Almost 13% of all social workers was authorised at the end of 2001. Two of the areas where the level of authorisation is highest (child and youth psychiatric teams and school social workers) are both examples where social workers are placed in multidisciplinary settings, perhaps indicating that authorisation is held to be more important there than in local welfare offices where social workers often hold a hegemonic position.

Research orientation (f) is based on an index constructed by the replies to five questions concerning the relationship between practice and research in social work. The variable is obtained by summing up the replies to attitudinal questions on 1. research as a source of competence, 2. familiarity with current research, 3. contacts with researchers, 4. belief in research as a means of improving future social work, 5. interest in applying for research education (Dellgran, Höjer, 2005c). A higher degree of research orientation is found among social workers in the child and youth psychiatric teams and among outreach workers. The research orientation is lowest among school social workers. One possible explanation for the latter is found in a content analysis of senior research in social work in Sweden. It was found that research that dealt with problems and interventions connected with school social work was much lower than equivalent research about other working areas (Dellgran, Höjer, 2003b). Research orientation also seems to have certain links to the social worker's degree of further education.

Of course the possibility of a social worker developing a research orientation differs depending on the standings of social work research in different European countries. In some countries there is a research discipline called social work. In others research about social work must be done within other disciplines – for information about the standings for doctoral work in the social work field in Europe, cf. Laot (2000); for Britain, Lyons (2002); for Finland, Karvinen, Pösö, Satka (1999); for Sweden, Dellgran, Höjer (2003c, 2005c).

One obvious purpose of professionalization is to obtain control, or at least influence, over the content of, and the conditions for, social work on a collective level and for the individual social worker. This could be examined in many different ways. In this study, respondents were asked to evaluate their satisfaction/dissatisfaction with nineteen aspects of their *working conditions* (g). TAB. 10.1 presents figures based on two indexes, one overall estimation encompassing all variables and the other an *assessment of autonomy* (h), including satisfaction/dissatisfaction with four variables: opportunities for creativity, degree of independence, control over daily work, planning and responsibility. One problem with such subjective opinions is of course that demands on working conditions might vary on a more systematic level. And since these demands are presumably affected by professionalization in terms of advanced education and occupational years, lower demands may very well stem from individual feelings of a lower degree of professionalization and therefore result in somewhat more positive judgments of actual working conditions. Nevertheless, we have found significant variations between different working areas. Both on the overall estimation and on the autonomy index, the specialised open-care workers are the most satisfied with their working conditions. Outreach workers also come out as a satisfied group while the child and youth psychiatric team, along with the local welfare offices, are less satisfied. Especially on the autonomy index these latter groups stand out as much more unsatisfied than the rest. Our tentative explanations for this follow somewhat different lines. In the child and youth psychiatric team we have along with earlier indicators very high figures for the degree of professionalization. In this case the expectancy might be higher than for other groups. The manager in this group is always a medical doctor and the group is formed with representatives from different professions probably decreasing the feeling of autonomy for social workers. In the local welfare offices, the situation is different. Here the social workers dominate the professional landscape, however many decisions (also on an individual client level) are made by local politicians, and consequently social workers have only a limited degree of discretion and autonomy.

Another important indicator of professionalization is the gaining of *status* (i) and legitimacy in the eyes of the State, other professions, client groups and the public. In another essay we have tried to investigate to what extent we have a status-oriented hierarchical stratification within social work (Dellgran, Höjer, 2003d). The reasons behind this are of course that the conditions for professionalization vary between different working areas. When the category status in TAB. 10.1 is applied to child welfare social workers in Sweden, it is an attempt to assess how social workers in Sweden understand the status of different kinds of social work. We let the social workers mark each working area on a five-grade scale (from 1 = *very high status* to 5 = *very low status*). In TAB. 10.1 the share of very high or high status is reported. Highest status is attributed to child and youth psychiatric team, following most of the other indicators. In this way, the lowest degree of internal status is given to outreach work and institutional care.

Finally, another way of indicating and measuring professionalization is to study the *income* (j) of social workers in various fields, a factor certainly linked to educational level, occupational years and management responsibility. Excluding social workers with management tasks, the average income in late 2001 was SEK 20,300 per month (2,200 Euros). As seen in TAB. 10.1, the incomes of the child welfare social workers are often lower than average. In the study on all working areas in Swedish social work the two highest paid groups were those dealing with social work education and research and with therapy, family law and counselling (126 and 113 using the same index). Perhaps the fact that child and youth psychiatric team social workers do not earn more wages despite their often very high educational level is another possible explanation for their low levels of satisfaction in the previously described indicator.

10.8
Career Patterns and Trajectories for Child Welfare Social Workers

In another study about Swedish social workers extra-emphasis is put into the career patterns and how they link to the concepts of professionalization (Dellgran, Höjer, 2005b). That study also indicates the existence of traditional trajectories and specific career patterns, although these are not described in detail in this chapter. They often consist of a strive for specialisation, investment in advanced education and upward mobility towards working areas with a higher status and degree of professionalization (measured in our terms), and higher wages. In child welfare it is obvious that there is a stream from the lower professionalized areas, such as local welfare offices and outreach work, towards higher areas, as work within child and youth psychiatric team.

The same pattern can be shown in other working areas, not connected to child welfare. In this way elderly, more experienced and higher educated social workers choose to work with research and education, with individual and family therapy and with counselling. In the US, as well as in many European countries, there has been a debate about whether or not this strive for higher professionalization, psychotherapy and private practice is an indication of social work losing its original values (Specht, Courtney, 1994; Lowe, Reid, 1999).

10.9
Outlook to Studies about Professionalization in Child Welfare in Other Countries

In a study about the impact of professional social work education in child welfare in the US, it was shown that social workers with a master's degree in social work performed better than those with only a bachelor's degree. The same study stated that, in the US, historically the social work profession has occupied a leadership role in the field of child welfare. However during the 1980s child welfare lost status amongst the fields of social work practices. This was connected to the fact that many of the people involved in child welfare had a limited social work education, although the tasks of child welfare had become more complex. Since then many schools of social work have engaged in collaboration with public child welfare agencies in order to improve the child welfare standings. These programmes are funded by the national State in order to improve professional performance. However they are very seldom evaluated (Scannapieco, Bolen, Connell, 2000).

A somewhat different picture is presented in a recent survey about the situation for social workers in Social Services Departments in England and Wales. Social workers are leaving their posts for alternative career opportunities. There is a staffing shortage, in some parts of London the vacancy rate is as high as 50%. Social workers are recruited from South Africa, Australia and New Zealand in order to fill posts. The reasons given for leaving social work include its low status, low pay, loss of professional autonomy and poor promotional prospects. The author believes that the new managerialism initiated in the late 1980s has had a big part in this. It has changed social work practice making it more bureaucratic and with an increased paper-work load. The teams specialising in childcare are suffering particularly badly because of this. The British government has initiated a number of measures to try to reverse this trend. Among other things, the government has invested in an advertising campaign that aims to educate the public about the role of social workers and to improve the image of social workers (Harlow, 2004).

10.10
Conclusions

The aim of this chapter is to analyse the differences regarding professionalization, status and career patterns within child welfare in Swedish social work. It is obvious that the different working areas in social work within child welfare show an unbalanced professionalization which follows certain patterns. It has been shown that this development is not limited to the child welfare part of social work, but is noticeable throughout the whole profession. This situation poses some strategic questions about the future consequences for social work.

A possible future scenario is that of an increase of stratification, perhaps to the extent that we may talk about a first and a second class of social workers. There are probably different views upon whether or not this is a menace to the profession. As of today it is hard to say whether or not different actors with an interest in social work oppose or advocate such a development. On the one hand, many actors have over many years tried to unify the profession, wanting the education to be a generalist one in order to maintain social work as a homogenous professional occupation. On the other hand, the union has lately begun to propose the introduction of different levels of competence in order to give more difficult jobs to the most qualified social workers, with a correspondence between wages and competence (and as incentives for individual social workers to invest in advanced education). The authorisation system could also be used as a step in this direction. It is however important to stress that we find no evidence that the more professionalized fields are more difficult, in terms of what kind of tasks follow assignments, than the ones held to be less professionalized. Secondly, it seems that the differences do not only reflect the qualifications needed for specific assignments. They also reflect the fact that more status is attached to work within psychiatric fields and within specialised open care in consultancy settings than to work closer to the client's own life, for example in outreach work, or in school social work, or in work with child protection issues in the welfare offices. If this trend continues it may be counterproductive to the profession since it may challenge its legitimacy in the eyes of the Swedish public.

Another question is to what extent the Swedish situation is comparable to other European countries. It has not been easy to find comparable information about the standings of the profession in other European countries. Therefore, it is our hope that the use of professionalization indicators, like the ones we have presented in this chapter, will make such comparisons easier.

Bibliography

ABBOTT A. D. (1988), *The System of Professions: An Essay on the Division of Expert Labor*, University of Chicago Press, Chicago.
BARKER R. L. (1999), *The Social Work Dictionary*, NASW Press, Washington, IV ed.
BECHER T. (1999), *Professional Practices: Commitment and Capability in a Changing Environment*, Transaction Publishers, New Brunswick (NJ).
CAMILLERI P. J. (1996), *(Re)Constructing Social Work: Exploring Social Work through Text and Talk*, Avebury, Aldershot.
CAMPANINI A., FROST E. (eds.) (2004), *European Social Work: Commonalities and Differences*, Carocci, Rome.
COLTON M., WILLIAMS M. (1997), *The Nature of Foster Care: International Trends*, in "Adoption and Fostering", XXI, 1, pp. 44-9.
DELLGRAN P., HÖJER S. (2003a), *En delad och ambivalent profession. Socionomers attityder till privatisering av socialt arbete*, in "Socionomens forskningssupplement", 15, pp. 17-36.

IDD. (2003b), *Forskning i praktiken. Om den seniora forskningens innehåll och socionomers forskningsorientering*, in Högskoleverket, *Socialt arbete. En nationell genomlysning av ämnet*, Högskoleverket, Stockholm, pp. 197-249.
IDD. (2003c), *Topics and Epistemological Positions in Swedish Social Work Research*, in "Social Work Education", XXII, 6, pp. 565-75.
IDD. (2003d), *Unbalanced Professionalization: On Status and Stratification in Swedish Social Work*, in "Social Work in Europe", X, 2 pp. 37-48.
IDD. (2005a), *Privatisation as Professionalization? Attitudes, Motives and Achievements among Swedish Social Workers*, in "European Journal of Social Work", in press.
IDD. (2005b), *Rörelser i tiden. Professionalisering och privatisering i socialt arbete*, in "Socialvetenskaplig tidskrift", in press.
IDD. (2005c), *Sources of Knowledge and Relations between Research, Education and Practice in Professional Social Work*, in S.-A. Månsson, C. Proveyer (eds.), *Social Work in Cuba and Sweden: Achievements and Prospects*, in press.
ERAUT M. (1994), *Developing Professional Knowledge and Competence*, Falmer Press, London.
FLEXNER A. (1915), *Is Social Work a Profession?*, in "School and Society", I, 26, pp. 901-11.
FREIDSON E. (1994), *Professionalism Reborn: Theory, Prophecy, and Policy*, Blackwell, Oxford.
GARRETT P. M., SINKKONEN J. (2003), *Putting Children First? A Comparison of Child Adoption Policy and Practice in Britain and Finland*, in "European Journal of Social Work", VI, 1, pp. 19-32.
GIERYN T. (1999), *Cultural Boundaries of Science: Credibility on the Line*, University of Chicago Press, Chicago.
GÖNCZ K. (2004), *Social Work in Hungary: Historical Situation and Current Issues*, in "European Journal of Social Work", VII, 3, pp. 352-5.
HARLOW E. (2004), *Why Don't Women Want to Be Social Workers Anymore? New Managerialism, Postfeminism and the Shortage of Social Workers in Social Services Departments in England and Wales*, in "European Journal of Social Work", VII, 2, pp. 167-79.
HESSLE S., VINNERLJUNG B. (1999), *Child Welfare in Sweden: An Overview*, Stockholm University, Department of Social Work, Stockholm.
HÖJER I. (2001), *Fosterfamiljens inre liv*, Akademisk avhandling, Göteborgs Universitet, Göteborg.
EAD. (2004), *What Happens in the Foster Family? A Study of Fostering Relationships in Sweden*, in "Adoption and Fostering", XXVIII, 1, pp. 38-48.
JANZE N. (1999), *A Comparative Approach to Public Childcare for Children Living away from Home in Germany and England*, in "European Journal of Social Work", II, 2, pp. 151-63.
KARVINEN S., PÖSÖ T., SATKA M. (eds.) (1999), *Reconstructing Social Work Research: Finnish Methodological Adaptations*, University of Jyväskylä, Jyväskylä.
LAOT F. (2000), *Doctoral Work in the Social Work Field in Europe*, in "Social Work in Europe", VII, 2, pp. 2-7.

LARSON M. (1977), *The Rise of Professionalism: A Sociological Analysis*, University of California Press, Berkeley.
LORENZ W. (1994), *Social Work in a Changing Europe*, Routledge, London.
LOWE G. R., REID P. N. (eds.) (1999), *The Professionalization of Poverty: Social Work and the Poor in the Twentieth Century*, Aldine de Gruyter, New York.
LYONS K. (2002), *Researching Social Work: Doctoral Work in the UK*, in "Social Work Education", XXI, 3, pp. 337-46.
MACDONALD K. M. (1995), *The Sociology of the Professions*, Sage, London.
RIGNÉ E. M. (2002), *Profession, Science, and State: Psychology in Sweden, 1968-1990*, Department of Sociology, Göteborg University, Göteborg.
SCANNAPIECO M., BOLEN R., CONNELL K. (2000), *Professional Social Work Education in Child Welfare: Assessing Practice Knowledge and Skills*, in "Professional Development. The International Journal of Continuing Social Work", III, 1, pp. 44-56.
SELLICK C. (1998), *The Use of Institutional Care across Europe*, in "European Journal of Social Work", I, 3, pp. 301-10.
SPECHT H., COURTNEY M. E. (1994), *Unfaithful Angels: How Social Work Has Abandoned Its Mission*, Free Press, New York.
SPRATT T., CALLAN J. (2004), *Parents' Views on Social Work Interventions in Child Welfare Cases*, in "British Journal of Social Work", XXXIV, pp. 199-224.
VLEMINCKX K., SMEEDING T. M. (eds.) (2000), *Child Well-Being, Child Poverty and Child Policy in Modern Nations: What Do We Know?*, Policy Press, Bristol.
WALDFOGEL J. (1998), *The Future of Child Protection: How to Break the Cycle of Abuse and Neglect*, Harvard University Press, Cambridge (MA).
WEISS I., GAL J., CNAAN R., MAGLAJLIC R. (2002), *Where Does it Begin? A Comparative Perspective on the Professional Preferences of First-Year Social Work Students*, in "British Journal of Social Work", XXXII, 5, pp. 589-608.
WINGFORS S. S. (2004), *Socionomyrkets professionalisering*, Sociologiska insitutionen, Göteborg.
YELLOLY M., HENKEL M. (eds.) (1995), *Learning and Teaching in Social Work: Towards Reflective Practice*, Kingsley, London.

II

Social Pedagogy: A Paradigm in European Social Work Education from German and Polish Perspectives

by *Günter J. Friesenhahn* and *Ewa Kantowicz*

II.1
Introduction

In context of the unification of Europe and globalization as a worldwide process, we are talking about both similarities and differences in concepts and theories in social work and in education for the social professions.

Our starting point is: the international relations between social services and social workers are increasing, impacts for social work in all countries will be more international and the language which is used mostly is English. The dominance of the English language in international contexts is evident – relevant textbooks, reviews and conferences are mainly written in English. The dominance of the language leads to the fact that technical terms have to be translated. The translation process is not only a matter of semantics; often terms lose their original sense.

At the same time it is quite evident that the work of social sector professionals is closely tied to the traditions, policies and to the national law of a given country. There are some scientific discourses on social pedagogy concepts and its influence on social work practice. They are mostly connected with a linguistic/semantics differentiation and the interpretation of social pedagogy/*Sozialpädagogik*, which have a certain meaning in a given cultural and social context. A scientific approach to social pedagogy/*Sozialpädagogik* has been not established in the English speaking countries in as strong a manner as in Germany and Poland, even it does arise in Denmark, the Netherlands, Switzerland, and other western and eastern European countries, especially in relations with community education, youth work, formation and social activation at welfare, tutelary and educational systems in general. The examples of the social pedagogy paradigm can be also found in concepts of education for the social professions across Europe. Taking into account some of these assumptions, the social pedagogy paradigm becomes a worthy issue for scientific comparison, both as a scientific discipline and as a practice.

However there are methodological dilemmas resulting from cross-national research in that field.

The differentiation between profession and discipline can be regarded as a standard of up-to-date scientific based social work. On the level of practical work, professional social work aims at efficacy; social workers wish to help, they want to assist and support other people. On the level of the discipline of social work, through research and reflection, and through the development of theories, aims to create new images of the world and of societies (Thole, 2002).

Similarly, argues Sunesson (2000, p. 512), in order to get a comprehensive picture of social work and other social professions it is necessary to answer the following questions.
1. What do those who work do when they say that they "work"?
2. How is the practice organised?
3. What are the thoughts behind practice? How it is explained, what reasons are given for it?
4. What are the outcomes of the practice? What are the results, for whom?

Paradigms can be seen as attempts to structure and frame a certain sector of reality. Scientific disciplines and the associated technical terms are just able to grasp a small part of reality, and on the other hand we have to be aware that through the associated terms a certain reality is constructed with a specific view.

Fook (2004, p. 88) points out that in all intercultural and international social work we have to ask ourselves about legitimate knowledge and how it is produced:

Questions about legitimate knowledge and legitimate knowledge production are at the heart of debates about paradigmatic differences in the research field, but can also be identified within different cultural systems or national boundaries. But they also lead us to think about political questions as well. Whose knowledge and ways of producing knowledge are regarded as legitimate?

Referring to the general methods of comparison, the discourse deals with elements of the structuring and functioning of concepts and understandings of social pedagogy/*Sozialpädagogik* for the social services and the education of the social professions. Drawing examples from research in Germany and in Poland, we consider how social pedagogy can be applied. This is a response to the idea of harmonising the concepts of professional training as well as improving the quality of social services in Europe. This is all due to European Union aims and declarations on co-operation.

11.2
Approaches, Concepts and Theories: Germany

11.2.1. Social Work

In order to understand the social pedagogy paradigm it seems to be necessary to look briefly at social work. Undoubtedly, in Germany there are differences between social work and social pedagogy with regard to their theoretical and practical references in history, and to their links with different institutions. The differences refer not only to origins and to respective roots, but are also represented into the recent past through different ways of training and training subjects and also partly within the different institutional competencies.

Social work has its roots in poor relief, in social movements, in the emergence of voluntary welfare work. It can be understood as a reaction to the social need which resulted from industrialisation in densely populated areas. Accordingly, social work is the answer to social predicaments, and it concentrates on that part of the population who has fallen out of the formal and informal social security systems. It is a matter of support, counselling, and assistance with self-help, and it aims at the promotion and stabilisation of humane living conditions; briefly, social work can be seen as intervention against psycho-social predicaments, or as organised assistance (Thiersch, 1996; Salustowicz, 1999; Hamburger, 2003).

From this perspective, the study of social problems is the object base of social work. With a view (or glance) at the connection between practice, theory and training Engelke (1992, p. 11) states:

Social work as science reflects and researches with scientific methods, social problems and their solutions. Social work as practice works with methods on the solution of social problems. Social work as training trains for the practice of social work. Again, differently phrased: social work as science is reflexive and social work as practice provides answer to social problems. Social work as training teaches the reflexive and active answers to social problems.

Also, other authors emphasise that social work theory deals with human action and social conditions under the following perspective: it focuses on the procedures and circumstances which lead to neediness, and it is concerned with the resources which individuals, families and groups use, or which they are missing, in order to lead a self-determined and independent life (Wendt, 1994). For Staub-Bernasconi (1994) theoretical statements in the context of social work refer to people who have problems in a certain formation of society, that is to say they have problems which could not solve by themselves.

The way in which social work theories and approaches have developed during the last hundred years (Lorenz, 1994, p. 81; Adams, Erath, Shardlow, 2001) shows "how dependent they are on external Zeitgeist and theory trends" (Staub-Bernasconi, 1999, p. 74). One can see, for example, a shift of influence from the sociological to the economical and psychological, from social policy scholars to social philosophers, then to sociological and psychological disciplines which are now being more and more replaced by representatives of business administration and management approaches.

One the other hand one can also detect a continuous line of thinking which is oriented towards the core concepts of the profession. According to Staub-Bernasconi (1999, p. 75) this thinking

transcends the national and language context. It can be described along concepts of needs, threats, learning, class and classism, gender and sexism, and racism, age and ageism [...] repressive versus participative organisation of social care, leisure and correction. They point in different ways to the European and international promotion of human and social rights (and duties) as an universal culture.

She comes to the conclusion that conceptual diversity of social work theories can be seen either as a terrible mish-mash of conceptions which can't be taken seriously or as an expression of pluralism and the liberty of academic teaching.

11.2.2. Social Pedagogy

The term "social pedagogy" was used in Germany for the first time around 1850 by Karl Mager and Friedrich Diesterweg and it drew attention to the new social problems that were emerging in the context of the industrialisation, and were summed up as the "social question". A new form of pedagogy, i.e. a social pedagogy, was supposed to help solve these problems (pauperism, neglect, the decay of family structures) through educational contributions/interventions. The cultural and social changes taking place at that time were understood as a loss of community as traditional norms and values disintegrated. The educational mainstream at the time was rather a-historical, was oriented towards the individual, and referred to the individual child. In contrast to this, Diesterweg recommended that education should interrelate with the lives of the children and adolescents and should participate in the improvements of living conditions. He also recommended that pedagogues – at that time primarily teachers – should become aware of the limits of pedagogy/education and the necessity for a political reaction to social emergencies (Konrad, 1998, p. 37).

Social pedagogy started its development during a historical period in which pedagogical reflections referred firstly to education and the schooling of children, but at the same time it became clear that outside the traditional educational institutions – family and school – society had to cope with new educational challenges (Müller, 1996; Hamburger, 2003). The new aspect to this perspective was: the reaction to social problems (like neglect, a state of destitution) was seen as a pedagogical task and not as matter for the police or other institutions involved in social control issues.

So social pedagogy was, since its early beginnings, always directed at the shaping/creation of the social dimension within society. On the other hand, since the beginning one inherent idea was to adapt working class people to the norms and values of the bourgeoisie. In that sense, social pedagogy was also an instrument to disguise the social contrast which had been produced by the capitalistic class-based society. At the end it should be an instrument to ensure the loyalty of the working class (Marburger, 1979, p. 24). Hamburger (2003, pp. 22-3) states that the term "social pedagogy" refers to a certain modus of action/intervention, which includes, apart from assistance and help, education, formation ("Bildung"), support, counselling and empowerment.

Paul Natorp (1899), one of the most famous turn of the century scholars, defines social pedagogy as an educational endeavour to ensure that the individual and society should be seen in relation to each other, and that they should refer to each other. Pedagogy takes place in the community, the individual only exists in the community; the community consists of individuals. The formation ("Bildung") of individuals is a condition of a real community. "The social conditions of formation [Bildung] and the conditions of formation [Bildung] of the social life, that is the topic of the theory" (Natorp, cit. in Marburger, 1979, p. 43). The education aimed at morality and sociality and these should enable the individual to improve the community. Social pedagogy in this sense was not seen as a part of pedagogy, but according to Natorp all pedagogy is social pedagogy. Konrad (1998, p. 45) indicates that this type of social pedagogy was an "approach without concrete practice" and Marburger (1979, p. 24) characterises this approach as an attempt to re-establish through social pedagogy the unity of the German nation. A similar background can be found in Poland, where up to now Natorp's ideas have played an important role in scientific discourses (Seibel, 2001; Lepalczyk, Marynowicz-Hetka, 2002).

In a textbook, thirty years later, Gertrud Bäumer outlined a definition of social pedagogy which represented a new view. The term "social pedagogy" does not indicate a principle (the rationale of pedagogy) which underpins the pedagogy as a whole, but a specific sector: everything which is education but does not takes place in school, nor within families. Social pedagogy stands for the embodiment of the statutory socio-educational provision and welfare work for children and youth, as long it is outside of school and family. Social pedagogy in this view stands for a specific working field, youth work and youth welfare services, in its double perspective: a proactive youth work seen as education in order to prevent abnormal behaviour and a reactive youth welfare in the form of intervention in cases where deviant behaviour has to be corrected (Marburger, 1979).

Following this perspective, in the 1960s Klaus Mollenhauer defined social pedagogy as the "theory of youth work and youth welfare services" and linked the responsibility of social pedagogy strongly to a specific age group. This linkage corresponds to a specific connotation. Social pedagogy has to deal with education, with formation, with learning, with support in developing and social integration processes. Social pedagogy in this sense is a scientific explanation and analysis of the living conditions of children and youth. According to Mollenhauer, social pedagogy indicates a specific sector in society, a set of interventions in order to assist individuals in the process of societal integration. This "assistance towards integration [Eingliederungshilfen]" emerges from and refers to social conflicts and critical situations (Mollenhauer, 1976, p. 13). For Mollenhauer, critical situations are those in which children and young people cannot cope with the expectations and opportunities offered by society, as a result, conflicts and problems emerge. Also, crucial to this perspective is the view of the German pedagogue Herman Nohl who pointed out in the 1930s that young people do not create problems but they do have problems.

The living conditions, the *Lebenswelt* of young people, and not just the adult's perspective on young people, then became a crucial starting point for conceptualising social pedagogy. One reason, amongst others, was that Mollenhauer and other authors were working in the context of the protest movements of the 1960s, and the discussion of the critical theory of the Frankfurt School had proclaimed a new approach. They named it "proactive social pedagogy" (Giesecke, 1973) in opposition to the so-called defensive social pedagogy which was in their view relying on traditional bourgeois norms and values. The proactive and critical paradigm sees the traditional social pedagogy as a part of the political ideology, as a symptom of society's contradictions and of the unsolved problems within society. The proactive social pedagogy required the maintenance of the rules of law, and the social rights of all citizens; the critical approach includes the critique of the existing social conditions and the demand for more democratisation, and above all the demand for emancipation. These are the aims and the object base of this critical approach. Following the philosopher and sociologist Max Horkheimer's critique in this sense, this approach has the task of confronting society with its own better possibilities/potential (Friesenhahn, 1985). And as a theory social pedagogy also has to be critical in relation to practice. A theory, when referring to social practice and social action as its main issue, must first analyse the case and not prescribe what the case ought to be.

11.3
Poland: Social Pedagogy as a Scientific Paradigm

Helena Radlińska was one of the first and the greatest of Polish social pedagogues, developing concepts, methodology and research related to social pedagogy as a socio-humanistic science in a worldwide perspective. Ewa Marynowicz-Hetka (2000, p. 80) writes:

The first form of the institutionalisation of education and the professionalisation of social welfare work/social work in Poland should be linked with social pedagogy and the education programme for social workers at higher education level organised by H. Radlińska in 1925 [...]. The next initiative concerning education for social work was also taken by H. Radlińska who organised the Chair of Social Pedagogy at the University of Łódz in 1945.

She defined social pedagogy as a practical science related to biological, social and cultural sciences with ethics, which is interested in human beings' attitudes to their environment and the influence of material surroundings and culture on people's lives. Helena Radlińska, defining the subject of social pedagogy, showed its interests in relation to human beings and social surroundings. She emphasised the influence of material and other aspects of the quality of life and the unique role of social pedagogy in creating life patterns and stimulating social activity (Radlińska, 1961, p. 361). Through her researches Radlińska wanted to evaluate the role of social and educational activity in improving the lives of individuals and groups in local communities.

In this context, social pedagogy has offered social work a few theoretical premises, and has also contributed some examples and directives outlining the possibilities for social action, socio-educational support and socio-cultural participation as a key in creating the life quality of a society. Finally – through qualitative research – social pedagogy has allowed more individual approaches and a more relative understanding of life quality, referring it to concrete, evaluating situations (Ciczkowski, 1996, p. 83). Important, practical repercussions issue from the theoretical assumptions of social pedagogy. At the level of pedagogical activity the tasks are concentrated on developing and fulfilling the needs and rights of individuals and groups – mainly through educational support, protection and activation of the potential possibilities and strengths which are inherent in the nearest surroundings of human beings (Kawula, 1996, p. 15).

In terms of social pedagogy, the basic criteria for the analysis and evaluation of social surroundings are: the opportunities for children, youth and adults to develop; the quality of co-operation; social links. Pedagogical diagnosis of the social environment becomes the first step in undertaking socio-educational work and in planning and projecting social work in accordance with improving the life quality of that environment. Exemplification of the theoretical approaches in Polish social pedagogy shows some normative and cognitive proposals for social work, which can be defined as (Przecławska, Theiss, 1995, pp. 19-23):
– ideas of *individuality*: the life quality depends on individuals and groups and their potential strengths, their "human power", because human beings are at least partly responsible and conscious of their abilities and their limitations;
– ideas of *equality*: individuals and groups have got equal possibilities for participating in social life through their inherent activity, and through equal chances/rights to education and socio-cultural services;
– ideas of *social education* in the context of education which can be an autonomic level of creativity and activity for individuals as well as an important factor of the creation of quality in socio-cultural life;
– ideas of *subsidiarity* (auxiliarity) which underline social responsibility and awareness in supporting all individuals, groups and communities "in need".

New approaches to Polish social pedagogy are represented by among others Stanisław Kawula (1999, p. 243) who emphasises that the pedagogical paradigm is important for community education and sociocultural participation. In the area of new dimensions of social work, pedagogical aims are related to developing and fulfilling the needs of individuals and groups.

Additionally, social pedagogy through qualitative research at its base allows for a more adequate understanding, evaluation and planning of socio-educational activities. Social pedagogy leads rather to a balance of individual and social needs. The welfare client is understood as a forming subject and the society as a democratic structure. The essence of pedagogical activity in social work lies in setting the "social strength" in motion;

in improving a social environment by the activity of dynamic individuals and groups through motivation, animation and guidance in educational and protective activity (prophylactic, compensation, and rehabilitation).

The unconventionality of the pedagogical approach to social work is expressed by at least a few features. Firstly, *totality* – a holistic interest in the full individual human being, taking into account the influence of living conditions and the sphere of culture in different phases of life (individual and social influences, providing a complex stimulation for human development and help in difficult situations). Secondly, *dynamics* – a creative, active and exploratory attitude to reality (progress and means of educational activity related to individual development and the value of the social environment in its quality). Thirdly, *compensation* – a strengthening awareness of the individual and social development (strengthening potential possibilities, stimulating changes). Fourthly, *valuation* – social pedagogy formulates universal values for individual and social progress, giving axiological bases for social work and defining categories such as: the individual, human rights, human needs, tolerance, responsibility etc. In social pedagogic theory, valuation holds the primary importance in terms of individual and social activity. Looking for valuable relations qualifies a specific pedagogical approach to welfare.

The last fifteen years have been characterised by socio-economic transition in Poland. During this time, the research relating to social pedagogy and social work has been intensified, particularly research dealing with different aspects of social problems (poverty, unemployment and their influence on development, social activity and the educational possibilities for children and adults). Contemporary social pedagogy in Poland concentrates on the social environment, especially on the conditions of individuals and groups living in different environmental conditions or in different institutional contexts. It analyses the factors which allow people to meet their needs and develop creatively in all phases of their lives and in all forms of their daily activity (Kawula, 1996, p. 29).

II.4
Current Developments

II.4.1. Germany: *Sozialarbeit*

According to Hamburger (2003, p. 106) a theory of social pedagogy refers to:
- a *reality*;
- a *practice*;
- a *discourse*.

A changing reality, a changing practice accordingly provoke a change in the social pedagogy discourse.

In former times *Sozialarbeit* (social work) and *Sozialpädagogik* (social pedagogy) were sometimes seen as parallel streams. As Lorenz (1994, p. 96) points out,

> The original differences – that social work training prepared students more specifically for positions in public social services which in Germany include welfare benefit functions, while social pedagogy was geared towards creative and therapeutic services – became less pronounced, and many courses now lead to a combined award. In Germany social work and social pedagogy are now more and more regarded as one functional section within society.

Without a detailed knowledge of the German discourses this categorisation is hard to understand. Also within the academic discourse it is nearly impossible to distinguish clearly between the terms social work, social pedagogy and *Sozialarbeit*. For about ten years we have been having a very intensive debate in Germany on the question of whether there is a school of "social work/social work sciences" and how this is different from social pedagogy (which belongs to the education sciences). As far we see it is a very German issue which is not presented here (Engelke, 1992, 1998; Wendt, 1994; Merten, 1998).

"Social work" is used as a general term, which in German is *Sozialarbeit*, and covers both social work (*Sozialarbeit*) and social pedagogy (*Sozialpädagogik*). The general use of "social work" in the broader sense for both professions indicates the approximation of both professions which has been visible in nearly all fields of practice. Training is provided by universities and universities of applied sciences (*Fachhochschulen*). Universities offer a four-year fully academic diploma, *Erziehungswissenschaft* (educational sciences), with an option in *Sozialpädagogik*.

To summarise, the term *Sozialarbeit* includes both strains, social work and social pedagogy, but nevertheless some scholars use still the term "social pedagogy". The developments mentioned above are important in order to understand the training and the practice of social pedagogy (social work). According to Lorenz (1992, p. 87),

> The most powerful and influential alternative to the case work paradigm is that of pedagogy and the derivation of social pedagogy. About half the German social workers hold a qualification in social pedagogy and there are more professionals working in occupations in France and Italy with a qualification in 'animation' or as 'educators' than there are qualified social workers.

In current theory discourse, social pedagogy/*Sozialarbeit* is not limited to work with young people. The function of social pedagogy within a society has been described as "assistance for coping with life" and "social integration". Yet, coping with life and its problems and challenges is not a task exclusively for children and young people, but for all age groups. With this connotation social pedagogy enlarges the functions/claims for which it is responsible and competent. In a classic perspective, social pedagogy claims its task in the tension (social integration) between individuals and society. Similarly, social pedagogy (social work, *Sozialarbeit*) is seen as a social service which can be claimed by all people in a given society. It is no longer crisis intervention but is presented as a normal actor for socialisation, support, and learning processes. The background for this enlargement is found in the changes in modern society.

Economic differences, inequality, and exclusion cannot be explained only by the way in which individuals belong to a specific class in society. For example, to analyse and explain inequality, categories like ethnicity, gender, cultural orientation etc. have to be taken into account. The new challenge is that the old and the new inequalities partly cross the traditional view concerning social classes and stratification with the result that social pedagogy (social work) cannot longer concentrate on social problems. Thole (2002, p. 47) writes in this context about a "generalisation of problematic cases". Not in reality but in principle, everybody can become a "case" or a user for and of social work.

To sum up, the current discourse on social pedagogy shows an enormous enlargement of perspectives and tasks. It involves specific help and assistance in particular life situations and proactive, preventive support in normal daily life. On the level of theory, social pedagogy is regarded as an academic discipline; it is also the profession for the social help system, and is responsible and competent for both learning and "Bildung". With this perspective we can meet the *Leitmotiv* of the social pedagogy approach. Obviously it has always to do with the "idealised" accordance/agreement between the individual's needs and interests and the interests of society, although this idea stands in opposition to empirical observations. After all, social pedagogy aims at the reconciliation between individuals and society. The classical scholars, from Diesterweg and Natorp to Nohl, Bäumer, and Mollenhauer, up to current authors like Thiersch, Hamburger and Böhnisch, have given different responses to this challenge. But they agree on the idea that through social pedagogy, through socio-pedagogical interventions and methods it should be possible to establish a relationship between the individual and society which is not dominated by conflicts.

11.4.2. Poland: Social Pedagogy as a Paradigm for Social Services and Social Professions

Nowadays, reflecting on the tradition in education for the social professions in Europe, we can observe some common trends related to academic and transdisciplinary dimensions in the training for social pedagogues and social workers. The social pedagogy concept in the educational process is influenced by other social and humanistic sciences. The original Polish social work and social-professional education was created by Radlińska through her research on social pedagogy as a practical sociohumanistic science, in which social work was a branch of social pedagogy. In accordance with Radlińska's ideas social work as a practical field of social pedagogy included a rich range of the helping, compensating, cultural and pedagogical activities for children, youth and adults. It was defined as systematic, intentional and skilful work that demanded extensive preparation for life activity (Marynowicz-Hetka, 1996, p. 134). At that time social work was directed to a multidisciplinary recognition of the phenomena related to social services and community education.

The concept then adopted of educating social educators and social workers has also been related to the thinking of Paul Natorp and has been similar to analogous worldwide and European solutions, so it still maintains its attraction (Marynowicz-Hetka, Piekarski, Wagner, 1999, p. 24). The continuator of Radlińska's ideas – Aleksander Kamiński – said that the improvement of social conditions could be achieved by the strength of individuals and society (Kamiński, 1978).

In that case the social worker or social educator role should be directed to supporting, stimulating and instructing social activity through educational and cultural work. When transformation started in Poland in 1989, social professions did not have to build the education system from scratch. At the same time the two concepts within social-professional education have developed two parallel educational approaches: namely the old Polish social pedagogy tradition and a "new" Anglo-Saxon social work.

Nowadays, reflecting on the European tradition in education for the social professions, it is implied as an optimistic assumption that an educated man of the 21st century should have the opportunity to become a person with different qualities. From a social pedagogy perspective, multidisciplinary and holistic academic education for the social professions have been referred to a complexity of roles and tasks within the social professions, and to many fields of social activities related to social work, e.g. childcare, protection, community education, socio-cultural animation and socio-educational work.

The process of education for the social professions aims to "encompass the types of activities which further the 'ability of individuals to function effectively' according to their needs and predispositions" (Kantowicz, 1996, p. 353). The educational profile of professional education must then reach beyond the confines of activities to intervene, save and provide therapy. Despite the variety of practice fields in social work, social work education based on social pedagogy refers to a set of ordered activities related to theoretical reflection in the areas of sociology, psychology, social pedagogy, and social policy.

The sociological background was very important in the genesis of social pedagogy and it supported this science with the fundamental methodology and issues dealing with social education (Auguste Comte, Émile Durkheim, Paul Bergemann, Józef Chałasiński, Florian Znaniecki and others). Sociology provides social pedagogues/social workers with a general framework for analyses of social phenomena: structures, norms, institutions etc. These schemes depend on the applied sociological theory. Consciousness of that fact leads to a relative understanding of our knowledge in the field of social welfare. Different sociological theories provide proposals for diagnoses of social processes and allow for a better understanding of the specific situation of human beings (social determinisms, values, attitudes). An analysis of situations in the context of individual conditions and dependences creates a possibility for the proper direction of undertaken actions. Sociological theories also allow the placing of social work in the social dimension, to justify the role played by a social worker and to estimate this role in aspects of further changes.

Social pedagogy as a humanistic science is connected with questions about psychological roots and principles of social relations and consequences (results) of socio-educational changes created by/through socio-educational work. The psychological approach includes the needs of individuals and groups for strengthening their autonomy. There is a certain scientific conviction that social work which is addressed to clients, but which is not accepted by clients, can fail. Psychological theories determine the concepts of educational activity and applied treatment in social work. The functioning of social pedagogues/social workers refers also to improvements in interpersonal interactions and to a modification of attitudes and social relations between people in their environment. A consciousness of the psychological dimension in social work education allows for a better understanding of human beings (their specific needs) and for understanding the social pedagogue/social worker as a person who acts in relations with other people.

According to Sunker (1996), Abramovitz in trying to answer the question "Whether all the students studying social work should be educated to social changes" thinks that "Social pedagogues/social workers' education should be steered towards individual, institutional and structural changes" at least for three reasons: to assure such standards of living which allow normal (correct) individual development; to prevent social work from becoming servitude for the conservative *statu quo*; to prepare social pedagogues/workers for being ready to take initiatives in the social background, for being able to initiate and create social changes and solve social problems (Sunker, 1996, p. 57). However, by applying scientific methods in the social welfare/educational activity area, students have to learn multistratified patterns of interpretation, which lead to better technological and methodological applications. In that case the professional social work and community work education oscillate around attitudes of knowledge creation as well as its adequate application (Dewe, 1996, p. 95). It means that open learning or education should lead to students (social workers, community educators) understanding the possibility of the application of social science knowledge, and anticipating its use in the context of solving social problems.

II.5
Conclusions

In accordance with contemporary perspectives in social work services and education for the social professions in Europe, which partly arise from the social pedagogy paradigm, we can found the ontological, epistemological and axiological sources of social functioning and acting, and thus provide competence in scholarly discovery dependent on complex situational expectations and subjective contextual meaning due to culture, language, time-space continuum, as well as in the objective determinants of existing and created knowledge of the social sciences.

Some years ago, the sociologist Norbert Elias stated the minimal consensus of what is now known as scientific work: to discover how experienced occurrences cling to each other. That means that the tasks of the social sciences are the empirical exploration of the social reality in which we are living, and the participation in the mastering of enormous social problems. This minimal consensus can be reached from both the social work and the social pedagogy path. A Polish colleague, Marynowicz-Hetka (2000, p. 73), describes the shared tasks of the social professions: "A common element is the goal of activity which is undertaking and organising activities, minimising concerns and hardships in the individual and their social dimensions, and anticipating the appearance of threats". And Thole (2002, p. 22) argues that social work has to do/to deal with the basic social assistance and help organised by the public/State, the task is help, support and "Bildung" provided by qualified professionals. Ways of acting in social pedagogy, the aims of the discussion and the arrangements with the living conditions of the target groups on different levels.

The pedagogical approach to social work connected with the social pedagogy paradigm promotes leading principles like "formation" and "individual" (the subjects of educational and social activity). These principles have a primary sense for social work, which gains self-awareness in the sphere of pedagogical thinking and in the humanistic as well as the hermeneutic tradition. Because the client's socio-educational problems are often considered in aspects of socialisation, social pedagogy enables us to a narrow understanding of socio-educational activity as an intervention in "abnormal" process of socialisation, and supporting clients in situations of pathology, depravation, poverty, social marginalisation or exclusion.

A short essay in the very first volume of "Social Work in Europe" (1994) illustrated this from another point of view. The essay was titled *Pedagogy! – Er... What Do You Mean by That Exactly?*. The author looking at the English connotation of pedagogy argues: "This concept is somewhat different from the English understanding of the term 'pedagogy' which tends to have connotations of dogmatism and pedantry". He then refers to a German book and quotes: pedagogy is "The entire process of guided growth and discovery which prepares young people for playing a meaningful part in society". He finishes with the consideration: "If then, continental Europe sees pedagogy as an activity concerned with nurturing, empowering and guidance, then all of a sudden it makes more sense to us that people doing social work should call themselves 'pedagogues'"(Anonymous, 1994, p. 10).

Bibliography

ADAMS A., ERATH P., SHARDLOW ST. (eds.) (2001), *Key Themes of European Social Work*, Rusell House Publishing, Dorset.

ANONYMOUS (1994), *Pedagogy! – Er... What Do You Mean by That Exactly?*, in "Social Work in Europe", 1, p. 10.

BERGEMANN P. (1900), *Soziale Pädagogik auf erfahrungswissenschaftlicher Grundlage mit Hilfe der induktiven Methode als universalistische oder Kultur-Pädagogik*, Hofmann, Gera.

CHAŁASIŃSKI J. (1948), *Społeczeństwo i wychowanie. Socjologiczne zagadnienia szkolnictwa i wychowania w społeczeństwie współczesnym*, Nasza Księgarnia, Warszawa.

CICZKOWSKI W. (1996), *Dziedzictwo pedagogiczne Aleksandra Kamińskiego*, Wydawnictwo Adam Marszałek, Toruń.

COMTE A. (1830-42), *Cours de philosophie positive*, 6 vols., Bachelier, Paris.

11. SOCIAL PEDAGOGY

DEWE B. (1996), *Wiedza i umiejętności w pracy socjalnej*, in E. Marynowicz-Hetka, J. Piekarski, D. Urbaniak-Zając (eds.), *Pedagogika społeczna i praca socjalna. Przegląd stanowisk i komentarze*, Interart, Warszawa.

DURKHEIM É. (1924), *Sociologie et philosophie*, Alcan, Paris.

ENGELKE E. (1992), *Soziale Arbeit als Wissenschaft. Eine Orientierung*, Lambertus, Freiburg.

ID. (1998), *Theorien der Sozialen Arbeit. Eine Einführung*, Lambertus, Freiburg.

FOOK J. (2004), *Some Considerations on the Potential Contribution of Intercultural Social Work*, in "Social Work and Society", II, 1, pp. 86-9.

FRIESENHAHN G. J. (1985), *Kritische Theorie und Pädagogik*, Express Edition, Berlin.

HAMBURGER F. (2003), *Einführung in die Soziapädagogik*, Kohlhammer, Stuttgart.

KAMIŃSKI A. (1978), *Studia i szkice pedagogiczne*, PWN, Warszawa.

KANTOWICZ E. (1996), *Selected Concepts and Standards in Education for the Social Professions in Europe*, in E. Marynowicz-Hetka, J. Piekarski, A. Wagner (eds.), *European Dimensions in Training and Practice of the Social Professions*, Slask, Katowice, p. 353.

EAD. (2001), *Elementy teorii i praktyki pracy socjalnej*, UWM, Olsztyn.

KAWULA S. (1996), *Studia z pedagogiki społecznej*, WSP, Olsztyn.

ID. (1999), *Inspiracje Aleksandra Kamińskiego wokół diagnozy środowiska spońecznego*, in I. Lepalczyk, W. Ciczkowski (eds.), *Bogactwo życia i twórczości Aleksandra Kamińskiego*, Wydawnictwo Adam Marszałek, Toruń.

KONRAD F.-M. (1998), *Sozialpädagogik. Begriffsgeschichtliche Annäherungen – von Adolf Diesterweg bis Gertrud Bäumer*, in R. Merten (hrsg.), *Sozialarbeit, Sozialpädagogik – Soziale Arbeit. Begriffsbestimmungen in einem unübersichtlichen Feld*, Lambertus, Freiburg, pp. 31-62.

KRONEN H. (1980), *Sozialpädagogik. Geschichte und Bedeutung des Begriffs*, Haag und Herrchen, Frankfurt a.M.

LEPALCZYK I., MARYNOWICZ-HETKA E. (2002), *Helena Radlisnka – Ein Proträt ihrer Person und ihrer Arbeit als Wissenschaftlerin, Lehrerin und "soziale Aktivism"*, in S. Hering, B. Waaldijk (hrsg.), *Die Geschichte der Sozialen Arbeit in Europa (1900-1960)*, Leske + Budrich, Opladen, pp. 65-72.

LORENZ W. (1994), *Social Work in a Changing Europe*, Routledge, London.

MARBURGER H. (1979), *Entwicklung und Konzepte der Sozialpädagogik*, Juventa, München.

MARYNOWICZ-HETKA E. (1996), *Koncepcje pracy społecznej w polskiej tradycji pedagogiki społecznej*, in E. Marynowicz-Hetka, J. Piekarski, D. Urbaniak-Zając (eds.), *Pedagogika społeczna i praca socjalna. Przegląd stanowisk i komentarze*, Interart, Warszawa.

EAD. (2000), *Socio-Pedagogical Dimension of Education for Social Professions in Poland – Anattempt at Analysis of Theoretical Approaches and Education Initiatives*, in W. Warzywoda-Kruszynska, J. Krzyszkowski (eds.), *Education of Social Workers on the Eve of the European Union's Enlargement*, Institytut Soccjologii UL, Lodz, pp. 67-86.

MARYNOWICZ-HETKA E., PIEKARSKI J., WAGNER A. (1999), *Issues in Social Work: An Invitation to a Discussion*, in Idd. (eds.), *European Dimensions in Training and Practice of the Social Professions*, Slask, Katowice.

MERTEN R. (1998), *Sozialarbeit – Sozialpädagogik – Soziale Arbeit. Begriffsbestimmungen in einem unübersichtlichen Feld*, Lambertus, Freiburg.
MOLLENHAUER K. (1976), *Einführung in die Sozialpädagogik*, Beltz, Weinheim, VI ed.
MÜLLER C. W. (1996), *Sozialarbeit/Sozialpädagogik*, in D. Kreft, I. Mielenz (hrsg.), *Wörterbuch Soziale Arbeit*, Beltz, Weinheim, pp. 503-6.
NATORP P. (1899), *Sozialpädagogik. Theorie der Willenserziehung auf der Grundlage der Gemeinschaft*, Frommann, Stuttgart.
PRZECŁAWSKA A., THEISS W. (1995), *Pedagogika społeczna – nowe zadania i szanse*, in "Forum Oświatowe", 1-2.
SALUSTOWICZ P. (1999), *Über die Akademisierung in der sozialen Arbeit in Deutschland – eine kritische Bestandsaufnahme*, in Marynowicz-Hetka, Wagner, Piekarski (1999), pp. 287-312.
SEIBEL F. W. (2001), *Soziale Arbeit in Mittel- und Osteuropa*, in J. H. Kersting, M. Rige (hrsg.), *Internationale Sozialarbeit*, Fachhochschulverlag, Mönchengladbach, pp. 145-67.
STAUB-BERNASCONI S. (1994), *Soziale Arbeit als Gegenstand von Theorie und Wissenschaft*, in W. R. Wendt (hrsg.), *Sozial und wissenschaftliche arbeiten. Status und Position einer Sozialarbeitswissenschaft*, Lambertus, Freiburg, pp. 75-104.
ID. (1999), *The History of the Object Base of Social Work Theory. Comparisons between Germany, Anglosaxon and International Theoretical Approaches*, in Marynowicz-Hetka, Wagner, Piekarski (1999), pp. 57-72.
SUNESSON S. (2000), *Dilemmas in Practice and Professionalisation. A Few Pages to Welcome a Young Colleague*, in S. Müller et al. (hrsg.), *Soziale Arbeit. Gesellschaftliche Bedingungen und professionelle Perspektiven*, Luchterhand, Neuwied, pp. 511-27.
SUNKER H. (1996), *Teoretyczne stanowiska, społeczno-polotyczny kontekst I profesjonalne perspektywy pracy socjalnej – dyskusja o pracy socjalnej*, in E. Marynowicz-Hetka, J. Piekarski, D. Urbaniak-Zając (eds.), *Pedagogika społeczna i praca socjalna. Przegląd stanowisk i komentarze*, Interart, Warszawa.
THIERSCH H. (1996), *Sozialarbeitswissenschaft: Neue Herausforderungen oder Altbekanntes?*, in R. Merten, P. Sommerfeld, T. Koditek (hrsg.), *Sozialarbeitswissenschaft – Kontroversen und Perspektiven*, Luchterhand, Neuwied, pp. 1-19.
THOLE W. (2002), *Soziale Arbeit als Profession und Disziplin*, in W. Thole (hrsg.), *Grundiss Soziale Arbeit. Ein einführenden Handbuch*, Leske + Budrich, Opladen, pp. 13-60.
WENDT W. R. (1994), *Wo stehen wir in Sachen Sozialarbeitswissenschaft? Erkundungen im Gelände*, in Id. (hrsg.), *Sozial und wissenschaftlich arbeiten. Status and Position einer Sozialarbeitswissenschaft*, Lambertus, Freiburg, pp. 13-40.
ZNANIECKI F. (1930), *Socjologia wychowania. Wychowujące społeczeństwo*, TI, Warszawa.

12

Supervision and Training of Professionals Working with Families and Minors at Risk

by *Alfonsa Rodríguez, Elena Roldán, Luis Nogués* and *Teresa Zamanillo*

12.1
Introduction

Social work involves working with people all of whom are unique, in situations which are complex, frequently messy and obscure, rarely easy to understand, and almost never to standardised responses. In social work training, experiential learning can take different forms; according to Yelloly, Henkel (2002) one is learning by doing in practice (Schon's practicum) involves a cycle of action and reflection; learning by observation and attention, and learning through reflection on the here and now (seminar groups, work with clients, staff groups). The last position best describes our approach and our experience of a supervisory and training group of professionals in which learning involves the power of holding back in order to reflect on what is happening almost instantaneously, and thus enables learning to take place, and transforms thoughtless action to thoughtful.

It is in this area in which a theoretical-practical process for social work professionals in Madrid has been achieved. These professionals have been working with Gypsy families who have suffered from many deprivations and long periods of social exclusion (multiproblem families). They are people who have had significant difficulties in life and for whom preferential and intensive intervention needs to be developed. This kind of professional activity requires a supervision space in order to help integrate theory and practice. For this reason, a supervisory and training group of involved professionals was created.

The main objective of setting up a supervisory and training group was to provide the possibility for the professional teams to be able to question their daily practices and share a common intervention methodology during their interventions with these families.

12.2
The Theoretical-Practical Training Process for Social Work Professionals

The work that is presented here is the result of the theoretical-practical training through supervision given to social workers, educators and teachers in IRIS's work teams from the year 2000 to 2003 (IRIS: Spanish acronym for the Institute of Social Integration and Re-Housing).

The training process involved 60 professionals, among them coordinators and members of the different professionals' teams. The group was split into three units of 20 professionals with whom three-hour meetings were held every two weeks. In each meeting, reading proposals were made allowing for the creation of a shared frame of reference. Creating common readings of the theoretical content and the supervision of cases allowed the integration of theory with practice, as well as the management of one's own emotions in the ulterior intervention process.

The main objective of setting up a supervisory and training group was to make it possible for the professional teams to be able to question their daily practices and share a common intervention methodology during their work with families. Of particular interest on this point is the approach of Hildebrand (2002) concerning the way to implement supervision as active learning, taking into account the interrelationships between trainees and the families they work with. Supervisors and trainees also have to recognise the influence on themselves of their family of origin, their professional context and of the training itself.

In the learning context of professional practice there are three interrelated elements: knowledge, the professional and the context. An integrated professional practice can only be learnt by converting the personal and concrete management of tasks into a topic of reflection; therefore, we understand supervision as a self-referential system. Thus, professional supervision is a particular form of research, whose objective is to provide certain keys to be exercised in relational reflexivity.

Intervention with families with serious difficulties demands a supervision space in which to articulate conceptual content with operative plans adapted to the requirements of the type of family; space, permits, furthermore, the critical review of aspects of the professional/pupil's own self which empowers him/her to be flexible and to enrich the quantity and quality of the answers that the professionals give to each situation.

In an intervention area such as that of multiproblem families, intense emotions are present on the part of the professionals. It is the key to the social intervention and research process to address these emotions. Theoretical structures help put emotions in the service of the process, thus avoiding acting out. Furthermore a solid knowledge of the organisational and legislative structures that affect evaluations and interventions is necessary. This knowledge will give protection not only to the professional but also to the family and the minor. The result of this process of reflection-action impinges not only on the quality of the attention paid to the families but also on the decrease in the number of risks that surround them.

The training activities are understood to be a process of action-reflection-action. This reflection involves becoming an observer of one's own acts and thoughts, in order to take stock of where one is and what is required of one. From this position, it is necessary to open oneself up to crea-tive acts, inventing new ideas and possibilities in order to improve one's actions and extend the process of capturing and transforming the reality. It is a constructive approach that emphasises process, plurality, possibility and the relational quality of knowledge (Parton, O'Byrne, 2000).

These training activities had a double objective: on the one hand, improving getting along with the families and, on the other, the provision of techniques and strategies for the professionals to help them properly face the difficulties they would come across in certain care scenarios.

12.3
Supervision and Training Activity Scenario: Gypsy Population and Institutional Framework

The professionals involved in this experience were working for the IRIS, which was created by the Assembly of the Region of Madrid by means of law 27 October 1998, n. 16. It is an organism that comes under the Department of Environmental Affairs and Territorial Regulation. Its objective is to provide housing for those people who currently live in shacks, sub-standard ground-floor housing or provisional housing and who are in situations of social exclusion, providing them also with an opportunity to integrate and progress within society. Almost all of the families with which IRIS works are of Gypsy origin, although this in no way implies that all of Madrid's Gypsy population answers to the characteristics of the shanty town Gypsy population, nor that all of the shanty town Gypsy population is in the same situation.

The social programme of the IRIS has a total of 84 professionals. The Institute's specific objectives are:
– that the 1,855 families who live in shacks and the 972 families that, in the past, were transferred to dwellings built in the Special Neighbourhoods have access to non-segregated flats;

- that the Special Neighbourhoods and shanty towns be demolished in the hope that the phenomenon of shanty towns will cease to exist;
- that there should be a full programme of social integration;
- that conflicts that arise in the new surroundings should not be dismissed, but should be openly expressed and dealt with by means of mediation so that the basis of intercultural coexistence can be established.

12.4
Profile of the Client Gypsy Families

IRIS professionals are working with families that, as has been said, have suffered from many shortages and long periods of social exclusion (multiproblem families), people who have significant difficulties in life and for whom preferential and intensive activities need to be developed. Their cultural training – in the sense of the acquisition of knowledge and skills, not in terms of their values, attitudes or life-styles – is much poorer than that of the majority of the population. There are still high levels of illiteracy, even in the younger generations. University education is incidental and the jobs they obtain generally do not require any qualifications, which means that to a large extent they dedicate themselves to non-regulated economic activities which lack any social recognition (despite the fact that in many cases they carry out necessary functions), a situation that helps sustain a stigmatised social image of Gypsies.

This population is undergoing an intense process of change, with significant differences between the generations in the way in which they behave and in their life-styles, a process that is reminiscent of the changes in the majority of our society one or two generations ago. Gypsy families use ways of structuring and organising themselves that are different from that of society as a whole. They establish their limits and their responsibilities from this different perspective. In order to understand Gypsy culture it is essential to consider the way in which they organise their extended family, where there is a strong culture of self-protection from external aggression that has allowed them to survive for many years. This culture is undergoing significant changes as families settle into different types of surroundings in which intercultural coexistence is a necessity. For various reasons they are being pushed inexorably into a different form of organisation as time passes by: the reduction in the number of children (currently between two or three) which makes it impossible to create large extended family groups; the progressive disappearance of segregated environments and their incorporation into environments with multicultural coexistence (schools, neighbourhood communities etc.).

The life cycle of a family of this kind is different from that of the majority of society when it comes to marriage. When their young people marry, there is no prior process of preparation for their life together as a couple. There is no previous friendship or even contact between young people of different sexes and there is no engagement during which they can get to know each other as a couple. It is difficult to get away from paternal influence in some marriages, especially in the case of girls. In the majority society, in general, there are some minimum requirements before a couple is established: where they will live and how they will support themselves. This process does not exist when a Gypsy family is set up: the newly married couple starts living with the groom's parents. The wife suddenly abandons her family in order to enter a new family environment in which she loses her personal space. The birth of the first child will rescue the wife from this initial situation of solitude. The child will bring recognition for the wife. From being "ordered about" by everyone she will start to be important and necessary.

For the husband, the arrival of the first child means that he has new responsibilities and these bring an end to his comfortable situation, even though the family may be able to support him if he doesn't earn enough. The arrival of the child will progressively help bring the couple together, so that in a few months or a couple of years they ought to look for their own place. The husband's acceptance of his responsibilities will mean that he will progressively start to make his way in life. He will make the most of his child, especially if it is a boy, and the child will become a figure in his life. He will take care of any economic responsibility and decisions that concern the child.

12.5
Supervision, Theoretical Frameworks and Epistemological Questions

As has been indicated already, the supervision of professionals working with Gypsy families aimed to integrate theory and practice. It was necessary, however, to slot epistemological and theoretical questions into the professional activity.

In the reflection process, the social work professionals delved into essential aspects related to decision-making, analysis of social reality, intervention methodology etc. Since the social work profession moves within an area of science that implies constant decision-making, this demands a prior analysis of the situation. This is the reason why the dialogue between theory and experience is inescapable for the progress of new knowledge. It should be pointed out that this call to eliminate practice in a vacuum is increasingly coming to the fore in professions involving social intervention: pedagogues, social workers, educators, promoters, and so forth, who note that vacuum in their decision-making knowledge. This was one aspect pointed out by professionals in the supervision groups.

A true perspective of social care must include the following factors in its reference model:
– the philosophical and ideological aspects or *principles* that guide any human action;
– the selection of the theoretical perspectives that will explain the field of professional care: this is an element that is also known as the *theoretical focus*;
– the *objective*: the selection of the facts or phenomena to be studied;
– the *method* as a procedure, guideline, or path to be followed during the care process: in social work there has been a generalised consensus for a number of years whereby it is accepted that this method includes stages within a procedure that should not follow a strict sequence (a study of the field of professional care; analysis/diagnosis; planning; execution; evaluation);
– the selection of the *techniques* set out in the theoretical focus and the method that has been decided upon;
– the *experiences in the field* as a reference point of the social reality, without which the required interaction between the theory and the practice cannot be completed – always bearing in mind that a model explains the reality but is never reality in itself.

And this should be so in the practice of social work because in social sciences a theory that is not linked to practice does not even attain the level of being a theory. It becomes an abstract and unreal speech. It also limits the possibilities of using the reference point for evaluation purposes. On one hand, practice is always a necessary alternative to the theory that serves as its base. On the other hand, because one of the characteristics of practice lies in its specifics, unlike theory that is generalised, it is necessary to adopt a theoretical perspective that will explain what is happening in practice, almost like a "map". But not all theory is practiced, just specific elements of it; furthermore, in social work the most common thing is to apply concepts for concepts which act as guides. Thus, we cannot sacrifice theory in the name of practice or practice in the name of theory.

It is with this starting framework that the supervision and training activity that is presented in this chapter has been developed and has been used as a reference for its application of the systemic model. This approach shows the complexity of the object of study: a phenomenon that is unfettered, either intra- or extra-familiarly, produces alterations of all types and in all orders. This is because the different elements of the system (individuals) are interconnected in such a way that changes to some parts affect all the others, and the whole. Incorporating complex elements and establishing connections between them makes the vast universe of families understandable.

In the supervisory and training group we look into the interconnections between the members of the family, and on those with different meaningful contexts: assistance, community of neighbours, housing conditions, extended family etc. The emphasis on the relationship and not on the intrinsic nature of the human beings is novel in itself and provides an optimistic approach to the intervention: it is more difficult to change people than relationships (changes in relationships will bring changes in individuals). Key concepts such as system, organisation, control, regularity and feedback are contained in Minuchin's work who states that the family is like an animals' colony with many different types of living organisms, which have different roles; however, all together 'the whole' itself composes an organism of a variety of individuals, and this in itself is a 'form of life'. The complex phenomena are those in which many interdependent elements in the various domains of the vital activities are implicated: biological, psychological, relational, cultural identity, institutional, structural etc.

The objective of this theoretical-practical process for social workers is to help introduce this view of the complexity in a phenomenon such as the mistreatment of children or at risk minors with families in serious danger of social exclusion. Understanding the social conditions that contribute to the vulnerability of particular persons, whose results are on occasion situations of poor welfare or active mistreatment of minors will permit the creation of a reflection space with the protagonists which will make change possible.

Cancrini (1999) outlines intervention with multiproblem families as: intervention, as such, and supervision. The latter, we observe, acquires the same range as the intervention. The author faces the process as a form of construction of a second level communicative situation in a context in which it is necessary to take into account the limits of objectivity and the implication/participation value, which are the elements of the therapeutic relationship. The theoretical-practical contents provided have to be the basis of the "hypothetical activity" guiding the social worker. This kind of activity will permit the introduction of reflexive questions that throw light on what happens.

Amongst the questions dealt with from a theoretical-practical point of view and which were involved in the work with the professionals are the following:
– basics of the systematic model: understanding of the phenomena from a relationship point of view;

- characteristics of multiproblem families;
- types of family-professional ties;
- situations where intervention is required and the possibilities of bringing about changes when there is no spontaneous demand;
- interinstitutional co-ordination (collaboration contexts);
- special emphasis on the definition of control contexts;
- arbitration and resolving of conflicts.

12.6
Significant Elements of the Supervision and Training Activity

In the supervised sessions with the group some of the ideas, beliefs or notions that the professionals may hold with regard to their work with people who have been excluded were exposed, and gave rise to the following points.

1. *Who is responsible for the family problem?* To a lesser or greater degree, professionals have preconceived notions about "who or what is to blame for the situation?". Is it a result of the intricacies of family relationships? Or the circumstances of poverty and exclusion? Or the characteristic traits of the Gypsy minority? The answers change, which means that, in general, there is no easy solution.

2. *Professionals' emotional involvement* The fact that the professionals are close to those with whom they are working is a definite advantage for one part of the group, whereas other parts of the group consider that it is precisely that closeness with the family that leads them to "delegate" their problems to the professionals. The degree of emotional involvement is the professionals' main concern.

3. *Intervention prognosis* There is a certain feeling of "tiredness", despite which the general feeling within the group is one of optimism: "we cannot expect immediate results; we have to think about the process". This thought about the processes that arise from dealings with the families, due partly to good ties with the professional, leads to greater hope and optimism that "things get better in the long run". Amongst the aspects that are decisive for care to take place is the "non-existence of demand" on the part of the families. It's important that "the families map some of the objectives out". The most satisfactory situations are those where the result of the work has been a long stretch during which the professionals have maintained the hope and desire that transformation will come about. They will have avoided *acting out* because of their sense of urgency. In fact, a wary relationship with the family will not lead to a working alliance. On one hand, a good parental relationship within a family that is characterised by mutual caring of the children is a factor

that augurs well. On the other hand, a deteriorated parental subsystem, i.e. drug-addict parent(s), psychological or mental problems, abuse of the children... will produce impediments against any working relationship between the professional and the parents. These situations result in *re-placement manoeuvres* by the professionals (Cancrini, 1999), which mean that they will have failed in their efforts to introduce improvements.

4. *Institutional co-ordination* Another good sign is that of good working relationships (co-ordination) with other organisations that have taken part in this initiative.

Turning to control-protection institutions (commission for the Protection of Minors) is an option that is used late in the care process, and is therefore viewed by the family more as a punitive act rather than an opportunity for restraint. The professional's explanation for this is based on a preconception that is more or less justified: "the law does not work for these minority groups". This subject leads to a discussion about the way in which the principle of the child's best interests is applied. It has always been a problem with the Gypsies in Spain to try to impose very strong legal forms on Gypsy families. Nowadays, a similar problem with immigrants can be seen. In Norway, for example, working with child migrants, professionals could see that sometimes the combination of a culture-blind and a context-free consideration of a child's best interests in the abstract primarily serves to justify increasing restriction of family action and thereby serves the State's best interests at the cost of the individual child (Engebrigtsen, 2003). Difficulties therefore arise when we split the objective of our intervention: we control the family by consciously not using this option of control-protection institutions as one of the guidelines of our intervention. We substitute intra-family roles and functions instead of understanding the reasons why the family does not get on or work together.

The problems of implementing a child protection system have been important in different European countries. In the UK, the White Paper *Modernising Social Service: Promoting Independence, Improving Protection, Raising Standards* (1998) puts forward some specific statutory changes to improve protection of children but it has been criticised because according to Jordan (2000), it "reflects doubts" about the usefulness and importance of social work as a professional part of social policy.

12.7
Implementation of Theoretical-Practical Care Criteria

The process of supervision has allowed the extraction of certain theoretical-practical criteria for caring for multiproblem families in excluded minorities: the situations of exclusion that these types of families are experiencing shut down their opportunities for creating relationships and don't allow them to respond to the outside world. These situations create a high degree of suffering, as well as organisational and emotional deficiencies.

In any social work environment it is difficult to come across families that have not been previously influenced by or are not in touch with different types of systems: health, education, legal, social services etc. The starting point that we put forward is that, just as we propose the analysis of the interdependence and interconnection between members of the family in order to find out how they work, we feel that there should also be an analysis of the influence of the various systems that interact with the family (Imber-Back, 2000). These systems establish relationship guidelines that are isomorphic to those of the family itself. If the family-operator link is built jointly, it is the responsibility of both parties to change the situation. The operators must adopt a meta-perspective that allows them to become part of the study, so that in this way they can evaluate the style of the relationships between the families and the services and vice-versa. It is necessary to carry out an exhaustive analysis of this relationship, as it will provide us with an indication of cyclical guidelines that produce barriers to the resolution of problems.

The analysis of the care system is of particular interest in the case of interventions with multiproblem families, where a family's limits with extensive systems are tremendously vague. We share Cirillo's (1998) view that the multiproblem family is already a multiproblem family before it comes into contact with a professional, but after this contact with the professional the situation can become chronic. An innovative working approach to break these situations of *chronic crisis in the care system* is to ask the family questions, in line with Imber-Back's theory, on the view that the family itself has of the services that are looking after them. "Of the care that you have received, which do you think has been the most useful?". "What do you think your family's opinion is of the different professionals?". "Do you think there are disagreements?". The response to these questions ought to be taken into account by the care providers.

Minuchin, Colapinto, Minuchin (2000) propose a focus based on family relations rather than work towards rescuing the individual. An exhaustive evaluation of the family relationship is required, and it must include the quality of the said relationship, the working guidelines that are generally followed and the intra and extra-family limits. It is important to avoid preconceived notions, a different approach is therefore required, one with an emphasis on interconnections. Creative practices following the analysis, which should be reflexive and critical, will allow us to gather information about the family itself, and thereby refocus on the complaint, explore alternative solutions, handle the conflict etc.

Inadequate parental activities, ill treatment within the marriage, negligence and neglect towards the children must not be justified on the basis that they take place amongst people that belong to minority cultures that find themselves in circumstances of exclusion. The characteristics with which these families are labelled should not stop legal mechanisms from being put into action. These measures (eviction due to non-payment of rent; guardianship of the children) would constitute a corrective feedback for the parents. In the same way, it is necessary to avoid glossing over situations that would not be permitted within wider society and considering them to be normal.

Only looking at the deficient aspects of the individuals: diagnoses that supposedly offer an explanation in themselves (drug addiction, for example) will not permit us to understand the relationship, which leads to a bias with regard to the phenomenon and the care project. Understanding is *only* possible if we have guidelines that provide a meaning for the facts: for example, addictive behaviour is a self-destructive process that can be understood in part as being "a remedy to a situation in which the suffering is greater". Having a different perception that takes into account the complexity of the phenomena rather than merely describing the facts, the problems and the people, will allow us to avoid moral judgements that do not help the caring process in the slightest.

The emphasis by the professional on transparency with regard to his or her proposals for the family will let him or her reach a consensus on the objectives and thus avoid the reluctance that many professionals have towards taking on situations in a unilateral manner. The use of a coercive or control context provides the opportunity, both for the professional and the family, to create a working framework from which they may be able to extract the motivation for change. It is always necessary to work with the extended family, especially when it is not advisable to differentiate between people, as this is not always a positive help in the care process.

Finally, care for families that belong to excluded minorities must stem from a position of action, of urgent intervention, of punishment and judgement, it must then move on to a situation of thinking and reflection. The challenge is to try to face up to a situation of enormous suffering in which the family is not asking for help, to base the care process on an examination of the complexities of the specific social context that surrounds the psycho-social difficulties that exist in the lives of the people, a process where the personal and social realities are brought together so that they can be looked at from a situation of critical awareness.

Let us include a few words to justify the objectives that guide us in the teaching-learning process of our discipline. If the help contexts, assistance, education etc. are guided by objective and technocratic procedures which do not introduce reflection about the contextual aspects of the lives of the persons, they convert their professionals' practice into stereotypes and a lack of ethics. The purpose that has guided our project with the professionals of the Institute of Social Integration and Re-Housing has been to avoid this.

12.8
European Approach

European social work is clearly involved in the two main subjects described here: family/child support and the role of social work and supervision. The renaissance of family support in different countries such as Britain, Germany, Italy or Spain is mostly perceived as an alternative to child protection, rather than part of a wider answer as different needs emerge. The literature on social work in Europe (Shardlow, Payne, 1998; Walker, 2002) acknowledges the difficulties of finding a common professional social work identity, and family and children support practice. The increasing problems in this field across an expanding Europe will demand new skills of professional, qualified social workers. The concern is that the lack of statutory social services to support families can lead to a retrenchment in professional social work.

In all European countries, Gypsies generally remain outside of society, in part by choice, in part through exclusion (Turner, 2000). The European Union has a compromise position of working for the social integration of the Gypsy community as well as respecting its ethnic identity. The European Committee on Gypsy Emancipation (1999) is one of the Gypsy organisations involved in the defence of Gypsies' human rights in the new European countries. Besides, at the moment there are different European projects for social action on Gypsies communities to achieve some aspects such as: networks between countries to implement good practices and exchange experiences, the implementation of training programmes, reports and guides elaborating the situation of Gypsies in different countries etc. (Fundación secretariado general gitano, 2003).

Further, supervision in the field of social work is taking a leading role. In 1989 the German Association for Supervision was created, which in the year 2000 had more than 3,000 members. Switzerland and Austria also have specialist associations. In the meantime, the Association of National Supervision in Europe was founded in Vienna at the end of 1997. Supervision in France, Italy and Spain is not as developed as in the Anglo- and German-language areas. Different studies in supervision application show – as well as what we have seen in our experience – very positive outcomes: social workers were able to improve their methodological and theoretical orientation in everyday practice (Belardi, 2002). They confirm the importance of supervision as a desirable form of further education. Clearly, supervision increases personal competence, promotes job satisfaction and improves the way in which people work in teams. The challenge remains to mainstream reflexive awareness throughout social work training, practice and research so that it becomes a part of the profession's habits.

Bibliography

BELARDI N. (2002), *Social Work Supervision in Germany*, in "European Journal of Social Work", V, 3, pp. 313-8.
CANCRINI L. (1999), *Las familias multiproblemáticas*, in L. Coletti, J. L. Linares (coord. de), *Intervención sistémica con familias multiproblemáticas en Servicios Sociales*, Paidós, Barcelona.
CÁRDENAS E. D. (1999), *Violencia en la pareja*, Granica, Buenos Aires.
CIRILLO S. (1991), *Niños maltratados*, Paidós, Barcelona (1991).
ID. (1998), *La intervención sistémica en contextos no clínicos*, in "Revista sistémica", 45, pp. 15-26.
DEPARTMENT OF HEALTH (1998a), *Modernising Social Service: Promoting Independence, Improving Protection, Raising Standards*, Stationery Office, London.
ID. (1998b), *Quality Protects: Framework for Action and Objectives for Social Services for Children*, Stationery Office, London.
ENGEBRIGTSEN A. (2003), *The Child's – or the State's – Best Interests? An Examination of the Ways Immigration Officials Work with Unaccompanied Asylum Seeking Minors in Norway*, in "Child and Family Social Work", VIII, pp. 191-200.
EUROPEAN COMMITTEE ON GYPSY EMANCIPATION (1999), *El fracaso de los gobiernos de Europa del Este para mejorar la base educativa de los gitanos*, in "Tchatchipen", 28, pp. 37-45.
FUNDACIÓN SECRETARIADO GENERAL GITANO (2003), *Documentación para coordinadores de intervención social*, FSGG, Madrid.
GUIDANO V. (1994), *El sí mismo en proceso*, Paidós, Buenos Aires.
HILDEBRAND J. (2002), *Learning through Supervision: A Systemic Approach*, in Yelloly, Henkel (2002).
IMBER-BACK E. (2000), *Familias y sistemas amplios*, Amorrortu, Buenos Aires.
JORDAN B. (2000), *Social Work and the Third Way: Tough Love as Social Policy*, Sage, London.
MINUCHIN P., COLAPINTO J., MINUCHIN S. (2000), *Pobreza, institución, familia*, Amorrortu, Buenos Aires.
NOGUÉS L. (2001), *Minorías étnicas, cultura y exclusión*, in "Trabajo social hoy", 31, pp. 49-61.
PARROTT L. (2002), *Social Work and Social Care*, Rutledge, London.

PARTON N., O'BYRNE P. (2000), *Constructive Social Work: Towards a New Practice*, Macmillan, London.
RODRÍGUEZ A. (2001), *Contextos de colaboración: entre el deseo y la realidad*, in "Trabajo social hoy", 31, pp. 73-83.
ROLDÁN E., RODRÍGUEZ A., SANTOS C., BARAHONA M. J., CASTILLO A., MOÑIVAS A. (2002), *Trabajo social con menores y familias*, video y CD, Universidad Complutense, Madrid.
SHARDLOW S., PAYNE M. (eds.) (1998), *Contemporary Issues in Social Work: Western Europe*, Arena, Aldershot.
TURNER R. (2000), *Gypsies and Politics in Britain*, in "The Political Quarterly", LXXV, pp. 68-77.
WALKER S. (2002), *Family Support and the Role of Social Work: Renaissance or Retrenchment?*, in "European Journal of Social Work", V, 1, pp. 43-54.
WALTERS M. et al. (1991), *La red invisible*, Paidós, Barcelona.
WATZLAWICK P. (1997), *Teoría de la comunicación humana*, Herder, Barcelona.
YELLOLY M., HENKEL M. (eds.) (2002), *Learning and Teaching Social Work: Towards Reflective Practice*, Kingsley, London.
ZAMANILLO T. (2002), *Teoría y práctica del aprendizaje por interacción en grupos pequeños*, tesis doctoral, facultad de Ciencias políticas y Sociología, Universidad Complutense, Madrid.

Authors and Editors

TOMASA BÁÑEZ, PhD, is a social worker and social anthropologist. She is a lecturer in social work at the University of Zaragoza. Her research interests are community work, gender and social work.

Dr. Dr. hc DETLEF BAUM is professor in sociology, with a special interest in social problems, poverty, youth and the sociology of urbanity at the University of Applied Sciences of Koblenz, Germany (Department of Social Sciences). His research interests are homeless people, the poverty of children and young people, social work with young people in deprived areas.

ANNE VAN DEN BERG is staff member and researcher at Zuyd University, Maastricht. She is a member of the MACESS (MA Comparative European Social Studies) team and a researcher at CESRT (Comparative European Social Research and Theory) research centre.

JANE DALRYMPLE, PhD, is a senior lecturer on the social work course at the University of the West of England, Bristol. She was a social worker with children and young people for over twenty years and was director of a national advocacy service prior to becoming a lecturer. Her research interests are focussed on the area of child and youth advocacy.

PETER DELLGRAN, PhD, is associate professor in social work at the Göteborg University (Department of Social Work). His research areas are social policy, poverty, consumption and welfare, social assistance and debt counselling.

WILFRED DIEKMANN is a senior lecturer in social educational carework/social work at the Hogeschool of Amsterdam. He teaches and researches social work methodology, especially in the field of child and youth welfare.

GUDRUN EHLERT, D.Phil., social worker and social scientist, is professor in sciences of social work at the University of Applied Sciences Mittweida, Rosswein (Germany). His research interests are the professionalization of social work, gender and social work.

JULIJA EIDUKEVIČIŪTĖ is assistant at the Social Work Institute, Vytautas Magnus University (Lithuania). She is a PhD student at the Social Work Department of the University of Lapland in Finland.

VINCENZO FORTUNATO is a researcher at the faculty of Political Science (Department of Sociology) at the University of Calabria, Italy, where he teaches sociology of organisation and social policies on the Sciences of Social Services degree course. Among the main research interests there are the organisation of social services in the Italian context and the organisation and structure of the third sector within the welfare State.

MARIA JOSÉ FREITAS is a researcher, a lecturer and student supervisor at Zuyd University, Maastricht. She is a member of the CESRT research centre and the MACESS teaching team.

GÜNTER J. FRIESENHAHN, D.Phil., is professor in European Community education studies at the University of Applied Sciences of Koblenz, Germany. He is head of the Department of Social Sciences, and his research interests are in comparative social work, intercultural communication and international youth work.

ELIZABETH FROST is a principal lecturer in social work in the faculty of Health and Social Care at the University of the West of England, Bristol. She lectures primarily in the sociology of identity and psychosocial studies and currently researches into identity and transition in children and young people. She is the director of International Development within the faculty.

STAFFAN HÖJER, PhD, is associate professor in Social Work at the Göteborg University (Department of Social Work). He has spent seventeen years in social work practice and in professional supervision, and he researches open-care treatment for youth. His research and publication field is professionalization in social work.

EWA KANTOWICZ, PhD, is assistant professor in social pedagogy at the University of Warma and Mazury, Olsztyn (Poland). Since last ten years she has been engaged in social pedagogues/workers training and researches in comparative studies of education for social professions in Europe. She is the author of many publications related to theory and practice of social work, protection on human (child's) rights and community education.

MARIA P. MICHAILIDIS, EdD, is associate professor in psychology at Intercollege (University College) in Nicosia, Cyprus. She is a psychotherapist and she also teaches courses related to social and clinical psychology. Her research interests include cross-cultural, multicultural and gender issues as well as stress and coping.

AGUSTÍN MOÑIVAS, doctor in psychology, is senior lecturer in psychology and subdirector at the Social Work School at Complutense, University of Madrid. He teaches psychology and researches into mental images, social representations, youths, and vulnerability and stress.

GÉRARD MOUSSU, doctor in sociology, teaches sociology at the Institut régional du travail social aquitaine de Talence (Bordeaux), and is head of the section of evaluation, research and development.

LUIS NOGUÉS holds a master of science degree in sociology, a B.Sc. in social work, and is associate professor in social work at Complutense, University of Madrid (School of Social Work). He researches in the field of social exclusion and is a civil servant in the autonomous Community of Madrid (IRIS).

ROLF H. PIQUARDT is professor in psychology at the University of Applied Sciences of Koblenz, Germany (Department of Social Sciences). His main subjects are: learning, developmental psychology, clinical and counselling psychology. His research interests include coping behaviour and achievement, counselling and sexual abuse, and youth and family.

ALFONSA RODRÍGUEZ holds a master of science degree in sociology, a B.Sc. in social work, and is associate professor in social work at Complutense, University of Madrid (School of Social Work). She is a family therapist and a member of the Spanish Association of Family Therapy. Her research areas are family intervention, professional supervision and social work practice.

ELENA ROLDÁN holds a PhD, a master of science degree in sociology, and a B.Sc. in social work. She is professor of social work and social services at Complutense, University of Madrid (School of Social Work). Her research areas are social policy, social exclusion, welfare and gender.

NIJOLĖ VEČKIENĖ, PhD, is associated professor and head of the Department of Social Work at the Social Work Institute, Vytautas Magnus University (Lithuania). Her research interests are social exclusion, social work development, community social work, qualification, standardisation problems of social professions.

TERESA ZAMANILLO holds a PhD, a master of science degree in sociology, and a B.Sc. in social work. She is professor in social work at Complutense, University of Madrid (School of Social Work). She researches social work methodology, and social work with groups and gender.